Naphtali is a hind let loose: he giveth goodly words.
—Genesis 49:21, KJV

To my beloved parents,
Wallace Raymond and Marjorie Hoban Neill,
and to my wonderful brothers and family,
who did not disown (but prayed for)
their rebellious son and brother…

and for Elia Neill Larson-Krisetya
and his beloved parents, Mathias and Karin,
who honoured me with a namesake.

Acknowledgements

Baruch HaShem Adonai Elohim,
Jehoshua Ha Messiach,
the name of the Lord God, Jesus the Christ,
lover of my soul (Isaiah 38:17),
who gave me a wonderful life.
Blessed be His holy name.

Preface	xi
Introduction	xiii

Thesis
1 Solitude	3
2 Identity	17
3 First Escape	23
4 The Second Escape	31
5 Our House	41

Antithesis
6 Revolution in Action	47
7 Koko	55
8 Psychiatry- The Perfect Fit	65
9 Europe	79

Synthesis
10 Close Encounter	87
11 Crash and Burn	95
12 Mountain Life	101
13 Magnificent Peril	111
14 Contrasts	121
15 Transistion	133
16 Jamaica Psychosis	141
17 Haiti	149
18 Cuba	159
19 Curacao	165
20 Full Circle	171
21 The Israeli Defence Force	179
22 Pilgrimage	187
23 Kosovo	197
24 Mashuginah Goy Joins the Navy	205
25 The Hurt Locker	213

Epilogue	217
About the Author	223

Preface

February 5, 2013

IN THE 50S, 60S, AND 70S, A CULTURAL AND POLITICAL EARTHQUAKE TOOK place in the West. I am of the generation that got "shaken." The true aftermath of that earthquake wasn't experienced at the time. We are experiencing it now.

Only in this place—the magnificent lands of the Americas—and only at this time in history could a life like mine have been lived: with freedom, vibrant economic growth, geographic expansion, peace in our land, opportunity of all kinds, explosive technological advancement, and incomparable human social development.

The revolution was intoxicating and hopeful, youthful and vibrant, rife with new music and art and politics and protest and revolution… creative and utterly destructive to the order which made it possible.

After several decades of post-revolutionary descent into cynicism, brutality, and the abandonment of the hopes of Woodstock, the 1960s revolution has sprung to life once again in 2008 garb, almost as though there had been no intervening years. It is the Hegelian dialectic at work: thesis, antithesis, synthesis. Prosperity and growth yield its antithesis (a cultural revolution) which undermines prosperity and growth—the seed of its own demise, creating another new entity.

But in the 60s, a revolution had indeed taken place—a revolution in mind and praxis—that changed the course of modern history. In this book, I seek to explore a typically unreported dimension of the revolution. Here, I will write about how the revolution looked to one boomer who was moving from the rustic new-world perfection of central New Brunswick to the Left Coast of British

Columbia—to mountain life, to Europe, to the Caribbean, to the Balkans, and to Jerusalem. It ultimately led to a revolution in mind that generated the most subversive activity in the world of the twenty-first century.

Introduction

I AM THE YOUNGEST SON OF A YOUNGEST SON OF A YOUNGEST SON.

Lack of insight can be a wonderful thing! In my early life, it manifested in my having no idea that I couldn't do what I ultimately did.

I grew up with a magnificent array of false assumptions.

The consummate baby boomer (born in 1946), I grew up in a Christmas postcard town as the third of three brothers. Fourteen and sixteen years younger than my two engineers-to-be brothers, I was for all intents and purposes an only child, born on the edge of Fredericton, New Brunswick, where rural met small-city urban. I had the best of all worlds: caring parents and brothers where the forest met town, and where the war met the self-indulgent 60s.

Born in a little red-and-white cape-cod house on the Woodstock Road, two stones' throw from the magnificent Saint John River, I wandered the bush and creeks, rode to school in a yellow bus, tobogganed and skied the hills of the Fredericton Golf Club, skated on the frozen river, and canoed the lakes. I did this mostly alone. I had no revolution in mind.

In rebellion, I took off for the Left Coast at age nineteen. I ended up in the Yukon for a summer and enrolled in "Revolution U" (Simon Fraser University), having no idea what I was getting myself into.

I married the tall, blonde, blue-eyed girl next door and became a fire-breathing academic Marxist. While revolting, I got a job in psychiatry with the provincial government, starting a thirty-year career. While in that exciting career, the true revolution came: the revolutionary faith of Jesus the Christ.

I then lost the beautiful tall blonde, blue-eyed girl next door, and with a broken heart I decided to turn the grief into productivity. Later, I came home to join my brothers in the loss of our mother and then burying our father before going off to Jamaica for seven years.

By God's magnificent grace, and under the stunning auspices of the Mennonite Central Committee (MCC), I ended up committing revolution within a democratic socialist state by getting innocent men out of Jamaican prisons, not having been informed that it couldn't be done.

Ultimately, I was led back into a new job in community psychiatry.

Three years later, I committed revolution against the international media establishment, eighty-five percent of the Christian Church, and my leftist comrades by volunteering with the Israeli Army's Sar-El unit. I then went for a visit to help Willingdon Mennonite Brethren Church missionaries in Kosovo, and two years after that I retired early to spend three months with the Israeli Defence Force for two years in a row.

In 2011, I committed revolution again (in print, this time) by starting a blog entitled "Donning the Yellow Star." In the context of the new, oil-funded version of global anti-Semitism, I stand in defence of the Jewish people's right to defend themselves against their enemies' latest extermination bid. History has shown us that defence of the Jews can only take place in the sovereign Jewish state of their ancestral homeland… Israel. For much of the world, this is considered subversive activity.

Thesis

1

Solitude

I WAS A FREE-RANGE CHILD AT A TIME IN HISTORY WHEN THAT WAS possible. I mourn for children today who can't even imagine it. They live in a prison of parental risk management, bereft of the joys of freedom I experienced.

My entire neighbourhood had open doors and kept an eye out for me (I was almost always alone), disciplining me if I got out of line. It was an era in which we lived in terror of our teachers' wrath and would heed our neighbours' reprimands.

Occasionally, another kid would be exiled by his parents to my idyllic cultural gulag, and we would live a Maritime Huckleberry Finn fantasy. Then he would move. I would mourn, then recover, and eventually happily carry on my avoidant existence.

One of these friends was a little Japanese kid whose parents lived in a tiny travel trailer at the side of the local service station. I don't remember his parents. They must have been very poor. It was barely 1950 and the resentments of the war remained.

I was insanely jealous of him, because I had the elderly neighbourhood women all to myself. When they fussed over this Japanese boy, I would ultimately find a way to take it out of his hide. He didn't seem to mind, though, and he enjoyed the attentions and treats of the older ladies.

One day, he was gone, and I knew nothing of why. Once again, I had to explore the streams and woodlands in solitude.

As I morphed into a pre-teen, hunting and fishing became my life. Mom and Dad and I would grab the steel telescopic fishing poles and wicker fishing baskets, jump in the '57 Buick, and drive up to Kelly Creek to fish Eastern Brook trout.

With respect to social skills, I didn't have any. With respect to worldview, it consisted of a perspective that everybody lived in nice houses with beautiful views; the men worked in order to hunt and fish and the women kept house in order to collect china, silverware, and crystal.

Outside Fredericton, there were two cities in Canada: Toronto and Montreal. Toronto was good and Montreal was bad, because it was Catholic and liberal and France and the Pope ruled there. I would grow up to go to university and become an engineer. I would marry a beautiful girl from high school and we would have two to four children. We would live in a little house with a used car and then, in two years' time, build a larger house and buy a new car. In two more years, we would build a summer cottage at Grand Lake and take winter vacations to Florida. Our children would go to the University of New Brunswick (UNB) and the boys would become engineers and the girls nurses or schoolteachers. When I got old, I would die of a heart attack and the children and grandchildren would come to the service at the Brunswick St. Baptist Church. Then they would all go home and watch TV. It was a wonderful life.

Outside, in the unreal world, there was talk of nuclear war, as well as war in the Middle East. But none of that had anything to do with whether or not the fish were biting in Kelly Creek.

Around age thirteen, my brother Bob took me skiing at the Royal Roads Hill on Fredericton's north side. This was where the university ski club resided, and it featured a ski jump and harrowing slalom course above the rope tow. This day changed the course of my life. I now lived to ski rather than hunt and fish.

Wooden skis, without steel edges, suicide bindings, and I was hooked. I went skiing every Saturday and Sunday until I got it out of my system ten years later. I would get up at 5:00 a.m. on school mornings and go across the road to the golf course hills and run down a little outcropping of rock that looked to me like K2. Then I'd rush home and have porridge cooked by my mom before catching the yellow school bus right at my front door. As I got more competent, I graduated to Royal Roads and the rope tow and I mixed with university skiers. They were such good skiers; I couldn't take my eyes off them.

I once got up at 5:00 a.m. on a Saturday morning and skied several miles across the Saint John River and up Stanley Creek to Douglas. In many places, the creek had open rapid water and I circled around the rapids into the bush and reaccessed the frozen creek upstream, blissfully unconcerned that I could have fallen through the ice, faraway from rescue. I skied all day and then headed back down the frozen creek and out into the river.

As the world turned yellow, and then pink in the sunset, the glistening lights of town and village emerged on the shores of the white-robed river valley. Exhausted, I saw the welcome lights of home, doffed the skis, showered, and fell asleep until Sunday morning and church.

My ski obsession turned into assisting the developers of a lovely eight-hundred-foot peak in central New Brunswick. I also helped with local racing and instructing, and finally I put in a season of full-time professional ski patrol at Mount Tremblant, Quebec in 1967, the Expo year. To this day, the sight of falling snow excites me. The intoxicating thrill of pushing off on my poles and taking the first skate down a steep pitch stirs my very soul.

It all started on a Saturday afternoon with my brother when I was thirteen. The day would cost me one dollar and twenty-five cents.

The ski hill ended my solitude.

Out the Hill

There's a book by the title *Out the Hill*, written by my cousin, Tom Myles. The homestead which it describes is a place of stunningly warm memories, though I spent very little time there. The images in my mind are like a Currier and Ives Christmas card.

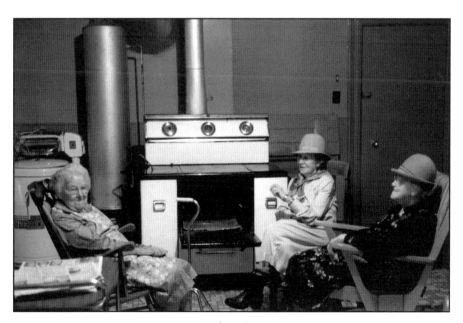

Family gathering

The big black-and-white heritage farmhouse where Dad grew up dominated the head of Neill Street. The rolling lawn out front swept around the house into endless pasture, until it reached the woodland to the north. The house had a stone foundation and shiplap siding with a big veranda where generations of rocking-chair meditation took place. Off in the distance stood the skyline of Fredericton, including the Christ Church Cathedral steeple (and half a dozen others). UNB swept up the other side of the St. John River valley.

My dad and his dad and his dad grew up in this big farmhouse. The house was replete with beloved children and dogs, ghosts and deaths, old men and young men, beautiful women and the men who courted them. It saw fights and romance, hilarious laughter and protracted grieving. It raised five generations and fed countless field hands, family members, neighbours, friends, and men looking for seasonal work in hard times.

More importantly, because of the very wise men (and women) who presided there, it was a place of meeting, not unlike city gates in biblical times. Men of integrity, courage, loyalty, and faith sat in that kitchen. The door was always open, day and night. A huge Franklin stove dominated the north wall, with a big steel warmer above the burner and huge oven. It was fed by a constant supply of firewood, cut on the river islands or from the property and stored in the shed just outside the big plank door. Cats and dogs would wait expectantly by the door to get into that ever-warm kitchen and its smell of bread and buns, beans and bacon, roasts and turkeys. Just inside the door was a slant-top wooden box, likely seventy years old, just like the door and everything else. A small kitchen table waited by the door. As people from the area clomped in, they got a joke and an unceremonious welcome, sitting down through an exchange of rural New Brunswick idioms. Coffee or tea was served and food set out on the table.

Slowly, after the warm, sarcastic chiding ended, family, community, and farming news began to flow. The verbiage was sparse and efficient, and much of the rich content dwelt between the lines. Much of importance was never stated. These chats pretty much always started with the weather and how it was going to affect the seasonal tasks at hand. Ploughing ground, ploughing snow, haying, planting, harvesting, milking, transporting, bucking, splitting, stacking, loading, unloading, irrigating, trucking in heavy snow, trimming hooves, cutting horn… not to mention the cost of feed, the price of dairy, the meaning of life, the goodness of God, and the intrusiveness of government.

News was filtered and corroborated from family near and far—who had called the vet for what and who had been injured and how, whose relatives had ended up in hospital, who was dying and who was recovering. Talk included government corruption, local and international politics, and how crazy the world was becoming.

The weighty and light topics always melted into sardonic laughter interspersed with significant periods of silent reverie as dry heat blasted out of the stove. The old dogs would roll over, sigh, and change position. Ghosts of old men and women in nineteenth-century dress might drift through the rooms coursing with images of a huge table surrounded by farm hands eating heartily and laughing at the end of an exhausting day.

Then there were the hunting and ghost stories told on snowy winter nights. The fire blazed and sunk in the firebox of the big old Franklin, and every now and then Doug (the oldest son) or Albert or Ron (his sons) went down the cellar stairs behind the rocking chair to stoke the furnace that heated all three stories of the house. The stories, though told hundreds of times, were always new: being charged by a big bull moose or a black bear, the twelve-point buck that appeared out of nowhere that no one seemed to be able to "down," and the huge brook trout that kept getting away after a strike. Everyone knew the endings, but it didn't matter. On the mantle above the fireplace in the den stood the oil painting of our great-grandfather, holding court over the proceedings. Below him were awards—cast-iron sculptures of champion Holstein cattle with bronze plaques. Year after year, Doug, Ron, and Albert took top prize at the agri-fairs, and each of the trophies had the animal's name and accurate markings.

On the wall above the roll-top desk, where all the business of the farm was conducted, hung a stunningly serene painting of a Holstein cow lying in the pale glow of a moonlit night. I would escape into that painting, hearing the deep breath of the massive animal and smelling the musk of her hide. I could smell the summer grass as the white and black of her coat melded with the moonlight of black shadow, white moon, and endless shades of grey. It was perfect.

Warm buns, bread, and donuts came out of the oven as stories flowed out of the men. The audience would ask clarifying questions as the women served or listened patiently. Thick seal skin coats and formal woollen ladies' hats with pheasant tail feathers lay on the bed in the bedroom off the kitchen.

After we were full to bursting, we would face the blast of cold air as we left the kitchen to head out to our vehicles, crunching across cold snow as we looked out to the warm lights of the barn, where at 4:00 a.m. Ron and Albert began milking, feeding, and cleaning. For most of the eighty years of their lives, at 4:00 a.m., and then again at 4:00 p.m., the relentless process of emptying the distended udders of those Holstein cows determined the clock. As a result, milk appeared on thousands of tables in the valley for over a hundred years.

The Skate

It cannot be done on the St. John River today, because of the hydro dam above Fredericton. The potential for rapidly changing water levels mean that new ice can end up unsupported. No kid gets to safely do what I did anymore.

One day while I was in high school, the river froze clear. Three or four inches of snowfall blanketed the valley, and then the temperature plummeted to about fifteen degrees below zero. I could see my reflection in the ice the next morning. As long as snow or warm weather didn't ruin it, after a couple of days of deep freeze I would sprint home from school, lace on my skates, and head out on the river.

The school day flashed by. At 3:30, I was out the door for the two-mile walk home. I saw the river as I passed the cemetery near the hermitage. It looked like a magnificent blue sheet of glass. I flew into the house, kissed Mom, grabbed my skates, and didn't tell her what I intended to do.

I headed down to the little rift in the riverbank where in summer I would launch my canoe and look across to the islands that adorned the middle of the river, a quarter-mile away.

Those islands were a source of wonder to me as soon as I could get to them. I would canoe across and fish the downriver points for perch and hunt duck in the fall. The islands were ringed with alder brush and hardwood stands with a barn for the cattle that were brought by barge and left to grow wild on grass feed all summer. In the winter, I would ski over the gently rolling hills of these islands, then through the woodlands, passing an ever-changing landscape of villages along the riverbank.

Amidst the magnificent colours that people come from all over the world to see: fire-engine red, brilliant gold, incandescent yellow, and orange, my best friend Ken and I ventured across the river to the first island. I had a sixteen-gauge Mossberg and he had a wonderful twelve-gauge pump-action Remington shotgun. There was a place where the trees and cattail grasses acted as a natural blind, presenting a view of the little pool in the river where duck stopped to feed.

Having beached the canoe, we would walk along the edge of the pasture, separated from the river by trees and alder brush. We were wearing red hunting jackets, of course, when over the small hill above us wandered a large bull. Being a "psychotic" adolescent, I jumped up and down, waving my arms in my brilliant red cagoule, just to see what he would do—and I immediately found out. With a blood-curdling bellow, the herd lifted their heads from grazing and followed the bull in a full charge toward us.

They were charging us toward the icy, swift-moving river. We crashed through the alder, and by the grace of God three large poplar trees grew just before the embankment. We ducked behind the trees as the lead bull roared through the alder brush, the rest of the herd in hot pursuit. It looked like he was going to find us, so in total panic we both let go a volley from our shotguns into the air. The bull stopped dead and the others piled up around him. We chambered another round as he stood snorting steam, his eyes red with rage, panting heavily like a steam boiler.

We didn't know whether another volley would further enrage him or send him packing, so we stood in a standoff. If he came further, we would end up in water-filled gum-boots in an icy river, and likely drown. I don't remember ever having been so scared.

We remained perfectly still. After five minutes, he probably wondered why he was there, so he turned and wandered back into the pasture. We loaded our gear into the canoe, abandoned the hunt for the day, and went home to do our laundry.

With these memories swimming in my mind, I cut through the snow in my skates and leapt onto the ice, gliding over the wondrous blue expanse.

It was stunning! I passed Aunt Doy and Uncle Artie's house, all the while peering into the lit windows and remembering the countless hours of delight I'd spent with them. Imagine skating for miles of open ice, between islands, and looking down through two to four inches of crystal-clear ice as the sun set on a perfect snowscape. I passed the tip of the island where I used to fish, then passed the island with the barn where we had been charged by the herd, passed the pool where my brother Allan and his wife and I had caught perch on one of their trips from Utah, passed the natural duck blind, then passed through a channel and into open river.

While the sun was still up, I looked down and saw a good-sized fish lazily swimming just under the ice. I couldn't see if it was a trout or chub.

When the sun dropped behind Mount Currie, the village lights glistened through the snow along the banks. My strides got longer and more efficient as I drank in the cold air and the beauty of my homeland.

Passing near open water where the currents were strong enough to prevent freezing, I decided this was an unnecessary risk. With a light breeze on my back, I turned back. As I rounded the final corner by the tip of the most westerly island, I saw the lights of my neighbourhood. Downriver were the Fredericton Bridge and a wide expanse of clear, smooth ice. This was a wonderful capital city of university and government; an old city of settlers, Loyalists, English, Scots, and Irish; of beautiful churches and warm, friendly, honourable people. I bathed in the cold air as they sat down at the tables of their wonderful nineteenth and early twentieth-century houses.

Exhausted, chilled, and filled with life, with senses overflowing with Christ's beautiful creation and intoxicated with freedom and safety, I walked into a warm home, a warm meal, and a warm bed.

Cabins and Camps

> Scholars have long known that fishing eventually turns men into philosophers. Unfortunately, it is almost impossible to buy decent tackle on a philosopher's salary.[1]

Until the age of thirteen, I spent my happiest days in cabins and at camps. Because it was a huntin' and fishin' culture, you needed a place to hunt and fish. Everybody had a cabin, or access to one.

Nowhere is this culture captured in more hilarious satire than in Patrick McManus' *A Fine and Pleasant Misery*. Amazingly, he proves that from the mountains of Idaho to the Canadian Maritimes, the culture is utterly homogeneous.

The Noonan Camp had been in our family for probably seventy-five years. It was a three- to four-mile walk off the Richibucto Road toward a beautiful little stream by the same name. The stream curved right past the front door of the cabin, and a hundred yards from it was a clear spring that provided drinking water. The log cabin served at least four generations of Neills for trout fishing and grouse, pheasant, and deer hunting.

> I became a philosopher at age 12, after a scant six years of fishing. One evening at supper I looked up from my plate and announced, "I fish; therefore I am." Perhaps awed by this evidence of precocity in a young boy, my stepfather turned to my mother and asked. "Is there any more gravy?" Thus encouraged, I forgot about philosophy until I went off to college.[2]

---

[1] Patrick F. McManus, *Never Sniff a Gift Fish* (New York, NY: Henry Holt, 1983), 20.

[2] Ibid.

Uncle Artie took me there in the fall nearly every year from the age of ten. Tragically, when I became "too cool" in my teens, I stopped going. Uncle Artie was a cook and loved to feed people until they needed their stomachs pumped, and that's what he would do at the Noonan Camp. At night, he would tell me and my cousins stories about the Dungarvon Whooper, and of Artie's escapades as a cowboy with his black horse, Midnight.

Of course, Artie was never a cowboy (rather, a grocery salesman and distributor), nor had he ever ridden a horse in his life, but until the age of consent I never knew that. He would make me furious by telling me that he would have to stop on his horse and wait for my dad (also a cowboy) to catch up. He would laugh lustily and infectiously as I loudly protested.

Artie was so dear to me. He had a twinkle in his eye and a love for life that was utterly intoxicating. Without him ever saying it, I knew he loved me and enjoyed having me with him. A staunch conservative, he used to cheat at Scrabble and cards (just to provoke me), tease me, feed me until I burst, and spin an endless trail of stories that kept me enraptured.

The Noonan Camp was your typical trapper cabin—rectangular, with a peak roof and a big plank door to keep the bears out. It had just two small windows, one on each long side, to let light into the wilderness home. The windows had heavy, hinged shutters to cover the glass (again, against the ingenious black bear) with a large, locked food box under the peak over the front door.

As you entered the only door and stepped onto the time-polished plank floor, you would see a Franklin stove to your right, a table and wooden chairs under the window, and pine bunk beds along the back and north walls, along with chairs and a bookshelf. Iron frying pans and burned pots were stored under a kitchen worktable beside the stove, and a massive tea kettle sat on the element. Kerosene lamps and lanterns vanquished the darkness from every corner of the room and the wonderful dry heat and aromatic pine, fir, and cedar smoke permeated every article of cloth. Then there was the stress-melting silence. An old wind-up tin clock graced the bunk-side table for those 5:00 a.m. awakenings. It ticked away lazily in the corner as the fire crackled, hissed, and banged in the stove and a warm, somnolent silence soaked into your bones.

On waking, the camp turned vibrant with old-man jokes, teasing, and the clump of boots on the floor. Bacon and eggs, pancakes, and onions sizzled in the iron pans. Coffee percolated from near-frozen spring water. As the glow of sunrise turned the frost to glistening drops against brilliant red, orange, and yellow leaves, we stepped out into the cold air, checked our shotguns and rifles, planned our paths in hushed tones, and filled the air with steaming breath.

Artie ultimately had an excruciating aneurism at the Noonan Camp and died on the way to the hospital. It is likely from this exact place, and with these exact beloved men, that he would have preferred to leave the world. He had been with my uncles, Don and Doug. When they learned he had died, it is said that the wailing from my uncle Don could be heard a mile away.

Grand Lake

Dad was the first in the family to negotiate a lakefront property from Roop, the sixty-year-old farmer whose family had grown raspberries, strawberries, and a range of root and leaf vegetables for fifty years.

Grand Lake was the largest lake in New Brunswick, forty miles long and three miles wide with spectacular winds and ice breakups. I was born three months premature and was kept alive in an incubator for an extended period. I was such an anaemic, sickly child that I nearly failed Grade One due to absenteeism. Dad, bless him, bought this property to try to build me up. Praise the Lord, the plan succeeded. I became robust in one summer.

With the help of my brother Bob, Dad, Roop, and I cleared and built a cute plywood cabin on the property with a wood-fuelled fireplace for heat, but electricity for light and cooking. It had just two small bedrooms with a big living room and kitchen area. Standing amongst oak, birch, and poplar on a promontory about twelve feet above the lake, it was extremely cosy. The shore consisted of a flat shale outcropping of rock and vertical cliff with little bays, and a beach right below us. Across the lake was the Roberts Point lighthouse. With wooded buffer zones between us and the fields beyond, we'd hear farmers shouting to their horses while ploughing, moving, and harvesting their fields. It was paradise.

I swam, walked, fished, paddled, water-skied, cycled, and eventually motorcycled myself to and from this happiest of places. Family would come and visit us all the way from Toronto. Dad sunk a well which Artie had identified (he was a "water dowser"), and my brother Bob built stairs to the beach, as well as swimming and water-ski floats. Bob fixed everything that Dad couldn't fix himself.

I lived a solitary existence there with Mom and Dad until other members of the family built places nearby—first my brother Bob and his wife Joey, and their kids; then our distant cousins the Manzers (Alder worked with Bob at Hydro);

then cousin Frank and Marie; and finally, cousin Brian would come to stay for a week before they built their own place and I would go nuts with the joy of having a partner in crime.

From wild central New Brunswick thunderstorms to blistering hot summer days when the lake was clear and warm, to the ten-foot mountains of ice that blew onto shore in the spring, the place was spectacular.

Once again, creative solitude defined my life. My family knew how to do everything and tried to teach me. The Neills were independent red Tories, suspicious of government yet lawful (due to biblical requirement). Having come from farming stock, they knew building, electrical, plumbing, mechanical, and business. I absorbed enough to survive later life despite my drift to the political dark side.

We had a little punt, with oars. With a mast and army cot, I turned it into a sailboat. I used to try to play my brother Allan's slightly bent trumpet on top of the rock outcropping, at least until Mom and Dad had had enough. I'd revive Allan's old canoe and walk down to an old steamboat wharf a few miles away. I had a spinning rod, and discovered perch and pickerel that no one else knew were there. I'd walk down to the harbour where pleasure boats were moored and talk with the old family who ran the store that served the local villages and tourist haunts. Mine was an idyllic life: safe, friendly, and surrounded by honourable, hard-working, salt-of-the-earth people in what was to become a rapidly changing world.

We used to get our water from Roop's farmhouse well. It was straight out of the nineteenth century—a stone-lined water well, four feet in diameter, with a wooden log for an axel. A rope dangled from the log axel with a bent-iron handle driven into the end, holding a bucket that rolled up and down into the well. We cranked it up to the surface to fill small-necked apple cider jugs. The well had a cedar-shingled roof over it and looked like something out of an English country garden. Roop would come out with a sweet, friendly, toothless grin. Though a man of few words, he would give us a warm country welcome. I didn't know until decades later that the poor man suffered from severe depression. He was durable, Canadian salt of the earth.

Then there was Dad's Mazerolle Settlement hunting camp. Dad was always able to find a terrific bargain. He had such a charming personality that he could get land and materials for nothing. Mixed with his construction skills, we could have just about anything we needed.

The Mazerolle Settlement was a rough-plank hunting cabin with a peaked sheet-metal roof, door on the side, and windows on the other three sides. The brightly lit cabin sat atop a birch-covered hill on an access road to the far side of a farmer's field. Down a steep embankment behind the cabin, in a gorge with a waterfall, lay the headwaters of Kelly Creek. It flowed approximately ten miles to the St. John River, far above where we lived on Woodstock Road. This was where I did my first serious hunting. When I was in university, my buddies and I would ride our motorcycles to the camp and stay several days.

Dad and the older boys had used it for white-tail deer, grouse, and some fishing. The camp had two stoves in it—a Franklin for cooking and a rectangular box stove for winter. The winter stove was so hot that it could drive you right out into the snow.

We had to cover the cabin's big divided windows with chicken wire, because when we came out to camp there'd be bear-claw scratches six feet high on the wall, all the way to the ground. Bears communicate with interlopers by putting reach-marks high on trees—or, in this case, a cabin—and a bear that cannot reach that high would be ill-advised to challenge the resident claimant. The chicken wire would penetrate the sensitive tissue between the claws and they would thus not break the windows. They could get into anything: cans, refrigerators, and metal boxes. They would ransack whatever they entered.

Once finished university, Allan left for Salt Lake City, Bob got married and started having kids, and Dad eventually lost interest in hunting and fishing. That meant I had the camp all to myself. It had big bunk beds and lots of firewood. We would go out in winter, crank up the stoves, eat like pigs, and hunt the beautiful rolling hills. Mom, Dad, and I went fishing in that area when I was younger, into the beautiful, meandering streams. I'll never forget the pungent aroma of the budding trees. We would scatter and fish before the evening light waned, then rendezvous and compare catches, driving home pleasantly exhausted. If we got home early enough, there would be a late supper of crisp and golden Eastern Brook trout.

In the fall, we would drive out on one of the country roads and walk around in the evening, looking for ruffed grouse or ring-neck pheasant. One evening, when I was about eleven, while standing and talking at the end of a road, Dad pointed out a grouse in the shadow of a low spruce. The folks were so proud of me when I bagged it with one shot from our old 410 shotgun.

The Mazerolle Settlement was eventually burned down by thieves who stole the stoves. Dad knew exactly who did it. He unapologetically walked straight into the guy's farmhouse kitchen and confronted him. Dad was fearless and had been fighter in his youth. He could have had the guy charged, but instead he made him pay and walked out with cash in hand. We never rebuilt. The deed to the property was given to me by my mom on one of her trips out west after I was married. I was so touched. It remains mine to this day.

Those were very different days. As a young kid, I recall coming into the veranda of our little house on Woodstock Road to find a deer hanging right outside the kitchen door. It seems like millennia ago.

These camps and cabins bear romantic memories of growing up, of learning construction, of picking up hunting and fishing skills, of firearms safety, and of the camaraderie of family and friends in the wondrous Canadian outdoors. We learned map and compass, stalking wildlife, camp life comforts, what to do when you get lost, how to help others in trouble, and loving the wilderness God had given us. We learned how to clean and cook wildlife, bonded with uncles and cousins, and shed the stress of everyday lives. This used to be part of rural Canadian life, and remains so for some today, but only for an ever-diminishing remnant.

Pity…

2

Identity

Allan's Canoe

A DEFINING MOMENT IN MY LIFE CAME WHEN MY OLDEST BROTHER returned from Europe in 1956. I seemed to have to wait forever for him to arrive. I returned home from school for lunch each day only to find he wasn't home yet. My heart would be crushed. I was ten years old and he was twenty-six.

I had given up hope when one lunchtime I came in the back door—and there he was, standing in the living room in front of the fireplace.

"Alllaaaaaan!" I screamed at the top of my lungs. I jumped on him and locked my arms around his neck, determined to never let him go.

Allan was a structural engineer and was in Europe during the Soviet take-over of Hungary. This caused the family no end of distress, but I was blissfully unaware and only knew that I had missed him. While he was away, I moved into his bedroom and would pour over photos he had left from his travels. I wandered and pondered. Except for him, we weren't a family of travellers. My mother had the wanderlust, and Dad did not. Bob wasn't born with it, either, but he travelled widely on business and holidays with his family. I believe it was those photos and my love for Allan that catalysed me into putting a pack on my own back.

Allan introduced me to cycling, canoeing, fishing with a spinning reel, and winter camping. Because of him, I developed an obsessive love for aquatic and field game birds, as well as deer. He used to draw wildlife. In the upper bedroom of our house, I would ponder over his drawings and look out the dormer window toward the river, often seeing ring-neck pheasant feeding along the bank. He gave me my love of the bush.

When he left for Utah and his wife-to-be, I was devastated. Something of himself was left behind, however: an old canvas canoe. There was some rot in the slats and cover, but the ribs were good and the gunnels sound. I used half-round moulding to glue and nail the top of the canvas to the slats. I applied spar varnish on the gunnels and interior and put several coats of red paint on the canvas. Then I had me a *canoe!*

Mom and Dad were used to boys surviving ricocheting 22-calibre rifle shells in the stone basement, as they tried to shoot the occasional rat that came in. Then there was the episode where one of them blew out the front window of the house with a twelve-gauge shotgun while demonstrating duck-shooting. Thus my paddling off into the lake, river, and stream in a renovated chestnut canoe was relatively mild.

Unbeknownst to me, Allan was running British Columbia's mighty Fraser River in a canvas-decked canoe equipped with oars navigated by a one-eyed cowboy from the Chilcotin.

My cousin Brian (who later became a well-known New Brunswick prosecuting attorney and successful venture capitalist) was easily talked into canoeing from Fredericton to Grand Lake, where our parents had cottages. I pushed the canoe into the St. John River from the familiar launch behind the house and picked up Brian on the pier at Fredericton. By 6:00 a.m., we were off down the mighty St. John, weaving through the monstrous booms of logs rafting up by the pulp and paper company.

It was a hot August day and we paddled hard down the lazy river, stopping only to take lunch. We had to make serious time if we were to get to the end of Scotchtown Road by dark, where our parents were waiting with a vehicle to pick us up.

When we got to McGowan's Corner, we had only a topographical map to locate where the arm of a huge bog came close to the St. John. At flood, it would be a raging stream, but it dried up during the summer drought, retreating through culverts and closed off in a large, meandering morass that no one we knew had ever navigated. At suppertime, we pushed and pulled the canoe up and over River Road, through the alder and muddy, nettle-choked streambed, finding water in a tree-shrouded slough.

Once we got into the huge bog on the edge of French Lake, the slough meandered back and forth like a channel of the Okefenokee Swamp. The light was getting dimmer and we could hear the narrow slough come close to the road.

We couldn't see the sky, with the trees forming a cathedral over the channel. At one point, a light rain came out of nowhere, making it even spookier.

We came upon an abandoned cabin along the channel, very deep in the bog. It was straight out of a horror movie, hanging with moss and vines. Its broken windows were just intact enough to harbour unspeakable terrors. Paddling ever faster and harder, we sweated profusely. When the mud grabbed the paddles, we came around one curve to see a herd of essentially wild cattle; they set out in the fields to forage for themselves for the summer, just as the farmers did in the islands of the St. John River.

The cattle roared and rushed into the water. The channel was barely thirty feet wide and we paddled like crazy to outflank them. As they began to bog down in the soft mud, they stopped thigh-deep and stared at us, bellowing. By this time, we could no longer hear anything other than the sound of our hearts beating.

After another half-hour of aerobic sprint paddling, we broke into the wide and deep channel that followed the road to the bridges at the narrows between French and Maquapit Lake. Seeing sky, we breathed something other than swamp air. The breeze blew the mosquitoes away.

Then we were into the wide marshes of the interval islands, paddling toward Indian Point. Our next terror was locating the right channel in the four-foot marsh grass. There were no landmarks and no compass fixes.

Somehow, we got the right channel, and at dusk we paddled into our familiar fishing ground, and into the arms of our anxious parents. We were conquering heroes, because in our families no one had ever attempted this trip.

Exhausted, we collapsed into our cabin bunks as a chop came up on Grand Lake. The waves washed the bog horrors out of our young minds.

Pickerel on a Bucktail

The genius fly fisherman of the family said it couldn't be done. From fighting Atlantic salmon to thirty-inch pickerel to Eastern Brook trout, Cousin Frank was deadly to fish. He was one of these practical, conservative family men, handsome, a highly successful insurance agent, and known and trusted by everyone in central New Brunswick. He had a small office in a heritage building right on the Devon side of the two-lane Fredericton Bridge. The wooden bridge that had preceded it had been built by my great-grandfather, who was reputed to have only used an angle and plumb-line for sighting. University engineering professors had said the wooden bridge wouldn't withstand the ferocious ice flows. He had also designed and built a rink in Fredericton with a non-posted span which the university professors said couldn't survive the snow load. I guess he didn't know it couldn't be done.

Uncle Frank married a beautiful woman (Marie) and had a son and daughter—his son, my cousin Brian, was one of my few summertime playmates at our self-built cottage at Grand Lake. Uncle Frank was reputed to see when the fished turned on the fly, and thus knew exactly when to set the hook. He got fish no matter where he was, even when no one else caught any. He had come to the conclusion that you couldn't get the thirty-inch pickerel that lay under the lily pads and reeds in the interval islands on a fly. But once again, I didn't accept that it couldn't be done.

On one of my long excursions through the wetlands, into the lakes, and up the rivers, I decided to find a way.

On a hot August day, I pushed through the reeds into an invisible pond off one of the main channels. I let the canoe drift, knowing that I could get any pickerel hiding under the lily pads with the irresistible three-hook, red-and-white spoon known as the "red devil," but the challenge was the bucktail fly. Standing in the canoe, I lay that bucktail right at the edge of every lily pad around the circumference of the long, grass-lined pool. No response. I just needed to know if the pickerel were there, so out came the spinning rod. One cast brought out a large dorsal fin. Strike and miss. I brought out the steel fly rod and laid the bucktail fly right at the edge of the lily pad I had seen him retreat to. Bang! Strike, and I had a problem. I had a very large pickerel on the end of a flexible fly rod while standing precariously in a canoe.

A half-hour later, I had tired him out, and he had tired me out. Miraculously, I hadn't fallen out of the canoe. I carefully netted him at the side of the canoe, removed the hook, and slid the living torpedo, the miniature barracuda, back into the water. He shot to safety.

Cousin Frank was a very wise man. He knew fish. When I told him what I had done, he understood but wasn't impressed. I had learned on multiple repeat attempts that you had to agitate them with the spoon before they would strike the fly. That wasn't real fly-fishing to Cousin Frank. Though he never said it, I saw in the twinkle of his eye that he was impressed with my ingenuity. That meant so much to me.

The Loser

I come from a brilliant family with Scot roots, conservative Baptists grown from the soil of central New Brunswick. My grandfather was the mayor of Devon for a time, and my uncles grew fiercely independent, with small business ingenuity; they took on construction engineering, insurance, high-tech genetic animal husbandry, and mill management. They were salt-of-the-earth folks in what at the time was a socially conservative environment.

My aunts were religiously faithful, observant United Empire loyalists which to me seemed strange given the Scottish heritage. On the other side of the family were the engineers who built the highways, bridges (many of them covered), and structural wonders of the time.

As a sucker-shoot on the family tree, I emerged as a free-range radical who voted for Pierre Elliot Trudeau in 1968. When I proudly told Dad on my first exercise of my electoral democratic right, he said gravely, "I cancelled your vote." Thirty years later, I was to learn how right he was.

My own brothers, fourteen and sixteen years my senior, knew the Second World War and went to university with the returning vets who were, of course, in Tom Brokaw's terminology , the greatest generation. Allan ended up being a structural engineer for one of the twin Bank of America towers in Los Angeles, then worked for Pan Am. Bob became one of the most prominent businessmen of New Brunswick, building a highly diversified engineering company (civil, electrical, chemical, mechanical, and forestry) with offices in seven countries, all from an office in his basement in 1964. For this magnificent accomplishment, he received the Governor General's Gold Medal for engineering business. Both brothers were athletes in high school and university—in skiing, boxing, football, and swimming.

Then there was me!

I was the ten-year-old kid who in softball threw the ball to the wrong plate (missing an easy out) and in track tied for last place in the 440-yard dash as the whole school looked on. In a championship rugby game, in front of the whole school I ran for the goal line rather than passing to the wingman, and then after being tackled I accidently "heeled" the ball with my toe, right into the hands of the opposing team at the goal line. I was the one who knocked down the girl who liked me and tore her nylons, then dropped my steady girlfriend in a mud hole in her long party dress as I tried to gallantly carry her in my arms after the Engineers Ball.

Looooooooooooooser!

I cut my head on a tin geometry set. I sneezed into my homework in Grade Two, then closed the workbook until the teacher came by to inspect. I embarrassed an Acadian family with theatrics when they asked me to play guitar for them. In a spastic attempt to be cool, I two-timed my steady girlfriend and got depressed from the guilt and shame when she started dating other guys. I started high school with high grades and was told by the dead-head "cool" guys (greasers) that I wouldn't get any girls if I kept that up, so I listened to them and stopped trying to achieve.

In my family, it was compulsory to go into engineering rather than an arts program, and I was miserable in it. I wanted to study the Vietnam War, the Middle East, and the Civil Rights Movement —not physics and math. Pierre Trudeau was my hero, with his sophisticated appreciation of law, politics, society, and an intellectual aplomb that I found captivating. Suffering through two years of mechanical engineering, in my second year I fortunately learned survey instrument work and drafting; those made me useful when I went west. In fact, my big brother's talk with me, in which he dissuaded me from going into an arts program, gave me an invaluable foothold in the West. However, I paid a significant personal price, one which the Lord knew would give me the necessary restlessness to search for alternatives.

Being unwise, socially unskilled, immature, and unintelligent in the art and science of engineering, I came to realize decades later that my discomfort arose from the brilliance of a highly respected family in which I was ill-equipped to find a role.

We were living in the Bob Dylan, Ian and Sylvia, Peter Paul and Mary era of folk music and protest. After failing spectacularly at piano, I picked up a guitar and became part of the expression generation, with a repertoire of on-the-road songs that helped me wail my way through my protracted adolescence. To survive, I had to get out of Dodge.

3

First Escape

If you miss the train I'm on, you will know that I am gone.
You can hear the whistle blow one hundred miles.[3]
—Hedy West

The Exploratory Phase

I SPENT A MISERABLE SECOND YEAR IN THE ENGINEERING DEPARTMENT of UNB. I still have nightmares about the math exam. In *the* major crisis of my adolescence, I was still working on the aforementioned seriously flawed social assumptions that, in fact, everything would just automatically work out. Remarkably, things were *not* working out.

My identity crisis emerged as I realized that I didn't belong anywhere. The elite students from Westmount, Ottawa, and Toronto (usually exiled by their parents to UNB from failed families and student careers elsewhere) were snobbish and looked at us locals as unsophisticated hicks. As for me? Well, I looked at my non-UNB friends from town as hicks; they were busy setting up businesses, getting married, having children, building nice houses, and starting to accumulate wealth. A rolling stone, on the other hand, gathers no moss.

I wasted my time trying to get sophisticated in science and letters. I learned from some of my engineering student colleagues that what we needed to do was to "bomb Hanoi" and "sick the dogs on them (n-word)." Somehow, that didn't seem right to me. I had no developed concepts to counteract the worldview of the "gears" (engineers).

---

[3] Hedy West, "500 Miles," *Peter Paul and Mary*, Warner Brothers, 1962).

As I proceeded through my "loser" existence, trying to pursue the good life without any money, I became quite isolated and unhappy.

From the midst of my isolation and unhappiness, an idea suddenly came upon me. I could become sophisticated if I travelled. Sophisticated people were well-travelled; ergo, if I went somewhere, I would become sophisticated.

Where was I to go? West, I thought. A close friend, who would later become a close enemy, had lived in Vancouver for a time. His parents were eminently sophisticated and very famous in Canada's artistic community. I said to myself, "Self, we will become worldly and sophisticated in Vancouver." So I sold my beloved souped-up 125cc Honda Super Sport road racer, on which I had nearly killed myself a couple of times, and bought a ticket for Vancouver.

It was the heyday of CN Rail. My buddy Ken and I booked an upper berth, which CN allowed us to share. For ninety dollars, each of us were able to go coast-to-coast with dining car privileges. That meant china, silverware, and linen in an observation car with an attentive steward. From New Brunswick to Vancouver, we slept in shifts.

Our parents and my steady girlfriend saw us off without fanfare or emotion. They either breathed a sigh of "Good riddance" or expected that we would be home in two weeks. In either case, we were off for the adventure of our short and sheltered lives.

In Montreal, we had the first taste of a cosmopolitan city. The Place Ville Marie, where the train disembarked, was unimaginable to a couple of Maritime Bob and Doug Mckenzies. I was constantly paranoid of being robbed, though I had nothing worth stealing. All the girls in La Place Ville Marie were drop-dead gorgeous and dressed to the nines; I might as well have been on planet Venus. We had an eight-hour layover before boarding the CN Transcontinental that night. Little did I know that in less than a year, I would be riding the rail as a dining car waiter on that very line.

I was always an aesthetic, but with such a seriously limited vocabulary, I embarrassed myself. After two tortuous years of engineering, all I knew was that force equalled mass times acceleration, and that you can't push a rope. One of our engineering professors used to say that *this* was all we needed to understand to get an engineering degree. Thankfully, I was never to find out.

I was overwhelmed with the expanse and beauty of "our native land." The experience initiated a change in me whose momentum continues to this day. It is embodied by what was to become my theme song in my secular years: Gordon Lightfoot's "Canadian Railroad Trilogy."

That was the beginning of an illustrious career of great escapes that, by God's magnificent grace, saved my life.

> Oh, there was a time in this fair land when the railroad did not run
> When the wild majestic mountains stood alone against the sun,
> And long before the white man and long before the wheel.
> When the green dark forest was too silent to be real…[4]
> —Gordon Lightfoot

The Yukon

I didn't know that by May, the students in Vancouver had already gobbled up all the summer jobs. There was so much I didn't know. In fact, my life was an *in vivo* field experiment. We just landed in Vancouver and then caught the ferry for Victoria in order to get as far west as the job market would allow.

After the Rocky Mountain high, the Gulf Islands acted as a designer stimulant. I was hooked. I had never seen such a beautiful place in my life and, indeed, I had grown up in a very beautiful place.

Ken and I hit the University of Victoria student placement office and learned that the job market in Vancouver was much more vigorous, but in any event we were at the bottom of the barrel because we had arrived so late. However, because of my engineering education and experience, I got offered a job out of Vancouver. I gave Ken all my leads and then caught the ferry back to Vancouver, setting myself up in the Blackstone Hotel. Now *that* was an education!

I'd never been in a seedy hotel before and didn't understand that various lucrative businesses were conducted out of its rooms and lobbies. Thus, when the girl in the room next door began suffering cardiac arrest or a seizure (evidenced by the sound of undulating mattress springs and pounding on the wall), I was ready to go and render first aid—until the lights came on in my tiny, rural New Brunswick brain. I decided that it was a job for B.C. Ambulance.

In looking for a park to walk in, I was told by the front desk that there was a "little" park due west. He was laughing as he said it. I walked and I walked and I walked and eventually found the sea wall, then English Bay, then the North Shore Mountains, then the Lions Gate Bridge. I walked to exhaustion until the sun went down.

---

[4] Gordon Lightfoot, "Canadian Railroad Trilogy," *The Way I Feel* (United Artists, 1967).

I was intoxicated, discovering beauty beyond description where the coastal range met the Pacific and salmon frolicked in the bay and people were cycling, running, paddling, and swimming. It was nearly midnight before I found my way back.

Along the way, a couple of older men were far too friendly to me, but I managed to politely disengage while attempting to ascertain their motives.

The job I had been offered out of Victoria evaporated, and my attempts to find other options didn't work out. The chill of fear gripped my soul as I lay in bed, hearing the squeaking next door and wondering what would happen if I ran out of money. I was determined not to call for help, but I knew that I could if I needed to; it would just be humiliating beyond measure. I wasn't about to contaminate my first bid for independence with a pathetic call for rescue.

I applied for unemployment insurance and harassed my worker until he got cranky. I have no idea what I was thinking. Was a job supposed to drop into my lap in three days? I had left with only a few hundred dollars and it was being burned up on my noisy Blackstone room. In my panic, I remembered where help came from. Though my adolescent rebellion and adoption of blasphemous language should have made me ashamed to ask, I nonetheless prayed—and it was very earnest. God answered my prayer.

The venture capital and resource-based industry end of town could be found in West Hastings. I went down to look for work and starting with the Marine Building. I took the elevator to the top floor and then walked down the floors, knocking on every door. After the prayer, fear evaporated and my confidence returned.

On about the fourth building, I found a door marked "Norquest Joint Ventures." The project engineer was in the office with a secretary, and miraculously I got ushered into his office. He told me that one of the student surveyors they had hired had taken another job; they were in need of a survey instrument man and draftsman. He asked if I could do stadia surveying, and I told him I could. After lunch, I was introduced to Gordy, a big, curly-headed kid who was a technical school student. He was to serve as the magnetometer tech. Together, we were off to Gastown and East Hastings to acquire boots, clothing, and gear. In two days, we would be heading to the Yukon.

The next day, I met Jim, the cook and all around jack-of-all-trades. He was an education student at Simon Fraser University. Later I was introduced to Bernie, a geeky education student from the University of British Columbia (UBC) who hailed from the Kootenays. I also met Bob, a nephew of hockey great Marcel Pronovost. Others were to join us. The camp was full of Cat skinners

(Caterpillar tractor operators), drillers, prospectors, and assorted tough, hard-drinking, poker-playing forest and mining workers. They introduced me to a fascinating world I would never otherwise have known existed.

Scotty, aptly named for his national affiliation and rich Scottish brogue, was a burly prospector who roamed the valleys and streams amongst the grizzly bears and moose. His hand had been butchered by a British army surgeon in the Second World War. He had been grazed by a bullet across the back of his right hand, and the resulting surgery had made it look as though a half-grapefruit had been sewn onto his skin. For the pain of disfigurement, whisky was his medication of choice.

By God's grace, after seeing the country coast to coast by rail, we set out to drive the full length of British Columbia—all the way to the Yukon. We had to deliver the four-wheel-drive survey panel truck to the worksite. It was an unimaginable experience for a Maritime kid. Total sensory overload. We travelled up through the Fraser Canyon, the Interior (cowboy country), and Peace River country. The Alaska Highway, I learned, was built to twist and turn, thus preventing strafing by aircraft. I also learned the legend of Ben Ginter, who allegedly marked the heavy equipment that disappeared into the bogs and tundra, then built a multimillion company out of going back to reclaim them. Between the gold-rush sagas and Billy Miner train robberies, I had no way to ascertain fact from fiction, but they were great stories.

One night at the magnificent log-built Watson Lake Hotel, my buddies decided that I needed to experience a loose barfly. As I headed up to my room, stepping over a passed-out drunk in the lobby, I heard the start of a fight. Jim's voice rang clear the din. He was protecting the questionable honour of a woman he had picked up at the bar; a falling-down-drunk guy had made the mistake of questioning her integrity. Jim shouted at and threatened him, forcing him to apologize. Then, for a laugh, Jim sent her to seduce me. Into my darkened room weaved an almost attractive thirty-something woman with a powerful smell of beer and stale cigarette smoke on her breath, suggesting that we "get it on." Even in those days, my diplomatic skills were finely honed and I managed, in my innocence, to talk her out of intimacy without insulting her—much to the amazement of my wicked colleagues.

We headed east from Watson Lake along the Cantung Road toward the Northwest Territories. Approximately a hundred thirty miles east of Watson Lake, we set up a tent encampment along the road at a large, wild creek filled with Arctic grayling.

A magnetometer grid had to be laid out in heavy alder brush along the road a few miles from camp. We slashed and tagged lines on a north-south grid between the road (which led to a major tungsten mine) and the Hyland River. We were looking for sphalerite (false galena) called "blackjack." It is indicative of the presence of other minerals; the magnetometer would tell us where to drill, and the cores would tell us what was actually there.

One morning, our semicircle of tents was the subject of a curious investigation by a huge cow moose and her calf. On another afternoon, after crashing through the hair-thick alder brush on the flood plain between the road and the river, we were having lunch in our four-by-four Chevy truck when a grizzly sow and her cub wandered out from the brush we had just been tagging. If we had run into her when crashing through the bush, we would have had our faces ripped off. We dropped our logging boots into her tracks and noted that there were several inches of space all the way around, not including the claws. Needless to say, we retreated to the truck very slowly and returned to work very late.

We then began a stadia survey of the old road to Blackjack Mountain. We did it as fast as we could, since the Caterpillars would be coming behind us to improve it for the big core-drilling rigs soon to follow. A burly, bushy-bearded First Nations guy joined the camp, and he was fearless with his Cat D-8. He would plunge the blade into the mountainside and then back it off with half the Cat's length hanging over the chasm. He played poker just as aggressively.

When we got to the high valley floor beneath Blackjack Mountain (elevation: four thousand feet), we set a large circular camp in the snow on plywood-covered joists and put woodstoves in the tents just as we had constructed in the lower camp. It was a magnificent setting. Rolling mountains ran parallel to the valley east and west, and Blackjack Mountain dominated a ragged set of peaks due west. Part of the peak collapsed into the valley just before we broke camp for the winter.

I tended to have screaming nightmares. My dad had taken me to the town doctor once when he and Mom weren't getting any sleep. Doc Chalmers, a family friend, just laughed and told Dad that I'd grow out of it. The most spectacular incident was the time we were at our Grand Lake cabin and Dad heard a crash from my room. He ran to my bedroom where the bed was under an awning window, hooked up to the ceiling with a screen over the opening. Dad turned on the light and I was nowhere to be found. Then he heard a knock at the back door; when he turned on the light, there I stood outside, still asleep, with the imprint of the screen on my forehead. I had taken a dive off the bed, tearing the screen off its hooks and accomplishing a perfect forward roll down to the woodpile and out onto the dew-covered grass. The next day, we were off to the doctor.

We had a high-strung Quebecois drill supervisor in camp. He was so acute that, while lying on his bunk one night, he looked through the stovepipe hole and saw a grizzly walk by on the mountainside two miles away. The rest of us had to find it with the transit scope. His senses were highly tuned! When at 3:00 a.m. I let out a blood-curdling scream, he'd had enough. This was the third time it had happened, so he walked out of camp. They could get another driller, but they couldn't get another instrument man and draftsman, so my two years of engineering misery at UNB helped me keep the job.

After the driller saw the grizzly (a beautiful, fat silvertip), one of the First Nations drillers, Samuel, grabbed a 30-30 lever-action rifle with only one shell in the chamber and literally ran up the mountainside, chasing the grizzly. As Samuel headed toward the bear, the grizzly took a detour, now sauntering straight toward the lanky, long-haired hunter. It looked like trouble until we saw the animal turn once again back. We lost sight of Samuel. These Native guys were amazing in the mountains. You couldn't come close to keeping up. They strode quietly and effortlessly straight up a mountainside at jogging speed without ever breaking a stride. They never seemed to breathe hard.

About half an hour later, we heard a single shot. It was getting dark and we'd lost sight of both the bear and the man. To take on a grizzly with a firearm like his was bravery to the utmost. To attempt it with a single shot was insane.

We waited over an hour and were discussing a search party when we caught a glimpse of Samuel. From a distance, we could see that he was carrying something heavy over his shoulder. When he walked into our circle of tents, he dropped a wolverine onto the ground. What an amazing creature, and what an amazing shot! The wolverine was about four feet from nose to tail and so muscular that it was difficult to lift with one arm. It had the characteristic stripes down its back, from shoulder to rump, and the most ferocious looking mouth of teeth I had ever seen. We now had the answer to why the grizzly had moved down the mountain toward the man and then circled back up. The grizzly, less concerned about the man, had actually been giving the wolverine a wide berth.

One morning, we awoke to a group of six caribou skirting the camp. Our water source was a beautiful mountain brook which grew into a cascade below us, surrounded by rich alpine meadows. We were camped on a cleared section of meadow. The fireweed, Indian paintbrush, blooming heather, and wild daisies turned the meadow into an English country garden by July.

In my need for solitude, I'd often take one of the camp's three Jungle Carbine rifles and a pack, walking off alone for a day. Not a wise thing, perhaps, but necessary for my mental health given that we were all suffering from cabin fever.

One time, while following the creek that disappeared into a valley to the north, I came across a magnificent waterfall. I then climbed up another cirque of mountains behind Blackjack. In the wonderful, open valley, I found a rotted circle of fencing that had obviously been used to contain horses. As I wandered the verdant alpine meadow, something glistened out of the carpet of flowers and heather —a beautiful, bleached caribou rack complete with intact skull. What a trophy! I put it on my back and carried it to camp to resounding applause. It ended up as a majestic adornment above the door of the cook tent.

Amazingly, we only got out of camp once from May to August, and that was for a day. We were a two-hour drive from the Cantung Road, with no two-way radio communication. By the time we left camp to return to civilization, we were bushed to the point of being homicidal. When the weather was good, we would work seven days a week. Because I was the draftsman, I was expected to map our daily results in the evening. We really earned our four hundred dollars per month.

When we arrived in the Yukon, the ptarmigan had been white, and when we left they were mottled tan, with markings to make them invisible even at close range.

The first snowfall came on August 9. Soon after, people began to leave camp. Poker was our evening entertainment. Surprisingly, I had a summer's entertainment and a constant place at the table with only a twenty-dollar cumulative loss to these skilled poker players. That made me proud. The herring-choker had now experienced a coast-to-coast trip, then up to the Yukon-Northwest Territories border. I would never be the same again.

The Second Escape—the Hedonistic Phase

BOB AND JIM FROM THE CREW AT NORQUEST CONVINCED ME TO APPLY to Simon Fraser University (a.k.a. "The Eye of the Storm"). I had made application and not heard a reply. Bob made a connection for me to find a room in a little house near the university owned by a friend's aunt and uncle. I moved into a bedroom of their little residential house in North Burnaby.

Across the street lived Amber, the blonde, blue-eyed only daughter of a Lithuanian couple. I was introduced to her by the buddy of one of the Yukon crew. She was gorgeous and friendly, only in Grade Ten, and had learned all the womanly homemaking crafts from her mom. Her mother was blonde and blue-eyed as well, and her father was a dour, rough-handed carpenter with bushy eyebrows who was fanatical about salmon fishing. He was a scary guy and only spoke once formally introduced. He wouldn't look me in the eye except for a brief glance.

They were European immigrants, conservative, hard-working, and practical. They had experienced the horrors that were meted out in the Baltic States during the Second World War as the Nazis and Russians wreaked havoc with the borders. The Soviets would occupy and slaughter German sympathizers, then the Nazis would regain the territory and slaughter all the Soviet sympathizers. They had been through hell and wouldn't talk about it.

Amber did the cooking, cleaning, sewing, and gardening so that both parents could work. When I asked her out, I was astonished that she said yes. On a student's budget, we went to movies and parks and bus rides all over the magnificent lower mainland.

The academic undertaking was much more of a challenge than I had realized. Because of my limited vocabulary, my lack of background in art and history, and the fact that I had only a superficial understanding of the sciences, I wasn't a strong candidate for success.

Surrounded by people who were articulate and sophisticated, some of whom were very well-connected (sons of diplomats and politicians), I struggled to hide my ignorance. These people seemed to have read everything that was ever written. It was extremely intimidating, but I decided to apply common sense to fields where sense wasn't common. My instructors seemed to think the approach was novel and creative.

Simon Fraser University had a unique educational philosophy at the time: the seminar system. One hour of lecture was balanced with three hours of seminar debate and presentations under the supervision of a teaching assistant (which I would eventually become). It demanded a lot of the student, and grading was based more on essays and presentations than on exams. One's debating and writing skills were immediately challenged. I have a lifetime of gratitude for that training.

Fascinating and varied people surrounded me in class, but surprisingly I was getting papers back with occasional A grades. This was a monumental encouragement for a country hick like me. However, my hedonistic gene remained dominant.

I got a job in the university library and was confronted with rebellious, long-haired radicals who insisted on making my life miserable by breaking every rule I was there to enforce. God put me in the library to learn how to find what I needed for my course work. It provided a foundation for a lifetime of learning. Though my methods were usually unconventional, I could throw myself into any task if I was allowed to do it my way.

Throughout the process of adapting to the arts and acclimating to the Left Coast, I had a girl next door to comfort me. Amber was wide-eyed and soft-lipped, sweet and sexy, unpredictable and expressive. For no apparent reason, she liked me. I had been introduced to beer for the first time in the Yukon, and my sweetheart's father, along with a neighbourhood friend whose husband was abroad on an acting career, introduced me to the joys of wine, hard liquor, and liqueurs. In the warm, fuzzy glow, Amber and I kissed, cuddled, and necked our way into a passionate love affair that lasted fifteen years.

At this phase in our relationship, I was beginning to embrace the delusional concept that I was a man of the world. All that sophistication I was going to get by traveling had been accomplished—or so I thought.

I met a very cool dude who went to school during the summer and fall semesters and ski-bummed all winter. He wore cowboy boots, and gorgeous girls chased him all over. I figured this was another dimension of being sophisticated. I once again had the urge to get out of Dodge. I developed an academic and cultural experimentation rationale: I would immerse myself in the French language, study Quebecois culture, and get practical experience in first aid. The pleasure of living on skis for a season was, of course, only incidental.

I had applied to various mountain resorts for ski patrol positions and got a response from Mount Tremblant, Quebec. This was the highest of the Laurentian Mountains and an old haunt of the Upper Canada and New England elite. The position required a first-aid certificate, so I acquired a St. John Ambulance course in the evenings and took it all very seriously.

My grade point average came back at 3.2—a miracle, given my ubiquitous ignorance and expectation of failure. I was getting interested in medicine, so now I had another reason to ski bum for a winter. I passed the first-aid course and booked a ticket to visit my brother Allan in Salt Lake City.

My sweetheart cried when I left.

Mom was planning to come out to Salt Lake for Christmas, making it a wonderful reunion after six months away from home. I took my guitar (which Mom had sent from Fredericton) and reconnected with the family as the new, sophisticated me.

Mom had been quite concerned when she heard that I wasn't returning home after the summer and had enrolled at Simon Fraser University. Dad was more philosophical about it and said that I had to do what I had to do.

In any event, it was a very sweet reunion. We had Christmas in a little gingerbread house surrounded by dry, desert snow. Allan and I went skiing at Alta. It was my very first time on a large mountain. The desert winds brought powder snow so deep that you could disappear in it.

I talked to Amber on the phone several times. When her mother answered, she told me I had better come back because Amber had been depressed and inconsolable ever since I'd left. When Amber came onto the phone, she said in a plaintiff, cute, sad voice, "Why did you leave me?" I had no idea I had made such an impact.

After spectacular skiing, the warmth of family, and the Mormon Tabernacle Choir singing Christmas carols in the brilliant surroundings of the Temple, I was pumped for the next leg of my life's journey.

I arrived in Montreal and travelled by city bus to a downtown hotel near the bus station. I left my guitar on the bus. When I got into the lobby and discovered the tragedy (that guitar was my very best friend at the time), I ran out to the street and couldn't believe my eyes. The bus driver drove off his route, around the block, late at night, to deliver my guitar to me. God bless him. This was my introduction to Quebecois hospitality in the era of "Vive la Québec libre."

The next day, I was on the bus north through Laurentian ski country, through towns whose names I had only ever heard of: St. Sauveur, Ste. Agathe, Ste. Adèle, and Val Morin. In the summer, national and international sports car races took place as urban cottagers converged on these magnificent valleys.

I suffered a lonely wait in the lounge at the bottom of the infamous Flying Mile downhill race course, all so I could meet the ski patrol director, Nelson. The strains of "California Dreamin" floated through the lounge as the beautiful people came in after a day's skiing, nursing their hot-buttered rum and dark ale.

It got dark and Nelson didn't appear. I didn't even have a place to stay for the night.

At last, a gorgeous, tall, blonde Aussie ski instructor came in and I mustered up the courage to ask her where Nelson Belmar was. She directed me down one of the snowy streets to a cottage. I knocked on the door and met the charismatic Nelson. He gave new meaning to the term "hedonist."

Nelson flew bush planes in the Caribbean and Central America during the summer and led a flamboyant playboy existence during the winter. He was a handsome, fit, and explosive French Canadian, charming and utterly unpredictable. He ultimately left me in charge of the patrol during his absences. However, acting director of ski bums (many of them travelling Aussies) wasn't an enviable job.

He assigned me to the dorm and introduced me to the other patrolmen. There was a European race-circuit competitor who was a UBC astrophysics student who had run out of money. There was a hippy kid from Toronto who just wanted to ski and subjected us to Beatles albums nonstop for three months. There was the dentistry student from Montreal who was taking a semester off for some unknown reason, who was really there to tumble as many visiting girls as he could meet. Then there was me—the pseudo-intellectual, very serious about the best practices of first aid and the only one who took the job seriously.

The buildings were all heritage design, with panelled wood and French windows. Mount Tremblant was a self-sufficient village of clothing shops, stores, restaurants, pubs, lounges, staff cottages, dormitories, and hotels. It was quaint beyond description, with a carnival atmosphere. Besides, when we passed New Year, it was Montreal Expo '67. The whole world came to our doorstep.

Every Sunday night, the departing tourists would look so disappointed that their time of ski ecstasy was over. For us, it just meant another week of constant skiing.

I'd be up early in the morning, before sunup, and head to the upper staff mess hall. Staff were class-divided into upper and lower staff, with the upper staff being the instructors, patrolmen, administrators, and managers (all bilingual or English-speaking), and the lower staff being the kitchen and cleaning workers, tow operators, and support staff, largely Quebecois-speaking.

A patrol meeting was held on the hill where coverage of all the trails was assigned. Then we went up the chairlift to the Rendezvous at the top of the mountain. It was a delightful, seventy-five-year-old octagonal log building with a crusty seventy-year-old resident cook. It had a huge copper funnel fireplace right in the centre. There was a stone hearth where people could sit and warm up while staring into the snapping, crackling, and highly aromatic pine log fire. The planks were smoke-stained. An old-fashioned crank speaker and headset telephone hung on the wall, to receive accident reports and locations for ski patrol responses.

Mount Tremblant got ferociously cold at times, but also had a January thaw (very brief) and times of heavy snowfall. These factors played in some key events in my time there.

Imagine skiing all day, attending four or five accidents per week, carrying a casualty down a moguled hill in a toboggan, being treated like a hero with every call, and then closing the hills at the end of the day… and being paid, fed, and housed to do it. Mind you, the pay was only $250 per month.

It was the best job on the hill, perfect except for the occasional ugly and complicated injuries, or the 250-pound men in a toboggan on ice, the substandard equipment, and often having to transport a casualty alone. The rescue toboggans had no braking mechanism; they were basically a smooth fibreglass shell with keels, and yokes of very thin aluminium attached to the fibreglass stretcher with rivets only. Bad news!

When I'd get close the Flying Mile, I'd stop at the top of the last pitch and look over the magnificent Laurentian valleys and the village lights along the winding mountain road. I could see the little circle of habitat buildings at the foot of the chairlift. They had warm, welcoming lights. We would clomp into those buildings with our ski boots, then put on our knee-high, fleece-lined après ski boots. We'd sidle up to the table where my buddies raised a glass in celebration of a successful day of snow-borne ambulance work. We'd slowly nurse our beer or hot-buttered rum and soak in the heat from the huge stone fireplace with wooden logs, smoke, and utterly mesmerizing crackle.

It got so that we walked poorly in street shoes because we'd become so accustomed to the lateral stability of a high ski boot.

Several memorable accidents come to mind.

One time, late on a very cold day as the light dimmed, I was called to an accident on a long beginners trail called the "Nansen." I arrived to find a group of stern friends and family surrounding a thirty-something woman whose left leg was literally curled around so that the toe of her boot pointed at her groin. Three people comforted her, and as I approached, one of them arose to preside over the rescue.

I could see that probably all the ligaments in her knee were torn and that the ankle was fractured—and most likely the tibia and fibula, too. She expressed discomfort but not excruciating pain, so I was afraid she might slip into shock. I had to move quickly!

We had a long ride to the bottom of the hill and the contorted limb couldn't be stabilized properly for a rough toboggan ride. I therefore made the prudential judgment to uncurl the leg and put it under traction. I explained to the family what I intended to do and that I would need their help. They agreed grimly.

We covered her and got her as warm as we could, then with her permission I put my ski boot into her groin for leverage and uncurled the leg slowly until I had a strong pull on the straightened leg. She only whimpered at what should have been excruciating pain. All we were issued were wire-mesh splints. I put significant pressure on the limb over the heel and instep once it was straightened. Having set the bandages in place, I then instructed the family to tie them off above and below each probable break site, as well as the knee. The triangular bandages went over the elongated splint to keep optimal traction.

We gingerly lifted her into the toboggan and the family escorted me down to the warming shack and a waiting ambulance. The family thanked me for the assistance.

Several weeks later, I learned that the people I had *thought* were the injured woman's family were actually doctors and nurses from a hospital unit and were there to observe me. The moment I had showed insufficient competence, they were about to take over. They didn't need to, however, and instead wrote a letter of commendation to Nelson and the Mount Tremblant administration, which Nelson read in front of the team. That's why he put me in charge of the ski patrol when he was away. Praise the Lord that I didn't know who they were, or it might have affected my confidence.

At night, I would arrive at the upper staff mess hall for supper and all the mail would be in a heap on a table by the entrance. One ski instructor would search the pile and call out the names of his crew, and a ski patrolman would do the same for us. Well, with all the studs in the room (as well as some striking female ski instructors, including the beautiful Aussie), our guy would call out "Roger" every third letter. I ended up with a pile of perfumed mail by my plate virtually every evening. What a blast!

Another spectacular, but medically insignificant, series of accidents that made us look like heroes came one day when the T-bar at the top of the North Peak[5] had a lazy retraction spring. When people stepped off the T, it would sometimes recoil and bop people on the head with the two protruding bolts, breaking the scalp. No one sustained any serious injury before we got it stopped. The scalp bleeds like a stuck pig, so these people would come to us with blood streaming down their faces looking like they were going to die. All we had to do was put two antiseptic fingers on the lacerations, and it would stop instantly. Then we would clean up their faces (many very pretty faces) and look like neurosurgeons. Such fun!

The day of the spring thaw was another matter. The temperature rose precipitously and a lightning storm came up, with yellow arcs licking up and down the chairlift cables. One of the tow operators was struck and burned quite badly.

I was in the Rendezvous when the call came in. I lifted the headset off the ancient crank phone when it rang, then heard the report. As I hung up the headset, lightning struck the wire and came down the log wall, blowing the phone off the wall. My ear had been attached to that phone only seconds earlier.

The storm cleared and the temperature dropped twenty degrees, turning the mountain to ice. We didn't have enough equipment to handle the volume of lacerations, sprains, and breaks that occurred. We rotated the toboggans as fast as we could to get people off the mountain. By the grace of God, no one got hypothermic before we got them down to warmth and medical care.

We had a manmade disaster when, on a warmish day, the Rendezvous fire could do nothing but smoulder. There must have been a downdraft in the flume

---

[5] This was a cable-pulled T-bar with a shock absorbing spring that the loader would hold. Two skiers would allow it to be placed under their buttocks, and it would pull them up the hill.

chimney. Someone decided to get it going with a can of kerosene, all while people were huddling around the stone hearth with boots and clothing on the ledge waiting to dry. As the resultant fireball tried to escape the funnel-shaped chimney, people screamed and boots and jackets were scorched. Only by divine providence did those tinder-dry beams *not* catch fire. The last I saw of the perp was him skating aggressively down a steep pitch off the Rendezvous hill, to avoid detection in the ensuing chaos.

One of my many fatal character flaws is that I suffer from an excessive sense of personal responsibility. I still feel guilty for the Second World War and my mother's pain at childbirth. One time when the director was away, a temporary patrolman hadn't done as I instructed him and covered a trail in the final sweep at the end of the day. In the previous year, rumour had it that a pregnant woman had been left on the chairlift when it shut down, and she and her infant froze to death. The prospect was a nightmare to me. I canvassed all the patrolmen and confirmed that all the trails had been covered. It was going to be a ferociously cold night.

For me, there was no alternative. I put on my snow boots and climbed the two-thousand-foot unswept trail after dark, calling out, "Ski patrol!" It was a beautiful, still night, but I was worried. I zigzagged up the trail in the event anyone had retreated to the bush. At about 10:00 p.m., I clomped into the Rendezvous and startled Charlie, the elderly resident chef. We checked the thermometer outside and it registered –50 degrees. The air was utterly still.

We had a drink and I walked back down the trail. I half-enjoyed the stunning beauty of the moon-bathed Laurentians, but then fell into my bed. I was soon up in the morning to act as director of the team again. Needless to say, I could have decked the negligent patrolman. But he didn't care. He was only there for the skiing.

As powder and ice turned to sugar-snow in the spring, we would sunbathe during our breaks. Soon, it was time to think of leaving.

I had a cousin, ten years older than me, who was a model in Montreal and had an A-frame in the Laurentians. When I contacted her, she said she was driving down to Fredericton the next weekend. She picked me up at Mount Tremblant and we spent a night at her lodge. In the morning, we drove her '65 Mustang down the beautiful St. John River to Fredericton.

I was going home as a new man, and all was well with me once again. This second great escape had been an unbridled success.

On the Trains

From small-town New Brunswick college boy to mining explorer in the Yukon to university student to Laurentian mountain ski bum, I had lived a lifetime in less than a year. After the mind-boggling trip back home, I caught the rail west for the second time.

Because of the Expo year in Montreal, I learned that CN Rail was hiring staff for the transcontinental run to Winnipeg. I immediately made application and was accepted!

I was trained for dining car and cafeteria duty. My class included ten other trainees, mostly students. One guy was an existing car steward, who I realize now was probably sent back for sensitivity training. He was a fanatical trainman and knew all the history and specs of the engines, but he had zero emotional intelligence—and probably was an obsessive compulsive. He understood locomotives, but not people.

Our bevy of college students learned about the proper presentation of linen, silverware, and china; how all the appliances worked; the hierarchy of authority on the railroad, which was almost paramilitary; proper dress; taking dining orders without a notepad; and other CN Rail procedures. My first run came only a few days later.

On a dining car out of Vancouver, I had another rude introduction to the raw and unforgiving real world. There was so much I didn't understand about a kitchen, let alone a kitchen on wheels going around corners in the Rocky Mountains at high speed. I didn't understand that there was class warfare in the kitchen, where the blue-collar cooks and sous-chefs deeply resented the often upper middle-class college student waiters.

I didn't understand that these middle-aged sleeping-car stewards and the conductors hated everybody below them and were determined to make their lives miserable. I didn't understand the physics of centrifugal force on rail cars as they went around curves, that the cars closer to the front were subjected to much higher G-forces. However, very soon I *would* understand.

The pressure on waiters was immense. At a breakfast, with four people per table, the permutations and combinations of eggs, bread, and meats was overwhelming without a notebook to refer to.

We were to serve the CN staff first—the aforementioned stewards, conductors, and engineers. What a nightmare! I was their test case. They made the order as complicated as possible and then cast icy glances later when I brought out their food, saying, "That's not what I ordered…"

Meanwhile, back in the kitchen, the cooks, who hated the college boys, put the plates in the oven to get white hot, then place them on the ledge next to two dishcloths, to be picked up by us waiters. They would scowl and yell at us, laughing when they turned away, as we screamed and dropped the orders on the floor. It only took one episode before we got the message.

There was a lot of competition among the waiters for the toasters, and trying to have the toast pop up just as the order came to the ledge without someone stealing it. We had to butter fast, then head off to the table. When my toast jammed in the toaster, the chief steward caught me trying to fish it out with a knife. Stupid! I caught heck for that… big time.

The job was solid, unremitting stress. If there was a mistake to be made, I made it on that first run. I succeeded in charming one of my tables, and they left a tip. As I lifted the plate, it stared back at the whole table. For some reason I didn't understand, everyone went to ice. The tip was small and I had left it visible when I lifted the plate.

It seemed that every time I had a tray of food lifted over my shoulder, we hit a curve. Praise the Lord, I never dumped a load, but it felt like running a gauntlet with six spinning plates over your head while at sea in a Force 3 gale. My greatest fear was that I would drop it on the heads or laps of the passengers.

At midnight, I went to bed in the car immediately behind the engine, which got the full force of the curves. It either plastered me against the outside wall or tried to throw me out onto the floor. At 4:00 a.m., I would be awakened to set tables. While preparing, there was, of course, competition for the showers and mirrors. I put on the compulsory grey flannels (I'm allergic to wool) and starched white shirt before going off to once again be humiliated.

The layover in Winnipeg was wonderful. It's a magnificent city of history, art, music, and dance inhabited by friendly, durable people. CN put us up in a small hotel downtown and we had two days to recover from the previous three on the rail. On the return run to Vancouver, I got my rotation in the cafeteria car, which was much less demanding.

I did my cycle and didn't get fired, which was no small miracle. Before my second run, though, Dad had a heart attack and my brother Bob called to see if I would come home to help with his construction supply business.

5

Our House

I WASN'T HEARTBROKEN TO LEAVE THE RAILROAD. DURING MY STAY IN New Brunswick, my mind was westward, where Amber had remained loyal to me. Her attempts at dating others hadn't sparked her interest.

I alerted her to my imminent return, to resume university for the summer semester. She was ecstatic. As for me, I had scratched another wish off the list: I had lived on skis for a season. However, I had decided that hedonism wouldn't be the way of my life. I could see in the eyes and behaviour of these folks that their lives were vacant. I boarded the transcontinental once again, but this time alone.

Amber and I, with her parent's blessing, got married by a Justice of the Peace in Bellingham on a Saturday in June 1969. We moved into a basement suite on Burnaby Mountain and I returned to school on Monday as she returned to work. I was twenty-one and she was eighteen. We led a passionate, sweet, intoxicatingly varied life as the world morphed—and we morphed with it. We were stunningly immature for different reasons and in different ways. She didn't know it, but I was on my way to becoming a student radical and she was on her way for a rough ride.

I joined the striking leftists at the university. When my name ended up in the press, her boss took it out on her. Thus I helped take over conferences, backed the occupation of the administration buildings at Simon Fraser University, wrote articles in leftist journals, and contributed to international causes. I became a joyless, angry, working-class rebel.

When I finished a first-class honours bachelor's degree, I took us out on the town with a credit card and devoured an entire Peking duck in a Chinatown restaurant. Amber and I rented a cabin accessible only by water taxi at Bamfield on the west coast of Vancouver Island, and cooked up a salmon I caught from my kayak. We camped at Manning Park and fished from our canoe, then kayaked on the local lakes. We drank beer and sang all night on my guitar with our hippy friends. We introduced some professor friends to the coastal mountains and the city of Vancouver city. We also skied Grouse and Whistler, alpine and cross-country.

My first job was at a residential treatment centre for emotionally disturbed youth whose trainers got into gestalt therapy, then primal scream, and then New Age religions. I ran the gamut and became depressed (a requirement of the training) as Amber continued to work with "normal people" in a bank. We travelled to Los Angeles and New Brunswick and attended professional conferences. We had passionate, loving, intoxicating times, followed by financial crises that took us to the bottom.

We moved into a little farmhouse in Maple Ridge and I got some academic papers and magazine articles published. When the residential centre became too weird, I resigned and was unemployed for several months. This left me free to take on the endless self-examination of pop psychology.

Then, by God's magnificent grace, the impossible happened: I got a bursary from the provincial government to conduct a study of residential care. It all hinged on a one-hour interview on the last day of applications for the newly opened graduate studies program in sociology at Simon Fraser University. Hallelujah!

On weekends, we rented a log cabin on Hollyburn Mountain as I adjusted to being a teaching assistant, another source of income. From the depths of depression and weird New Age religion, I rose to become a graduate student and teacher in a rational and mentally challenging environment. Because of the bursary, I came out of my master's degree with, for me, the best job on the best team in the best community psychiatric service in the country.

For the first time in our lives, we were going to high-level cocktail parties and receptions with prominent people from the university and psychiatry. We moved from Maple Ridge to a condo in Port Moody to a house in East Vancouver to a suburban three-story house in Fraserview. Amidst lovely neighbours, we had a big backyard with fruit trees and a garage. I began to be known in the field of psychiatric social work, and we even bought a recreational property in the mountains near Chilliwack Lake. I paddled white-water in the river and climbed mountains. We enjoyed the mountain life all four seasons. It was a fast but unsafe life on credit, with cycles of crisis and recovery. I had put us at risk physically and financially on many occasions and dismissed Amber's practical attempts to get me under control.

Then I became a Christian. Can you imagine? She had met me as a rural, conservative student and seen me morph into a fire-breathing Marxist atheist, then a pop-psych existentialist, then a social-democrat grad student, then a clinical supervisor on a community mental health team, then a minor published author, speaker, and researcher, and then a mountain-obsessed builder and renovator, paddler, and climber. Then I did the one thing that was right: I came to Christ. It must have seemed like just another gig to her, but He was the only *truth*. Everything I did intruded into her life, because she loved me. As a new Christian, I was naming the Name, but not walking the walk. She saw the hypocrisy, I'm sure, and finally the "light" went out!

I had carelessly snuffed out her love in my self-absorption. I didn't realize that I had emotionally abandoned her, deeply embarrassed her, and destroyed our precious, fragile love with a sledgehammer.

My mistakes were horrible and I said things that make me fall on my knees in tears to this day. I was so insensitive and neglectful. My life was taking off and I'm sure she must have thought she had no part in it. We had decided not to have children, but I realize that it was never settled. I was emotionally gone and she was left all alone. Everything I did must have terrified her and convinced her that I no longer loved her. Nothing could have been farther from the truth.

I loved her from the very core of my being, but I stopped expressing it. I focused on myself and not on her. I abandoned her. I never thought it was possible for her to be unfaithful to me, because it wasn't possible for me to be unfaithful to her. The guilt would have killed me. What I meant as trust, she experienced as disinterest, neglect, and being taken for granted.

She had said to me that she felt unsafe in our marriage, that she felt lonely. I dismissed these tender cries. Had I heard them, it might have saved our relationship. I was in denial and paid the ultimate price: the light of love went out of those beautiful eyes.

There are few horrors worse for a man than coming into your home and finding that the love is gone, that it's an empty house, that it has no meaning. I squeezed the love out of that beautiful young woman by self-preoccupation, insecurity, and pride.

The grief that consumes you when you lose the one you love can only be described as open-heart surgery without anaesthetic. I have seen men who hate sharks because they drive away salmon. Such men rip a shark's belly and dump it back into the water. It swims away with its entrails exposed.

That's what it's like. The woman I loved was gone.

I'll be alright if I don't have to face the world again.
And if I never love again, I'll be alright.
And if I never love again, I'll be alright.[6]
—Gordon Lightfoot

---

[6] Gordon Lightfoot, "I'll Be Alright," *The Way I Feel* (United Artists, 1967).

Antithesis

6

Revolution in Action

SIR GEORGE WILLIAMS UNIVERSITY WAS TO ERUPT IN 1968–69, AND SIMON Fraser University was soon to follow.

The B.C. Social Credit (Socred) government created a university of spectacular futuristic design by architect Arthur Erikson.[7] The movie industry was to have a heyday making sci-fi flicks onsite. With its elevated quadrangles and prefab concrete-and-glass austerity, not to mention its open concourses and Parthenon staircases, it was a perfect backdrop to the twenty-third century.

Sitting atop Burnaby Mountain with vistas of the Burrard Inlet and Indian Arm Fjord, it was probably Canada's most spectacular university setting, with the North Shore Mountains dominating the skyline.

I was almost a charter student when I registered in the fall of 1966. During my first semester, I would leave the library at 1:00 a.m. and hitchhike to the bottom of the mountain. Mule deer would frequently be feeding just down the bank from the bus stand. The shoulders of the mountain provided a habitat for bears and cougars. People often got lost on the north side and perished from falls and hypothermia. The Lower Mainland Archery Association Range was located there. While running their bush circuit, you might as well have been on the Sunshine Coast. It was so wild.

---

[7] "Global architect, Arthur Charles Erickson was a passionate advocate of cultural awareness, and a fervent explorer of human and natural environments. His buildings, though remarkably diverse, share deep respect for the context, incomparable freshness and grace, and the dramatic use of space and light. He has brought to his work an understanding of the community of man that, when filtered through his insightful mind and fertile imagination, gives birth to a singular architecture that is in dialogue with the world" (from "Arthur Erickson, Architect," *A Portrait of the Visual Arts in Canada*, December 17, 2010 [http://fredericks-artworks.blogspot.ca/2010/12/arthur-erickson-architect.html]).

For a small-c conservative government, the Socreds were remarkably tolerant and risk-taking in approving SFU's structural and academic design, which I'm sure they deeply regretted later when an academic Marxist was installed as chair of the Social Sciences department. Dr. Tom Bottomore, an eminently honourable and courageous man, split the department evenly between right- and left-wing teachers and professors. This was to allow the dialectic process to generate a vigorously emergent synthesis: truth. What it, in fact, did was blow the department apart in just three years. The explosion generated a flash of intense heat and light, leaving many "dead and injured" amongst the metaphorical rubble.

Up until that time, it was the most vibrant learning environment one could ever imagine. Halls were filled with union leaders, Communist Party chairpersons, gorgeous female students in see-through blouses, and radical feminists. There were political visitations from the left-wing superstars of our time: Herbert Marcuse (New Left political philosopher), Jerry Rubin (liberation theatre), and representatives of Eldridge Cleaver of the Black Panther Party.

The unimaginable phenomenon taking place throughout this social upheaval was a Christian outreach to the hippies and beach bums in Southern California by a pastor by the name of Chuck Smith. The mainline churches tended to reject their presentation and behaviour, not seeing them as a culture to be reached. After the Spirit moved through this man, thousands of long-haired, foul-smelling, barefoot hippies were waiting to become Calvary Chapel pastors and conservative talk show hosts. Today it reaches the tattooed, drug-addicted, body-pierced, green-Mohawk youth with the love of Christ. But I digress.

The Vietnam War was going badly and the Soviet-sponsored Communist bookstores in Vancouver were standing-room only. There were revolutions in Latin America, Africa, and Asia. Mao's "great leap forward" (actually backward) was taking place amidst what seemed to be a global phenomenon. In other words, *we were winning*. It was a carnival atmosphere of drugs and sex and rock n' roll to the glory of the revolution. Now this was a religion I could believe in!

The once hated and feared Russians became our comrades, and life in the Soviet Union and Cuba wasn't the way Radio Free America portrayed it. The gulags were a myth and the Chinese Cultural Revolution cleansed the Communist movement of bureaucratic control, returning the revolution to the people. We were later to learn that it was a genocidal orgy of rape, torture, and mutilation that rivalled few others in history.

We "useful idiots," as Lenin called us, were ready to rally and riot, protest and occupy at the drop of a hat. Every woman, black, Vietnamese, or Hispanic psychopath who got up on a soapbox was a victim of white imperialist racism and couldn't be confronted, even if they were dead-wrong. In the film *Forrest Gump*, Tom Hanks depicts the internal abuse and exploitation of idealistic individuals so well. I got progressively angrier at my government, my nation, my race, and my relative prosperity.

This was Bill Clinton's youth: an epoch of life uncomplicated by humility, integrity, or shame. He injected these characteristics into the White House for eight years to the applause of a significant proportion of the nation.

My classes were extremely exciting, often taught by a Jewish Rhodes scholar who once marched us into the faculty lounge just to embarrass his colleagues. We learned about guerrilla warfare, anarchism, and Mao's brave march. We learned about the courageous comrades of Leningrad and how the U.S. government was really fascist and not democratic at all. We learned about Marx's early work and the theorists who sponsored the Marxist-Christian dialogue and wed Marxism to existentialism and psychoanalysis.

None of this is shocking today, since we have a seventies radical in the White House and listen to the same left-wing railing in the universities and on CNN, but in *those* days there was a price to pay.

In the build-up to a student and teacher's strike at Simon Fraser University, I was quoted in a newspaper article, and received film coverage from a rally at the university. My wife's boss recognized my name and asked her about it, whereupon he allegedly pulled out a file drawer, dumped it on the floor, and told her to get down on the floor and refile it.

When we went on strike, we lost all our student loans and bursaries and had to be reinterviewed and sign a disclaimer in order to reregister. My East Coast family was very worried. Their idiot, hedonist son had become a fire-breathing Marxist atheist. My wife's mother and father, who had survived both Nazi and Soviet occupation during the war and had seen relatives summarily shot before their eyes, were terrified. I was labelled a Bolshevik by one of their relatives and essentially expelled from the house.

We tried to barricade the classrooms from the gears and jocks. Fights broke out in the concourse as the jocks organized to remove the barricades. Chairs flew, there was screaming and bloody noses—not part of one's normal coursework—and students occupied the administration offices. Ultimately, the president of the university slapped a trusteeship on the PSA department.

As all this was happening, a mild-mannered, sweet-tempered Argentinean from Buenos Aires landed in Vancouver to take a teaching position in Latin

American politics. His colleagues had neglected to tell him what was afoot. As soon as he approached a department in chaos, he was asked, by the left-wing professors, to go on strike before receiving his first paycheque, while the conservative faculty petitioned him to maintain classes. He and his wife were devastated. We became fast friends and Amber and I literally saved their mental health by befriending them in the second greatest crisis of their lives.

Pickets were set up and the university was awash with plainclothes RCMP, CSIS (Canadian Security Intelligence Service), NARCS, and newspeople. I had come for an education in the social sciences and found myself bouncing around in a bubbling beaker atop a Bunsen burner set on high heat.

When the Canadian Association of University Teachers (CAUT) slapped a censorship on the university for its handling of the department, it created a hiring moratorium. But a radical Maoist revolutionary who had fought with the MPLA[8] in Angola took one of the positions; he didn't care about any of these bourgeois political activities—like strikes—that promoted academic freedom. He knew that power grew from the barrel of a gun (Mao) and that he needed money. In an American university, he had allegedly failed an whole class just so they could "experience Vietnam" and learn the truth about the soon-coming "dictatorship of the proletariat." He was my instructor. He would hold his classes in the Caribou Pub so the working class could see us studying Mao's "Little Red Book."

It was a madhouse, with faculty assigning shoplifting as homework, sleeping with students, carrying on open marriages, committing suicide, and forming communes. Students were dropping out. There were New Age gurus, and people were embracing transcendental meditation. Even the Beatles were going Maoist. Everywhere, you could hear the theme of the soft radicals: "Imagine…"

In other words, it was just like today!

We were dangerous radicals on the social perimeter of an essentially conservative province, nation, and continent. However, we never really knew how dangerous we were. We now know we were being sponsored and encouraged by remarkably grotesque totalitarian regimes who would have incarcerated us first… had we actually been successful. Menachem Begin chronicles this in his book *White Nights*,[9] where in Lithuania the first people the Soviets imprisoned were their allies in the revolution: the Communist Party and labour leaders.

---

[8] The People's Movement for the Liberation of Angola.
[9] Menachem Begin, *White Nights: The Story of a Prisoner in Russia* (New York, NY: Harper & Row, 1979).

Just as now, thirty-five years later, the Obama White House reflects the same political opinions as we had through people like Bill Ayers, Jeremiah Wright, and Juanita Dunn. Just like Obama's foot soldiers, we had "one of ours" as prime minister in our own federal government—Pierre Trudeau. He, too, loved snorkelling with Fidel and hated Republicans. Thus, we had an ideological ally at the highest levels.

Meanwhile, our comrade brothers were committing unspeakable acts of genocide, abortion became a major medical industry, and HIV/AIDS and other rampant venereal diseases spread as a result of free love. There were the Chicago Riots, the Civil Rights Movement (as a bright light), the Weathermen (a left-wing U.S. domestic terror group), the Symbionese Liberation Army, and the kidnapping of Patty Hurst. There were the Kent University shootings, Bobby Kennedy's assassination, and that of Martin Luther King Jr. While America convulsed, the Soviet Union and China gobbled up vast territories in Latin America, Africa, and Asia; they had thoroughly infiltrated Europe and the United States.

I was working nights as a childcare counsellor at a residential mental health facility and going to classes during the day. After the trusteeship and the signed disclaimer, things settled down. With the exception of negotiations with the Canadian Association of University Teachers, to lift the state of censure, classes resumed and I set about finishing my BA. As this was happening, the Biafra War came to an end in Nigeria and the first commercial flight of the Boeing 747 put history's most successful commercial airliner into the air.

Our revolution had failed, but only in a manner of speaking. The trumped-up charges of racism against the professor who catalysed the Sir George Williams riot were dismissed, but students were brought into the university decision-making process. Five of the Chicago Seven, who were charged with conspiracy related to the 1968 Chicago Riots at the Democratic National Convention, settled in favour of the lesser charge of incitement across state lines. The Nuclear Non-Proliferation Treaty was signed, to the benefit of the predatory Soviet Union. Three Weathermen blew themselves up trying to assassinate service personnel at a military dance; the survivors didn't know they were to become frequent flyers in the Obama White House.[10]

The My Lai Massacre in Vietnam seriously discredited proponents of the Vietnam War and appeared to give the left the moral high ground. The propaganda

---

[10] The Marxist Bill Ayers, author of *Weatherman*, was to become one of Barack Obama's mentors and advisors.

war waged by the Soviet and Chinese-Communist-sponsored American and European left proved highly successful. Labour unrest in the United States Postal Service required the intervention of the military. The Japanese Red Army hijacked JAL Flight 351, and the Concord made its first supersonic flight. Apollo 13 was launched, the first Earth Day was celebrated in the U.S., and America invaded Cambodia, setting off a firestorm of international protests. China launched its first satellite. The Kent State shootings created martyrs to the anti-Vietnam War cause.

There was, indeed, trouble in paradise. As has always been the case, the leftist denominations fought for power. Labour had its own interests in the West. Many union members were patriotic veterans and knew on which side their bread was buttered.

In New York, unionized workers attacked anti-war protesters in May as the U.S. labour movement's ideology was challenged by the "New Left." Patriotism and group interest collided with the New Left's globalist ideology. The Tupolev Tu-144, the first commercial airliner to acquire Mach-2, represented a coup for the Soviets, who were in competition with the Chinese in determination to defeat the West.

Thus, after the heady days of the prosperous 1950s, the 1970s introduced domestic and international terrorism. Woodstock kicked off a cultural revolution and the Cold War risked becoming hot at any point. Unimaginable technological accomplishments were competing with news of tribal war, international war, civil war, terrorism, and an internal cultural revolution which successfully undermined the West's resolve to survive. Moral and cultural relativism infected the universities and the left, which couldn't produce viable economies, democratic freedom, or independent technological innovation, succeeded monumentally at what it did better than anyone else: propaganda.

The cumulative effect of this short list of political and social forces manifested in the 2008 election of Barack Obama, bringing the ideology I believed in into the most powerful office in the world. The road was paved by the disastrous Carter and Clinton years, but the *coup de gras* was delivered by Obama.

In the hands of the left's historical revisionists (the rewriting of history in the interests of propaganda), the Vietnam War and Watergate represented coups which live on in the mythology of today's media. Few have the intestinal fortitude to confront it, since the days of free speech and free press have vanished, with a few notable exceptions. People who believed what I did then now fill university teaching positions and the media. The scandalous propaganda-driven demonization of Ronald Reagan, Margaret Thatcher, George W. Bush, the Tea Party, and Sarah Palin—combined with the "immaculation," as per Rush Limbaugh, of Barack Obama—may well represent the demise of American democracy.

My 1970 dream was fulfilled thirty-nine years later. Now it is a nightmare.

7

Koko

AMBER AND I HAD DECIDED TO HOLD BACK ON HAVING A FAMILY UNTIL I finished my bachelor's degree. We needed something small and cuddly to nurture, so we had the dog vs. cat debate. Since her family had owned a nasty miniature Doberman Pincer and my family always had dogs, we headed off to the pound.

Because we lived in a basement suite on the north side of Burnaby Mountain, close to Simon Fraser, we thought a smaller dog would be best—but no Chihuahuas or miniature poodles for me. We agreed.

Workers at the pound led us down the aisle for the heart-breaking choice, and we came to a cage near the end with a cute, fuzzy puppy of unknown breed and a three-year-old terrier-Chihuahua cross. When we looked at the puppy, Koko (he came with that name) stood on his hind legs and crossed the stall with his front feet raised in the air, just like a circus dog. He had us at hello!

As we were soon to learn, he was really a tiny human in a fur coat. He had a little bandit-mask like a raccoon, he was black and tan with a curly tail over his back, and he was terrier size. Energy? Boundless! Intelligence? Utterly remarkable! He had the heart of a lion.

We took him home to my in-laws' place for an introduction. They had a clapboard fence that enclosed their backyard. We let him into the yard and he ran around looking for an escape route. When there wasn't one, he jumped six feet to the top of the fence, hooked his front paws over the clapboards, and used his hind claws to propel himself over the fence and into the neighbours' yard. We heard yelling as he pursued their beloved cat.

Great! We had sprung a juvenile delinquent from death row.

When we tracked him down, he did come to our call, probably being intelligent enough to know where his next meal would come from. That was the beginning of a long life of crime. I was like the father in the film *A River Runs through It*. The father was a pastor who turned fly-fishing into a philosophy of life. He especially loved his psychopathic son (played by Brad Pitt), who heroically landed the prize salmon, then went on to disgrace the family and be murdered at the hands of thugs he had stung in his gambling addiction. Nothing he did could dissuade his father's love and admiration. So it was with me and Koko—and metaphorically, so it was with God's love for me.

Little Koko had a ferocious growl and was very fast. He could put much larger dogs to flight. Perhaps because of this, he was sexually grandiose—no matter how large the female, he was there. When the biggest dogs in the neighbourhood came into heat, Koko would claim them, whether German Shepherds, Dobermans, or Samoyeds. We knew when they were in heat, because he wouldn't come home. If we didn't catch him in time, the city pound would arrest him and we'd have to bail him out. This happened repeatedly, to the point where we didn't know if there would be groceries on our own table for our next meal. But we would have sooner starved than give up Koko.

Eventually we had to consider taking away his "reason for living." Neutering him was a difficult decision, especially for me, because I could identify with the problem and the ramifications of its solution. However, Koko took it well and didn't grow fat and lazy. He would still get arrested protecting the females in heat. It didn't seem to matter to him that he couldn't consummate these relationships.

Koko could smile and keep time. His ears "broke" like a terrier's, with the little flap facing forward. His tan mask made him extremely cute. If you embarrassed him or teased him, though, he would turn his head away with an embarrassed smile.

I know this is anthropomorphism, but remember, he was really a little human in disguise. He had a perfect internal clock. We would let him out the door before we went to work for the hour when we showered and had breakfast. In this time, he explored the neighbourhood, checked in on his buddies and girlfriends, got petted and fed by the neighbourhood ladies, chased a cat or two, and exactly at the time we had to leave, he would appear at the back door and stay in all day. Except on garbage day!

One morning, he didn't appear. We were going to be late for work and we couldn't afford another arrest, so we drove around looking for him. On a median near the house, there he was, munching on garbage. We drove up beside him and didn't say a word. He didn't hear us approach. Then, looking into my eyes while munching a chicken bone, he smiled a hugely embarrassed smile. I started to laugh hysterically. I then reached back and opened the back door, saying sharply, "Get in here…" He jumped into the back seat sheepishly and would smile every time we looked at him. It was scary.

When Amber and I drove across the country in 1968, we bought a little brass "hippy bell" in a craft store in Ontario. They were popular with the Woodstock generation and we attached it to Koko's collar with several strands of bailing wire. We did it so that when he took off into the bush, he wouldn't actually catch a squirrel or grouse, and we would know roughly where he was.

One year later, he came home from his morning jaunt without the bell. The wire had worn through. It was wild enough outside our suite that deer, bears, and cougars had been sighted there. Several people had died by falling off cliffs and down ravines in the coastal jungle above after wandering off the deceptive trails from Burnaby Mountain Park.

A year later, Koko came in from his marauding and had something in his mouth. I was always worried about what he carried in his mouth because of the gross things that interested him. When I reached for his jaw, he spit out the hippy bell. He had recognized it somewhere in the bush, knew it was his own, and brought it home to us. Simply amazing! Dogs don't like having metal in their mouths.

This little guy wasn't only an endearing criminal, sex addict, and serious fighter… he was also a hero. One evening, he came home after travelling his circuit with a tag attached to his collar. It read, "Call the Sheriff," and then had a phone number. Oh no! He had obviously dug up somebody's prize rose beds or hurt someone's dog or cat and we were about to be sued.

With fear and trepidation, I made the call. The male voice on the other end was not hostile.

"That's the smartest dog I've ever seen," he said. The man then recounted the story of how he had been having a party at his house a few doors down from us. His swimming pool didn't have a ledge like most pools. While they were in the house eating and drinking, their poodle fell in the pool and couldn't get out. It had swum itself to exhaustion. It was about to go under when Koko went to the back door, scratching and barking. He created such a ruckus that the dinner guests came to the door. He then led them to the pool, where they rescued the poodle. Our little rebel wasn't just a cute dog; he had significant communication and problem-solving abilities. The smile was for real.

Diamond Head, north of Squamish, was a mountain that eluded me. On one attempt to climb it, I drove up the road with Don, my first and best Vancouver buddy, toward the abandoned ski resort. We ventured as far as we could with the vehicle, then walked to the lodge. Koko was with us; he always was, because he loved to hike. He would travel ten times as far as we did because he'd run a quarter-mile up the trail and then all the way back to check on us every ten minutes before racing off again. It was so cute: he would come to the top of the hill above us and perk up his terrier ears. When I'd say "okay," he would run off up the trail again.

When we got to the only partially constructed lodge (there was nothing but foundation, frame, and plywood), we discovered a four-by-four truck with a juvenile German Shepherd running around.

Koko was a little irritable that day and the big, clumsy German Shepherd kept trying to play with him by knocking him down with his front paws, straddling him and jumping over his back. Koko issued his menacing growl, baring his wolverine teeth. I warned the owner, who said dismissively, "Oh, he won't hurt your dog." I expanded on who, indeed, was at risk. The owner responded, "He's got to learn his lesson." We then continued to talk about Diamond Head and the abandoned lodge.

Suddenly, we heard the most excruciating screech and yelp—there was the poor young Shepherd, with Koko hanging off his upper lip. I yelled at Koko to let go, leaving the Shepherd to run off at high speeds with his tail between his legs, blood dripping from his upper lip. I gave an "I told you so" glance to the Shepherd's owner, and he just laughed, saying, "He learned!"

Another time, in the fall, I decided to try Diamond Head solo with Koko. I rented a little dirt bike, rode it up to the trailhead, stashed the bike, and hit the trail.

I pushed harder and harder to make it, but the early November sunset overtook me. As the sun turned the tortured, glaciated, and saw-toothed Tantalus Range to gold, I lost the trail. I ended up plunging down a brush-filled gulley, because if I couldn't find the bike in the darkness, I'd be stranded for the night, causing Amber untold anxiety.

When I began to recognize my surroundings, a frightening thing happened. Without hearing the bang, a bullet shot the legs out from under me. With excruciating pain, I fell backward, rolled, and began sliding down the gulley on my back, head first. Koko thought I wanted to play, so he jumped on my chest and started licking my face so I would stop screaming.

Once my momentum ceased, I felt for blood and discovered instead a baseball-sized knot of muscle behind my left leg. Amidst the push to get to Diamond Head, I hadn't consumed enough minerals. Likely, a salt depletion cramp had hit me.

I managed to find a stick for a crutch and hobbled down to the logging road and the pile of brush at the switchback where I'd hidden the bike. I worked out the charley horse behind my knee; it remained painful but functional. It was now quite dark, but the last vestiges of sunset gave me some light at this elevation. Unfortunately, I now had to plunge into the darkness of the valley.

I rested Koko between my knees on the tank of the bike and we started down the mountain. When we got into the forest, all I could see was a groove in the darkness where the road was supposed to be. It seemed like we rode forever. Whenever we hit a big pothole or gulley, little Koko bounced over the handlebars or off to the side. I would call to him, he'd come back to me, and I'd lift him back onto the bucking horse. Only by the grace of God did he not break a bone or tear a muscle or tendon. Like I said, he had a lion's heart…

We eventually found the car, and I lifted him onto the front seat. He slept all the way home. When I got to Squamish, I called Amber, who was frantic. Little Koko (a.k.a. Rubber Bones) and I got home without injury.

One warm September weekend, I decided to hike the Cheakamus Lake-Black Tusk-Microwave Tower circuit in Garibaldi Park. Koko and I would take three days and two nights, solo. We rode the hand-operated gondola over the wild Cheakamus River and switchbacked up the pine forest into the lake-chain meadows below the prominent basalt spire called Black Tusk. Koko romped happily and chased mice in the meadows, but he never kicked up a ruckus to draw the wardens.

In the morning, we walked up the buttress, approaching the Tusk (a volcanic plug). I climbed the "chimney" and out onto the narrow ramp to the peak of the Tusk while Koko yelped and barked, trying to find a way up for himself.

It had been a dry summer and the Forest Service had just finished fighting a fire along the Microwave Tower Road. I didn't relish getting conscripted into fighting a fire, but I saw—and smelled—the smoky haze. It looked like the fight was over. As I rejoined my grateful little buddy at the foot of the Tusk, the summer sun hovered just above the horizon. I had intended to camp at the top for the night and walk out in the morning, but it hadn't been a hard day and I still had lots of energy. I started down the Microwave Road, which was very long. As the sun set, I saw the glow of control brush piles and decided it would be a good story to tell.

With the haze, the smell of smoke, and the glow in the darkness, my surroundings were delightfully spooky. But the fire was obviously under control, as there were no firefighters around. They had likely moved on to more imminent threats.

It was nearly 2:00 a.m. when Koko and I got to the bottom of the hill, and we still had a three-mile walk up the Cheakamus Lake Road to where the car was parked. My legs didn't have three more miles in them, so I found a nice flat spot just off the road, threw out the groundsheet, and collapsed in exhaustion.

When we were backpacking together, Koko had a habit of marauding around the camp and setting his boundaries. He would then come to the head of my sleeping bag and whine until I dutifully unzipped it and climbed inside to curl up against my chest. About half an hour later, he would begin to pant from being overheated and whine to get out and relieve himself. When he got cold, he'd whine again to get in… and so it went all night. I so loved the little guy that I didn't mind. He also slept at the foot of our bed at home and never misbehaved.

This particular night, when he got out I heard an ominous, low-pitched, salivating, teeth-bared growl. I was too depleted to be concerned.

My buddy Ian, who knew everything about the bush, told me that the First Nations people bred a dog about Koko's size that kept bears and big cats away from the children in the camp. It was reputed to be so fast that it could "worry" a bear to death—namely, bite and retreat, bite and retreat. The bear could never touch it and would eventually expire from exhaustion and stress.

The next morning, I woke to a wonderful summer day feeling completely refreshed, every muscle sore and yet totally satisfied at another night in the bush. Koko was off harassing the local wildlife. When I went to do what guys do, I saw something through the trees in the distance. I walked toward it and stumbled onto a five- to ten-acre garbage dump. It would have been full of black bears all night; my little bear-dog had kept them eating garbage, instead of me and my pack food.

When we got back to the car, I stowed the pack and boots and put on my moccasins. I called Koko into my lap and he helped steer me down the road, clear of squirrels all the way home. When I would carry him somewhere, he'd sit erect in the crook of my arm with his paws in the "sit up" position. Koko could look into your eyes and read your expression. He was not at all uncomfortable with eye contact, so when I looked at him lovingly in my arms, he would look back, smile, and lick my face.

I had two incidents of near cardiac arrest regarding our beloved Koko. One was when Don and I took him to the Lower Mainland Archery Association Range on Burnaby Mountain, just a mile from my house. It was really wild, and vacant except for the organized shoots. They had a course set where every type of shot was arranged into a bale of hay. It was a hunting-training exercise: you shot through the bush, uphill, across gulleys, downhill, and through stands of trees. Because of the bell, we always knew where Koko was. Don loved Koko as much as we did.

One night while we were at the open shooting range, Koko came out of nowhere just as I released an arrow, converging with the arrow across the front of the target. I froze in horror. Time warped to slow motion as the arrow sailed straight toward his ribs. The arrow went into the grass between his front and hind legs. Don and I both collapsed on the grass, hyperventilating and unable to speak. Koko stopped and looked at us with perked ears, then carried on, blissfully unaware that he had come inches from death.

To this day, I shudder when I think about it.

The second incident happened when Koko was across the street in the bush and saw me. Stupidly, and without looking, I whistled. He ran toward me just as a car came careening down the street. I put out my hand and stepped into the path of the car. The driver slammed on the brakes just as I saw Koko disappear under the driver-side wheel. My breathing stopped, my heart stopped, time stopped. I heard a thump and wild yelping as he came limping out from underneath the car. The driver felt terrible, but it was all my fault.

I knew that Koko had to have been badly injured and was running on adrenalin. I ran toward him. He shied away from me, afraid of the pain of my touch, but then he reluctantly limped over. I checked him and could find no injury. I had seen his little body disappear under the wheel. It was a miracle! Miracle? I didn't believe in miracles! I was a Marxist. I meditated for days over that event. Had Koko died because of *my* stupidity, I never would have forgiven myself. Would anyone?

Maybe I should believe in miracles, I told myself. More importantly, where did forgiveness come from in a Marxist world?

If ever we needed entertainment, Amber and I would put peanut butter on the end of a finger and plaster it to the roof of his mouth. He would lick and lick and lick and lick with exhausting pleasure until the two of us would collapse in tears on the floor. He didn't appreciate the mirth at his expense. He was smart enough to know what was going on. Afterward, he would turn his back on us and retreat to his bed in disgust.

Koko was sixteen years old when he started to have medical problems. He had arthritis in his knees, a pinched nerve in his back and an inoperable tumour the size of an orange in his abdomen. He was on constant medication for the last three years of his life, but he had a lion's heart.

With his daily dose of medications, we could only get it into him with peanut butter, and he stoically complied. Our little black-and-white cat, Cynthia, seemed to know he wasn't feeling well and would climb into his little bed in a cardboard box in the kitchen. She would curl up at his stomach. He would get so hot that he was panting, but he didn't dare move because she would extend her claws onto his front leg. We would have to remove her to give the poor little guy a break.

The poor little soul would lie on our living room couch and groan. Everything hurt. At seventeen years old, he was still bright-eyed, though he had hearing loss and cataracts. But all I had to do was say, "Koko, let's go for a walk," and he would propel himself off the couch and bounce to the door, wagging his tail. He would run and bark and sniff and leak, and when we got back I would have to carry him up the stairs and lift him onto the couch because he could no longer get there on his own. He would resume his painful vigil, trying to find a comfortable position.

When Amber left me, my world collapsed. I had to move into an apartment with Koko, who was very ill. He was so intelligent that I knew our separation would kill him like it was killing me. One morning, I took him for his walk, gave him his favourite food, loved on him, and put him in my lap for a drive to the vet. There had been lots of such drives.

He'd had plenty of needles, but he always became agitated when he smelled the vet. He would lean back and put his head behind my neck; he knew it was going to hurt. The distress he saw in me on this day wasn't new, either, since I had been grieving since Amber had announced her departure. Through his pain, he had tried to comfort me in every way he could. He would come to me and look into my eyes as we cuddled and I cried.

After receiving the shot, I held Koko in the crook of my forearm as his beloved body relaxed from its pain. He looked up at me as I sobbed convulsively, patting his head and caressing his perky little terrier ears down the back of that intelligent black head.

Then he was gone. His jaw relaxed and the light went out of those loving eyes. That tongue that had licked my face so tenderly now lay listless. I tell the story through tears.

This little dog was such a gift. Like so much that God gives, he came from nowhere, undeserved, enriched my life immeasurably, loved unconditionally, and captured my heart forever.

Little hiking buddy

8

Psychiatry– the Perfect Fit

The heart is deceitful above all things, and desperately wicked: who can know it?
—Jeremiah 17:9, KJV

MY CYNICAL, BITTER, GUILTY, SELF-LOATHING, CAPITALIST-LOATHING, government-loathing, prosperity-loathing self had no expectations. My professors had taught me that we were overpopulating and polluting the earth and that an apocalypse was inevitable. It was very religious, all the while claiming that it was anti-religious.

The left lives in a parallel universe of highly structured religiosity. Everything they accuse conservatives of applies to them. In psychiatry, this represents a dynamic called "paranoid projection." One projects all one's socially unacceptable thoughts and feelings onto the other, who is the object of one's vitriol.

Speaking as a recovering leftist, I can state that they are the most highly religious of all faiths, with the least evidence while vigorously denying that they are religious. While claiming scientific objectivity, they make utterly ridiculous ideological assumptions that drive their evidence-gathering, totally distorting the resultant findings. The statistical impossibility of accidental formation of organic matter from inorganic matter should have killed the theory of evolution in its adolescence. Instead, the left burned the witches. Then along came the genome project and the problem of information and complex multibillion-line codes in the genome. This required *design*. They demonized and exiled the opponents of their evolutionary fantasy into their preconstructed gulags.

Then came ideological terrorism, through the apocalypse of global warming. This bleak and preposterous eschatology causes our children night terrors. Once again, they demonize and dehumanize the "rebels" who dare think otherwise, pumping their propaganda through the sewers of the state-sponsored media. Contrary evidence is systematically suppressed and the propaganda machine kicks into high gear. Just as in the 70s, truth is the first victim of an ideological war.

As with all propaganda machines, the evidence is irrelevant. The testimonies of multiple Nobel-Prize-winning physicists who confirm that the theory of evolution doesn't bear evidential fruit get buried alive, just like Saddam Hussein's political victims. After all, we cannot be morally accountable to anyone but our own carefully fashioned gods. Our "gods" look and act just like the phallic and animal-human hybrids of old—ruthless and genocidal like Marxism and Islam, sexually obsessed like our pornography mill, and infant-sacrificing like our multibillion-dollar abortion industry.

I was thus temperamentally and ideologically prepared for the secular priesthood: psychiatry.

During the strike at Simon Fraser University, I needed work. I had a wife, a dog, a cat, and student loans to support. An ad appeared at the Student Union Building about the provincial government hiring childcare counsellors for residential treatment. I applied and waited forever to get an interview, which I blew. Then I waited forever to get the rejection. Then I was told I got the job.

The job was night-shift supervisor, and the staff I had to supervise was me. It was a magnificent introduction to community psychiatry (as opposed to hospital psychiatry) in the best-funded residential facility in the province. The staff was largely comprised of young Turks like myself, some having finished degrees, some working on graduate degrees, some with young families, and some career psychiatric professionals. It was an exciting social-psychological experiment destined to go wrong. But it was, indeed, *exciting*.

We all worked with emotionally disturbed adolescents, surrounded by psych nurses and psychiatrists, but we were all anti-psychiatric in our ideological positions. Go figure!

This was the era of Ken Keysey's *One Flew Over the Cuckoo's Nest*,[11] Thomas Szasz' *The Myth of Mental Illness*,[12] R.D. Laing's *Knots*,[13] and Laing & Esterson's

---

[11] Ken Keysey, *One Flew Over the Cuckoo's Nest* (New York, NY: Signet Books, 1962).

[12] Thomas Szasz, *The Myth of Mental Illness* (New York, NY: Harper and Row, 1961).

[13] R.D. Laing, *Knots* (London, UK: Tavistock Publications, 1970).

Sanity, Madness and the Family.[14] Fritz Perls was up from California, and earlier from the U.S. East Coast, and influential around Vancouver Island.[15] His book, *Gestalt Therapy*,[16] had taken British Columbia by storm, and his disciples flooded into the area. Those who hadn't jumped off the cliffs at Esalen, California—or rather, stepped into the "existential void," as Fritz called it—now enrolled in Cold Mountain Institute as pop psychology was wed to eastern religion and occult practice on the fertile ground of the youth-cult revolution.

Aimless, morally confused, culturally relative youth like myself found that the socialist revolution didn't come immediately, as we expected. Evil capitalism didn't collapse with our dope-smoking, fornicating, Age-of-Aquarius attack on it. The revolution must have been taking place in the empty space between our naval-gazing ears. Over one generation, we retreated from the unsuccessful socialist revolution into the psycho spiritual "garden of earthly delights," brought about by the products of modern drug labs, eastern religion, and psychological technology.

> *…that we should no longer be children, tossed to and fro and carried about with every wind of doctrine, by the trickery of men, in the cunning craftiness of deceitful plotting…* (Ephesians 4:14)

Since the existential void of gestalt therapy was frightening, sometimes life-threatening, and less than productive, a less ethereal technology was required. Enter Arthur Janov and *Primal Scream*.[17] Our colleagues spent fortunes sitting in oversized chairs and getting in touch with their inner child, re-entering the latex birthing canal in California, Vancouver, and on Vancouver Island. John Lennon and Yoko Ono were allegedly among Janov's patients.

After a decade of making promises of empirical research that would prove Janov had found the cure for neuroses, the peer-review-authenticated research never materialized. The limelight disappeared.

Well, the void hadn't done it, and screaming your guts out in a plastic womb hadn't done it. The God-shaped hole remained. Enter Subud, an Indonesian

---

[14] R.D. Laing and [First Name] Esterson, *Sanity, Madness and the Family* (London, UK: Penguin, 1964).

[15] Martin Shepard, *Fritz: An Intimate Biography of Fritz Perls and Gestalt Therapy* (New York, NY: Saturday Review Press, 1975).

[16] Fritz Perls, *Gestalt Therapy* (Gouldsboro, ME: Gestalt Journal Press, 1992). Originally published in 1969.

[17] Arthur Janov, *Primal Scream* (New York, NY: Dell Publishing, 1970).

Muslim technique whose *latihan* resembled Janov's primal scream. It provided technical "abreactive therapy" which had continuity with Janov's teaching. More importantly, it filled the religious void, the need for structure and models of behaviour, and a foreign cultural identity for over-indulged, guilt-ridden, self-loathing, middle-class North American young adults fresh out of Woodstock.

> We are star dust, we are golden,
> But we've got to get ourselves back to the garden…[18]
> —Joni Mitchell

With Subud, that was *it* for me. I had become depressed seeking my true self in the internal garden of personal emotion and religious fantasy. Finally, my neo-Marxist, analytical mind kicked in. I was out of there after two years. I had completed a first-class honours bachelor's degree in political science, sociology, and anthropology. I'd also picked up experience and credentials that would provide, unbeknownst to me, the foundation for a wonderful career.

A year after I left residential care, Jack Webster, a crusty old Scottish investigative journalist and talk-radio host, got wind of some of the anomalies at that very expensive provincial residential facility, and blew the lid off it.

By that time, I was in a brand-new phase of academic pursuit, one that came out of a miracle God performed when I didn't even believe in Him. That miracle, against all odds, started a career at the Greater Vancouver Mental Health Service (GVMHS), and eventually at British Columbia Provincial Mental Health Services.

The miracle began in a Simon Fraser academic department administration office and later unfolded over a hospital bed at Burnaby General Hospital.

After leaving residential care, I found myself between jobs for a few months. In my search, I wandered into the admin offices of my old university department. The administrator, Pauline, who had been in place since long before the strike, remembered me. What I didn't know was that these were the very last hours of the very last day for applications for a newly reactivated graduate studies program.

Pauline asked me what I was interested in and I told her—political philosophy in nature. She told me that the last position with the most prestigious professor in the department hadn't been filled, and he might be interested. The professor, Dr. Ernest Becker, was a prolific author with encyclopaedic knowledge. He had pretty much read everything in art, science, and literature, and wove all aspects

---

[18] Joni Mitchell, "Woodstock" (MCA Records, 1970). Released as a single.

of it into his writing. He was truly a renaissance man. He lived in a heritage house in Shaugnessy, built magnificent classical furniture to perfection. Becker had been caught in the crossfire of the revolution on campuses in the States and moved to Vancouver. Allegedly a victim of S.I. Hayakawa's[19] house-cleaning at San Francisco State, he was a genius who had written remarkable summary analyses in the fields of education, psychoanalysis, social science, and philosophy.

When Dr. Becker interviewed me, he was understandably unexcited about my topic (Marxism, existentialism, and phenomenology), though he was intimately familiar with the controversies. What he *was* interested in was my experience in psychiatry, about which he had also written extensively. I told him of the conceptual dilemma I had observed in the social psychiatric model of residential adolescent treatment. I formulated the ideological contradictions between the tenets of social psychiatry (Maxwell Jones[20]) and gestalt and primal therapy (Frederick Perls and Arthur Janov). This captured his interest. He stated a profound truth: "Do empirical research in your thesis, not theory." Before sending me away, he told me to read everything Erving Goffman had ever written. He then agreed to be my senior supervisor, and within days I was a graduate student with a teaching assistant position, about to study something that might be of enduring significance to the fields of psychology and psychiatry.

After my first supervisory meeting at his home, I never saw Dr. Becker again. He went into rapid decline with cancer and died during my studies.

Once more in my life, the God of creation performed an impossible eleventh-hour miracle for me. I wasn't even a believer—but I had a problem. I had no job, no money, and a wife, but I seized the opportunity, as I had done so often in my life, not having the foggiest idea what I would do next.

At the residential treatment centre, we young Turks gave the lovely nurse administrator a perforated ulcer. Somehow, God bless her, she didn't see me as

---

[19] "Samuel Ichiye Hayakawa (July 18, 1906–February 27, 1992) was a Canadian-born American academic and political figure of Japanese ancestry. He was an English professor, and served as president of San Francisco State University… During 1968–69, there was a bitter student and Black Panthers strike at San Francisco State University for the purpose of gaining an Ethnic Studies program. It was a major news event at the time and chapter in the radical history of the United States and the Bay Area. The strike was led by the Third World Liberation Front supported by Students for a Democratic Society, the Black Panthers and the counter-cultural community, among others" (from *Wikipedia*, "Samuel Ichiye Hayakawa," October 24, 2013 (http://en.wikipedia.org/wiki/Samuel_Ichiye_Hayakawa).

[20] Maxwell Jones (1907–1990) was an enthusiastic developer of the therapeutic community concept in Britain, as well as the U.S. Additionally, he made an attempt to extend these concepts outside the world of formal psychiatrics. His book, *Social Psychiatry in Practice* (Middlesex, UK: Penguin Books, 1968) was reference reading in residential care.

one of the perpetrators responsible. Amber and I came to visit her in hospital. By this time, I had already resigned, over which she expressed regret, having seen me as a voice of reason.

She so appreciated our visit and gift, and that was its own reward. But there was to be another. Visiting her at the same time was a psychology consultant for the provincial government's Mental Health Services.

The consultant was very interested in my thesis and my senior supervisor. He told me to write a proposal for a provincial government bursary. I expected a one-time bursary of a few hundred dollars, but in fact the funding was continuous for the course of my studies. In exchange, I had to commit to work for the province an equivalent number of months. That stipulation guaranteed a job for me at the completion of my studies.

Money problem solved! The teaching assistant salary and the bursary meant I wouldn't have to work full-time. It was a remarkable gift from God, and I didn't even know Him yet.

I so enjoyed my education, and it showed in my grades. I got to study what I wanted and apply it to my life, something most people never get to do. My first graduate paper got published, and so did my second graduate paper. These weren't big psychiatric journals, but it was a start. An abridged version of my thesis was published in an international psychiatric journal, and several of my short stories appeared in local magazines.

Every master's degree and every PhD I've ever heard of has ended up being an acute political nightmare. Mine was no exception, but I loved the topic, and all but one member of my supervisory committee were impressed with the thesis. The one antagonist brought my thesis into his political conflicts with the dean, but they were solved relatively easily.

Praise the Lord, I got through it and received accolades from my chairman at the completion of my defence. I came out of university to get what for me was a dream job. The psychiatric team I worked for was university-affiliated and designed very early in the community-psychiatric movement by a well-known American psychiatrist and researcher, Dr. John Cumming.

Greater Vancouver Mental Health Service was the envy of the nation, because it was a carefully designed, integrated, deinstitutionalization model in which we partnered with the provincial mental hospital, general hospitals, community mental health teams, and relevant non-government organizations (NGOs) toward achieving community rehabilitation and reintegration of the seriously mentally ill as they were released from the provincial mental hospital.

We were studied by some of the most prominent researchers in North America, with frequent tours from Europe and Asia. Vancouver hosted a series of high-profile international conferences after the National Institute of Mental Health (NIMH) declared war on schizophrenia.

Brain-imaging technology was showing remarkable promise, and psychotropic medications were improving exponentially. The clearly neurodevelopmental, biochemical, cerebral-structural, and physiological substrates of schizophrenia were vanquishing the myths that had been driving the field for decades. Schizophrenia was now dignified with major medical discoveries, and those who worked with them and their families were no longer considered the "losers" in the field, but rather an elite group who believed there was actually something we could do to change the duration, course, and outcome of schizophrenia.

Some of the best and brightest young medical minds were getting interested in large-scale epidemiological studies, such as the International Pilot Study on Schizophrenia (IPSS). Practical psycho-social interventions—such as the clubhouse model from Fountain House in Manhattan, skills training, and psycho-educational models from the University of California at Los Angeles (UCLA), the University of Southern California (USC), London's Social Psychiatry Unit, and Toronto's Clarke Institute—were achieving impressive results in controlled psychiatric research. Money was becoming available for genetic markers and predictors studies. Brain post-mortem studies in England yielded fascinating structural, functional, and biochemical findings in the understanding of this enigmatic condition.

Provincial Mental Health Services, in concert with Vancouver's municipal government, decided that we might have a marketable product, since our integrated inpatient, outpatient, and community-care system constituted an enviable model at the same time the U.S. was reviewing its own service delivery system. Our province and city could benefit by drawing the world to its doors.

Thus the Schizophrenia 1990, 1992, and 1994 conferences brought the world's best neuroscientists, epidemiologists, psycho-pharmacologists, research psychologists, and biochemists to Vancouver, along with NGOs, patient and family support groups, and treatment professionals. This was quite remarkable in that it was the first time researchers, practitioners, administrators, patients, family members, and decision-makers brought their best knowledge and experience to bear at an international conference on the heretofore neglected condition of schizophrenia.

I had the privilege of presenting multiple workshops over these three conferences, rubbing shoulders with those who had written the books I read. It was intoxicating. It was the heyday of psychiatry in British Columbia.

This field was perfectly suited to the optimization of my strengths and minimization of my weaknesses. I was invited to the research committee, audit committee, and geriatric services committee of the GVMHS and various advisory committees of my professional association. Yet I badly needed the reality-verifying hands-on work that informed my supervisory role. We were doing individual and family psycho-educational groups, training for our non-profit partners, as well as individual reality-adaptive-supportive psychotherapy while monitoring medical health, medication, therapeutic efficacy, and side-effects. We also arranged emergency admissions to hospitals and set up housing, volunteer, education, and rehabilitation placements. The case managers were the hub of the wheel and took very personal and professional responsibility for forty to sixty seriously disturbed adults usually suffering from refractory psychotic or major mood disorders. Our mandate also applied to those with challenging psycho-social needs such as poverty, the loss of housing, the absence of social networks, and addictions.

Because we did outreach into the community, we had some very interesting incidents. For example, one day a call from a distressed wife came to the office, and as usual we dispatched a psychiatrist and mental health worker. As they walked up the front stairs of a house, they saw that all the slats had been kicked out of the veranda railing. Allegedly, the worker (a nurse) heard a click as she spoke to the terrorized wife who was talking through the chain on her door, hearing her say, "Uh-oh, he's got the gun." The nurse was tall and slender and the young psychiatrist who accompanied her admitted that when he heard the dialogue, he said, "We'll be going now." He backed slowly down the stairs, assuring that the nurse was between him and the door. The team went into uproarious laughter when they heard him tell the story with self-deprecating good humour. He was short and portly and the imagery was hysterical since the nurse would have afforded no protection at all. The story ended well, with a psychotic husband successfully apprehended and treated and no injuries resulted.

Then there was the time I attempted to do a preliminary assessment on an elderly eastern European man who had just lost his wife. According to the neighbours, he was exhibiting signs of dementia. I knocked on the door and rang the doorbell for about twenty minutes, then shouted the man's name through the mail slot. After another wait, I heard scuffling on the other side of the door as the dear old man tried to let me in. Since he didn't appear to be succeeding, I leaned down to look through the mail slot only to see distinct anatomical features of an elderly naked man. Another successful intervention got him into care.

On another occasion, I nearly got "smoked" by an elderly Baltic lady who had just lost her husband. Her landlord had reported hearing strange sounds and screaming from the apartment at night. Due to some miscommunication, the psychiatrist didn't arrive at our rendezvous. Without him, it was very difficult for the Mental Health Act to be brought to bear on the situation, even if there appeared to be "danger to self or others." I walked up to the door and prepared to knock, then hesitated. I didn't have the papers to do anything without the doctor, so I walked away.

It likely saved my life.

The next morning, an Estonian-speaking community nurse came to the door and declared her name through the closed door. The dear old woman who lived there opened the door and allegedly said, "Yes, dear. It is so good you spoke my name and didn't knock. I've had a shotgun and rifle aimed at the door all night, and if someone had knocked, I would have fired…" Surprised, the nurse looked and, indeed, at the end of the apartment hall was a chair leaning against the wall with a loaded twelve-gauge shotgun and 22-calibre rifle. Not long afterward, as the nurse had tea with the sweet old lady, the police arrived. She was admitted to the hospital. She became floridly psychotic at night after having been a pleasant and sweet little old lady all day long.

The mentally ill in the community commit fewer crimes of person than the so-called normal population and are more likely to be recipients of acts of violence than commit them. Unfortunately, when a rare incident does occur, it ends up as front-page news, giving a false impression.

Most exciting was seeing people get well, people who twenty years earlier would have had the proverbial trip to Riverview (the province's psychiatric hospital). Though the work at Riverview during the 1980s and 90s was excellent, with the young Turks working in concert with the old guard to turn it into a centre for excellence, it had a foreboding appearance and has since been the set for many Hollywood horror films.

To me, the practice of community psychiatry brought satisfaction beyond measure. In one instance, a young man who was self-medicating with marijuana had been hearing voices since his early teens. He had become somewhat wild and rebellious, ultimately deteriorating into a serious psychosis which put him in a psych ward for several months. After discharge, he came into licensed residential care, to a twenty-bed unit that I was responsible for.

Licensed residential facilities had nurses on shift during the day, a nurse administrator in charge of clinical care, and a solid complement of experienced mental health workers for monitoring symptoms and engaging the clients in active rehab. The environment was casual and normalizing. We made efforts to have clients spend as much time in the community as possible.

Residents had their medication administered until they were able to administer their own under supervision. Then, as they approached discharge, they received skills training in independent medication management.

Once acclimatized to living in a social environment with nineteen other residents, they began in-house activity programs which included psycho-educational programs on the nature of psychiatric disorders and their management so that they could take responsibility for it from an informed position.

Then there were skills-training programs in stress management, social interaction, conflict resolution, addictions, and work-preparedness. After what was often an arduous process for psychiatrists and team members—trying to find the right combination of medications in the right doses to maximize therapeutic effects and minimize side effects—clients began to improve and return, in stages, to real life. When the clinical and behavioural problems stabilized, clients returned to ever-increasing personal responsibility.

The NGOs (for example, the Canadian Mental Health Association, Lookout, the Coast Foundation, the Schizophrenia Society, the Mood Disorders Association, Pioneer Community Living Association, and New View) played a crucial role at that point. They provided community life experiences through clubhouses, where everyone chipped in to maintain the work crews for the house and did community construction and repair projects on a contract basis. They also provided thrift stores and government-funded programs with volunteer jobs and rehabilitation placements.

Once the people had returned to life successfully, more independent living became possible, including competitive housing or transitional housing. These were usually small single-family dwellings in residential neighbourhoods where clients, who still visited the mental health centre for monthly follow-ups, had their own rooms in a normalized environment, living with three or four others with only four to eight hours per day of paraprofessional input. The remainder of the time, they maintained the house independently, which demanded significant interpersonal cooperation and daily living skills. There were no nurses on-site and an in-house staff would attend from 8:30 a.m. until perhaps 3:00 p.m. They were supported by special and general emergency numbers but able to maintain themselves over evenings and weekends. Success usually depended on reliable medication compliance.

After an average of two years, these individuals usually demonstrated the skills necessary for them to maintain their own subsidized apartments with only occasional visits from a mental health worker. Clients maintained routine mental health centre visits, and eventually the goal was that they be supported in finding employment, and perhaps even cancelling the subsidy.

The entire enterprise was highly demanding and satisfying work. Watching someone progress from active psychosis to successful symptom management, and then to active community engagement and ever-decreasing support, was wonderful for both the client and the worker.

I had clients who were dead in the water, floridly psychotic for four to five years, and still made the transition through the residential options. Over a period of two or three years, they moved into competitive employment and independent living. One very delightful but symptomatic individual kept an immaculate apartment and held a warehousing job where he never missed a day's work in six years. He had previously been living in his car, filthy and psychotic. While in residential care, he appeared nonresponsive for over five years. He then emerged from the darkness.

Having a resourceful, insightful, and supportive family was a major positive prognostic indicator. Basic pre-morbid functioning and personality traits were also predictive. One young man progressed through three years of residential care directly into subsidized housing. After a couple of close calls with alcohol, he landed himself an apprenticeship which put him in line for a six-figure salary. He was highly successful at all features of his work, including handling fragile raw materials worth more than ten thousand dollars apiece.

After a terrible decade of poverty, untreated paranoid psychosis, and raising a daughter on her own, one middle-aged woman progressed to the point where she procured an apartment, disability pension, and part-time job. Her daughter, who understandably had episodes of drug abuse and acting-out behaviour, stabilized with extended family support. Our client supported her through school and technical training, and she became a skilled worker in industry. After five years, our client attended a family function and her sister reported (in tears) that she was unrecognizable from her period of active psychosis, thanking us profusely for giving her sister back to her.

Progress most often didn't occur in a straight line. We would have to assist clients through terrible setbacks with periodic medication noncompliance, followed by descent into active psychosis, episodes of drug and alcohol abuse, and occasional loss of housing. There would be certifications under the Mental Health Act, restabilizations, and legal charges. Given the standard load of forty to sixty seriously and persistently mentally disturbed individuals per case manager, when several clients got into distress at the same time I would be running my feet off trying to find enough hours in the day. But the outcome was profoundly influenced by a long-term trust relationship with the client.

One client whose brother also suffered from schizophrenia (and ultimately committed suicide) maintained a professional position in a major corporation for twenty years, and the company stuck with her through episodes of acting out, police chases, and certifications to Riverview. She was ultimately pensioned. One client had been a commercial airline pilot until symptoms became evident to his crew. He had completed all his flight training and functioned well for several years but nonetheless suffered from a major psychosis which he was able to hide. The JAL Flight 350 crash in 1982 demonstrated that it could happen, but safeguards are now so rigorous that the travelling public is kept nearly perfectly safe.

So many times, a client would call me and I would determine, because I knew him or her so well, that they had gone off their medication and were headed for trouble. The client and I were a team, but only if we had a trust relationship. Building such trust took time. They would call me because they knew I would *know* what was going on with them. Though they would fight me, many would relent, and thus repeated hospitalization could be prevented. The challenge was to intervene sufficiently early to help them get back on track before the psychosis so interfered with their judgment that they no longer trusted us.

The whole system functioned on trust. The psychiatrists and physicians came to trust our judgment because we knew the clients so much better than they did. We spent on average ten times the number of hours with them than the psychiatrists did. The psychiatrists had to cover all six hundred clients at the centre. We would see them in a natural, non-clinical environment. I came to realize that the client in your car or the client in a coffee shop was a different person than the client in your office.

When we had to ring the alarm, psychiatrists were would respond like lightning. They had the authority and skill with the client to prevent an unnecessary crisis, certification, hospitalization, or retreat to the dumpsters (literally). We, on the other hand, could trust the remarkable skill of that unique breed of psychiatrist who loved to see the client in a normalized context and bear the responsibility and risk of being called on the carpet for what a client had done. This could involve anything from self-harm to a suicide attempt to disturbing residents in their apartment to breaches of the law.

When the system worked, nurses, social workers, physicians, psychologists, and occupational therapists all worked together in carefully orchestrated choreography. Community services, NGOs, the welfare department, hospitals, and outpatient departments were committed to preventing deterioration and the need for unnecessary hospital days in general or provincial mental hospitals. In most cases, neither families nor clients were happy with long-term hospitalizations.

However, the need for closed facilities and locked wards remained for a small proportion of psychiatric patients, and access had to be assured.

It was such a joy to see people "melt" from suspicious, aggressive, withdrawn individuals into delightful, warm, and productive people. But, of course, it didn't always happen! Basically, a third got better, a third stabilized, and another third had a deteriorative course. However, the third that remained symptomatic had a much higher quality of life and vastly fewer hospital days. The third that deteriorated could be supported through the process so that the consequences were less catastrophic. Our goal was to have the smallest number of people end up on the streets or in prison.

The heartbreak for professionals and family members when clients couldn't kick an addiction, which kept them chronically depressed, mood-cycling, or psychotic, was tragic. Drug-dealers would prey on these folks and could spot them in a crowd. Dealers would hand out home-delivery cards on welfare-cheque day. The dealers were skilled marketers and manipulators, and their skill could confound all treatment efforts. We clinicians couldn't find the line between symptoms of drug use and symptoms of an endogenous psychiatric condition; further, we couldn't use pharmacology to solve a drug addiction. In some instances, misdiagnosis and the wrong psychoactive medication could be fatal. The utmost caution was necessary.

Then there were the refractory folks who didn't respond to treatment. They often had no insight into their illness, or judgment. If a person was missing both, they were in deep trouble. I had clients with terrible psychoses who, despite being stabilized on medications, refused to accept their illness in the face of spectacular evidence to the contrary. They would take their medication for irrational reasons and do very well at work and social functioning. Others would understand their illness but have extremely poor judgment in relationships and everyday decisions; if they relied on us to help with the decision-making, they would do quite well. Others continued to act using poor judgment and would crash and burn repeatedly, despite successful symptom management through psycho-pharmacology.

In this pressure cooker, it was imperative that colleagues watched your back. We would take up the slack for one another, becoming a well-oiled machine. It was exciting, varied, and rewarding work—but exceedingly stressful! The information technology, clinical recording, and legal demands increased daily, as did the caseloads and caseload acuity.

Unfortunately, the era of relationship-based psychiatry has come to an end. The loss was a fiscal, ideological, and socio-political phenomenon.

As for my thirty-five year career, I loved it and volunteered countless unpaid evenings, weekends, and vacation days without regret. I enjoyed the satisfaction of seeing clients emerge from the darkness and horror of psychosis or mood disorders, of seeing families relax from carrying an insufferable burden. The experience cannot be adequately described in words. I appreciated the immense gratitude of families who had in the past been blamed for these terrible medical conditions or watched their young people languish and end up on the street. That was the bonus for endless unpaid overtime. When the families, psychiatric professionals, and clients became a team, the outcomes were astounding. But when we failed, families broke up, siblings left home prematurely, parents succumbed to drug or alcohol addiction, and a psychiatrically vulnerable individual ended up on the streets—or prison.

I loved it for thirty-five years, working shoulder to shoulder with others who devoted their lives to it and loved it.

But had I stayed another day, I would have hated it.

9

Europe

IT WAS THE OPPORTUNITY OF A LIFETIME… AND I ALMOST DIDN'T TAKE advantage of it.

I had put aside the grief of my failed marriage to work on a family psycho-education project for those suffering with schizophrenia. Because the research showed the uniquely powerful effects of such programs, they had to be duplicable. Videotape had become affordable, and three-quarter-inch tape was still being used in the broadcast media, so committing the program to videotape was a fairly revolutionary idea.

A young neighbour of ours was attending Emily Carr College of Art and Design and needed a class project, so I did a partnership with the Schizophrenia Society to tape a public forum. This included interviews with patients and their families, as well as a behaviour family management package using Emily Carr student actors to demonstrate the skills.

Using student producers, directors, and actors was highly creative both for budget purposes and community education and involvement. Copies of the tapes were sold widely across Canada, with a few copies requested abroad. The project was also written up in *Canada's Mental Health*.

Dr. Louise Jilek-Aall, an internationally renowned Norwegian-Canadian psychiatrist, anthropologist, and epilepsy researcher, submitted it to the Fourth International Congress on Psychiatric Rehabilitation as a forum for presentation in Orebro, Sweden. It was accepted. Greater Vancouver Mental Health Service, who had sponsored the project, paid my airfare, and soon I was off to Europe to deliver a presentation to those who had written the books that inspired the venture.

I was determined to present the paper and do a quick turnaround back to Canada, but Dr. Jilek-Aall told me that I *had* to see Europe. She was very convincing, for which I am eternally grateful, because one month of touring Europe changed my life.

She met me in Amsterdam. After booking into a bed-and-breakfast, she taught me how to navigate the European rail system and visit the best sights in each city. She, her husband Wolfgang Jilek (a well-published and experienced Austrian psychiatrist and Anthropologist), and their daughter had become dear friends of mine and they even visited my mountain home. We were colleagues in the GVMHS and they brought a European perspective into the clinical care of our mandated population. They were very stimulating to work with.

Near Piazzo San Marco, Venice

Thus, I learned the routine of arriving at a city's train station, stowing my luggage in station lockers, checking the city's accommodation listings, changing currency, getting maps, locating bed-and-breakfasts, checking the bus and streetcar schedules, and riding out.

She knew exactly what was most important to see. In Amsterdam, we started off with the Rijksmuseum. As we walked in, before us was the two-by-five-meter Rembrandt *De Nachtwacht*.[21] I was transfixed. In this timeless museum of the Dutch masters, I realized how different the deep historical timeframe of Europe is versus the short frontier history of Canada and the United States. I was breathless, looking at Rembrandt's paintings of the *Neue Kirche* and the *Oude Kerk*. The depiction came complete with period dress, with dogs and kids in the congregation as the pastor preached in the famous church. We later visited that very church and stood in the place where Rembrandt had stood to paint the scene. Five hundred years later, the building was unchanged.

As we went from gallery to gallery, we plunged through time and expressions of faith. I would absorb the emotion of each artist—the Inquisitions, the wars, the political upheaval as Europe emerged from the Dark Ages, the Renaissance, the Reformation and colonial wars, then the Napoleonic era, the passage from medieval social organization to the industrial revolution, and the horrors of the twentieth-century bloodbaths. When we left the museum, I was so profoundly moved that I felt physically ill. These world-renowned sculptors and painters had captured the romance and trauma of their subjects, the luxury and poverty, in light and darkness, colour and texture. I experienced European history in my very body.

We met a friend of Louise's who was an art student. She toured us through the canal houses, artist sections, specialized small museums, and stunning landmarks. The history was captured in architecture and she analysed what made the Dutch "Dutch" in economy, social structure, character, and artistic expression. I had been thrown into the deep end, but with watchful instructors.

Then we caught the EuroRail through Germany to Copenhagen, Stockholm, and eventually Oslo. Magnificent ferries, bridges, and rail stations transfer large numbers of multilingual, multicultural, and artistically, musically and historically educated citizens. It was a place so different from my own, though my cultural roots were there.

In Hamburg, we walked the mall and saw the Institut für Gewerblich-Technische Wissenschaften (the science and technology institute). A generation ago, this superb city had been a pile of smoking rubble, having experienced firestorms and near total destruction from Allied bombing. It was now an ultra-modern international city, a centre for science and technology, research and development.

Next up was Copenhagen, with its ponderous architecture. Louise and I climbed the spire of St. Peter's Church on a cold and windy May Day and saw the

---

[21] The painting has since been attacked with acid and restored.

city spread beneath our feet. The top of the tower's staircase was extremely small. With the wind, it was not a place for the even mildly acrophobic. Stockholm is a magical city, a secular paradise with a strangely high suicide rate. When you see it, you wonder how that could be. The people are stunningly beautiful. All the women, from their teens to their sixties, are fit, blonde, blue-eyed, and gorgeous. It drove me crazy to see how many of them dyed their hair black or red, just to be different. Our bed-and-breakfast had an outstanding spiral staircase with a tiny elevator in the centre; the woodwork and brass metalwork was magnificent.

The bed-and-breakfast was located on a small, closed alley just off an ancient street. On Sunday morning, a brilliant church clarion of hundred-year-old bells chimed out the Lutheran Hymn "A Mighty Fortress Is Our God." I nearly wept.

We toured Skansen, ascending and descending through the historical architecture, from small, sod-roofed cabins dug into hillsides to relatively modern rural accommodations. The harbour lay below us. I was struck with the tangible spiritual vacancy of this perfect Scandinavian city of beautiful people, amidst living history and vibrant culture.

This tour represented a mental collage of spectacular sights, sounds, and aromas—a Viking ship, a royal tall ship, a marine museum, churches, cathedrals, and orchestral and chamber music events under the stars in cobbled squares. We saw sophisticated people, stone sculptures, brass sculptures, wooden sculptures, palaces, and prisons, all infused with art, science, technology, administrations, languages, and worldviews.

We attended an organ concert on a Sunday afternoon in Stockholm featuring two impresarios and acoustics playing in a four-hundred-year-old cathedral. The music soaked into my bones, causing me to weep uncontrollably. The massive pipe organs turned the sanctuary into a reverberating "lung" of praise to the magnificent God. I sobbed convulsively. There were only ten people in the audience.

Right in the heart of Stockholm, I saw a white-water kayaker walk with his kayak over his shoulder. Slalom races were held on the Norrstrom River, gates hanging down over a white-water drop through an ancient bridge. The river curved among the ancient streets and spectators looked down on the paddlers from the street railings.

I was terrified during the presentation in Orebro. As I mentioned, the audience included several of the authors of the books I had cited in the bibliography of my videotape package, and also in several of my published articles. They were the big guns from the London Social Psychiatry Research Unit, the University of Pittsburgh, UCLA, the Clarke Institute, and the University of Southern California. Louise was a stabilizing influence and spoke with confidence; after all, she was very much among peers.

The event was quite a success. A reception for the presenters took place in the prominent Orebro Castle (the fourteenth- to sixteenth-century House of Vasa fortification), complete with banquet tables and staff from Sweden's psychiatric rehabilitation system. I practically floated out of the auditorium after the stress had lifted.

After Orebro, we met up with Louise's brother, a well-known country physician and foreign medical-aid doctor. Together, we caught the train for Oslo, and then Roa, where we went up into the hills. I was permitted to accompany her brother on his rounds through the isolated farms. We then returned to the traditional log *hytte*, where he and Louise had grown up during the Nazi occupation of Norway. The chair I sat in at the kitchen table had once held a Nazi officer who came to visit Louise's famous ethno-methodologist mother (because of her prominence), putting the whole family at risk of being labelled collaborators. They were persecuted as a result and watched by members of the Resistance. They were clearly under duress, and the Resistance officers unequivocally corroborated that fact.

After our time in the mountains above Roa, Louise dropped me off at the train station in Oslo. I was on my own for the next three weeks, to tour Europe solo.

With my rail pass, I planned to spend the night on the train to save hotel bills. I would spread out the map to decide which city to reach next on the overnight run. I planned to see Munich, Vienna, Innsbruck, Salzburg, Venice, and then return to Amsterdam to catch the plane home. During the trip, I lived off the blade of a Swiss Army knife I bought in Innsbruck, as well as a loaf of hard bread, a brick of cheese, tomatoes, onions, and European sausage. I took a cable gondola to the top of a mountain in Innsbruck, then attended a chamber ensemble concert at the Archbishop's Palace in Salzburg.

The train wound through the Austrian Alps, and ultimately took me to the coast of Italy, as a beautiful world rushed by my window.

I found a tiny bed-and-breakfast just across the canal from the Central Train Station in Venice. A young family sang through the passageways of the Venice streets, pushing their little girl in a wheelchair over the cobblestones. I visited Piazza St. Marco, and then enjoyed a pasta dinner and bottle of wine on the waterfront while a lovely breeze rolled over me from the bay. I walked back through the narrow cobblestone streets and over a bridge, hearing the gondoliers sing Italian classics to love-struck couples on the canal below as little lanterns swayed to and fro from the gondola's ornate prow and stern. It was an impossibly romantic city that could pull moments of loneliness from the heart of even the Lone Soldier.

Because I didn't want to risk missing my plane, I took the train straight back to Amsterdam and booked into a small canal house. I had a relaxed day or two to wander the magnificent canals and parks. The park lakes had islands on them with flocks of sheep and towering eight-hundred-year-old church steeples in the background. Gorgeous Dutch girls sunbathed topless in the public parks.

I came home a changed man. I realized that the free-range cowboy existence I lived in the North American wilderness was a dream. I spent every spare moment of my off-work existence building, felling, bucking, splitting, paddling, and backpacking in my beautiful wilderness. For Europeans, this kind of life was nothing but a documentary. I had limitations in language and living—including knowledge of history, art, and music—that comes naturally to Europeans, but they could only imagine my life of pickup trucks, chainsaws, dogs, and bushwhacking through alpine meadows and unvisited mountain lakes. On the other hand, I could only imagine their lives surrounded by antiquity and the most magnificent expressions of the Renaissance Era.

© Synthesis

Close Encounter

AS A BOOMER AND CHILD OF THE 60S, I LIVED THROUGH THE BIRTH OF rock and roll and the attendant idol worship of Elvis Presley, the Beach Boys, and the Beatles. The Beatles' globalist hedonism was much more attractive than the biblical proverbs and reformation hymns. James Bond broke new ground with amoral indulgence in tumbling girls, killing unarmed bad guys with impunity, and drinking exotic alcoholic beverages at every respite from the violence. Sean Connery was cool beyond imagination. Pastors were not.

Thus, in high school, my defection to the world began. I learned to swear, spit, live for fun, date girls, snow-ski, water-ski, go to parties, ride motorcycles, and try to be cool. I failed at the cool part but succeeded in the fun part. The Christian life appeared crushingly boring by comparison.

My advanced degree in the dark side began when I became a fire-breathing political radical and atheist, trying my best to dissuade Christian university students from believing in God. I should have burned in hell for that. One mature student told of how Mao's Red Guard had crushed the hands of her grandfather, a Catholic priest who refused to stop praying. He ultimately died of the injuries they inflicted on him. I was sympathetic but rationalized the sadistic and genocidal Great Leap Forward and Cultural Revolution just as today's students once again wear Che Guevara and Mao T-shirts, dismissing the 120 million deaths attributed to the quest for a global workers paradise.

I remember relishing the blasphemy and stating, "Once you die, that's it. There ain't no more…" Existentialist authors celebrated the freedom of suicide, which always provided a way out if things got tough, while the Marxists praised the brutality of the liberation movements that were coming to enslave a quarter of the world's population. I proudly studied the strategy of urban and rural guerrilla warfare. Stalin's slaughter of twenty million of his countrymen and Mao's genocidal romp through sixty million of his own were just examples (we were told) of CIA propaganda. The propaganda was, in fact, coming from our own side—a profusion of lies told often enough that they are accepted as truth in today's urban mythology.

Thus I signed onto the world's second most genocidal impulse in human history. Today, the first and second most genocidal movements have formed an alliance. Neo-Marxist groups and Muslim jihadists are championed by Lenin's proverbial "useful idiots," who are my age and teaching in the universities of Western Europe and North America. David Horowitz, himself a recovering leftist, has documented it chillingly in his book, *The Unholy Alliance*.[22]

But an ember still smouldered within me. Somehow I reacted when my comrades spoke ill of Jesus. Something about the Bible made it different from all other literature, though my professors put it on reading lists with Marx's *Das Capital* and Mao's little red book.

> *So shall My word be that goes forth from My mouth; it shall not return to Me void, but it shall accomplish what I please, and it shall prosper in the thing for which I sent it.* (Isaiah 55:11)

There was no strength of character or goodness in me that explained why the Christ (Messiah) wouldn't just let me go. All He had to do was put a Communist party membership card and gun in my hand and send me off to die for the revolution like so many others had—uselessly and tragically. It was such a waste of human life and creativity, like those who died for the glory of the Third Reich.

I see it happening again as youth all around the world convert to leftist causes and jihadism as though no history has transpired in the preceding thirty-five years; as though Soviet communism had succeeded; as though the betrayal of Che Guevara and Carlos Cienfuegos by Fidel Castro and the uncovering of the Cambodian and Chinese genocides had never happened; as though the Islamic crusades of the seventh, tenth, and nineteenth centuries didn't leave a river of blood all the way from North Africa to India to Europe—and today, Indonesia to New York City. It's just as though it had never happened.

---

[22] David Horowitz, *The Unholy Alliance: Radical Islam and the American Left* (Washington, DC: Regnery Publishing, 2004).

I speak from experience. When evidence is irrelevant and irrational propaganda is taken as fact, the blindness is spiritual, not ideological.

Professing to be wise, they became fools… (Romans 1:22)

But the dark side doesn't only manifest in the violent excesses of jihad or communist revolution. Our North American and Western European kid-glove fascism makes us think we are good and decent human beings.[23] Those who justly accuse me of pathological naïveté forget that the blood of fifty million unborn is on our hands. Also on our hands are the ravages of pornography, the enslavement of women and children throughout the world to serve our sexual fantasies, venereal disease, Hollywood's celebration of sadistic and masochistic sex, and the plague of divorce and subsequent poverty. These are the diseases of prosperity and possessive individualism gone mad. As decent, middle-class suburbanites, we will stand before God for these monumental evils. I stand in corporate condemnation for these sins, as well as my atheism and revolutionary intent. I have not been willing to actively risk life and career to fight these Western democratic evils.

> *And even as they did not like to retain God in their knowledge, God gave them over to a debased mind, to do those things which are not fitting; being filled with all unrighteousness, sexual immorality, wickedness, covetousness, maliciousness; full of envy, murder, strife, deceit, evil-mindedness; they are whisperers, backbiters, haters of God, violent, proud, boasters, inventors of evil things, disobedient to parents, undiscerning, untrustworthy, unloving, unforgiving, unmerciful; who, knowing the righteous judgment of God, that those who practice such things are deserving of death, not only do the same but also approve of those who practice them.* (Romans 1:28–32)

The Lord is never conventional or predictable. Thus He used my unbelieving wife, a cult horror flick, a communist guerrilla fighter, and unmitigated life success to bring me to Him.

When I was finishing my bachelor's degree, I took a course from an American Marxist who had just come from West Africa, where he had been active with a guerrilla movement. His Marxism was absolutely religious. He had a Maoist

---

[23] Jonah Goldberg, *Liberal Fascism: The Secret History of the American Left from Mussolini to the Politics of Meaning* (New York, NY: Doubleday, 2007).

vocabulary that could compete with any ecclesia-babble or psycho-babble I had ever heard. He was ruthless, self-sacrificing, and disciplined beyond measure. He was ready to kill both heretic and infidel. Missionary zeal was his motivation and a little red bible was his truth. You wouldn't want him watching your back unless you had shown yourself to be a "true believer." He was my hero until I started asking myself: would I be willing to give my life for this?

When *The Exorcist* came out, people were vomiting, fainting, and running out of the theatre. Those days are gone now. We are a generation desensitized to sexual sadism and horror. Every new horror movie bumps up the gross index.

I was unimpressed with *The Exorcist*. I went to the movie and it was very good and I got scared, but it was just a new level of sophistication on an old theme. One night, I came home from night-skiing on Grouse Mountain with one of my professors. I was in graduate school and had been teaching that day and was quite tired. Amber was asleep and I turned on Johnny Carson before going to bed. William Blatty, author of *The Exorcist*, was the guest. He had audio tapes of the actual exorcism which had inspired the book. It was horrifying beyond measure and chilled me to the bone. He played the tapes, and I heard a rapid, back-masked speech with proper rhythm and cadence and a sound that was utterly inhuman. Johnny Carson was visibly shaken, as was I. I couldn't dismiss it.

I spent the night in fits of nightmarish horror and soaked my pillow with sweat. That had never happened to me before. Was there a dimension other than the material world? Was there a spiritual evil? If that was the case, how vulnerable was I to that kind of power? The Bible spoke of literal demons; maybe it wasn't just a metaphor for human evil, as my teachers had stated. My philosophical materialism was shaken, but I soon forgot and returned to homeostasis.

But the idol was fractured.

After completing my master's degree, life was *so* good. I had a beautiful wife, a job I loved (and at which I was excelling), two academic degrees, professional registration as a social worker, and some publications. I was paddling and climbing, and after a long period of student poverty, Amber and I were travelling, laughing, loving, and drinking deep of literal and figurative wine.

Our life was like the Crosby, Stills, Nash & Young songs "Our House" and "Summer Breeze."

Our house is a very, very, very fine house
With two cats in the yard.

> Life used to be so hard.
> Now everything is easy, cause of you…[24]
> —Crosby, Stills, Nash & Young

I knew that with my fundamental lack of character and intelligence, an innate ability couldn't explain this outcome. I was filled with gratitude and had no one to thank.

> Summer breeze makes me feel fine
> Blowing through the Jasmine in my mind…[25]
> —Seals and Croft

One Easter, Amber said to me, "You should take a look at this. It's something called *The Shroud of Turin*."[26] I did, and I was rapt!

I came to learn the stunning accuracy of the biblical account of the crucifixion in the disciplines of forensic medicine, botany, anthropology, archaeology, and history. Christianity, unlike the other major faiths, wasn't just raw belief. In the nineteenth and twentieth centuries, incontrovertible evidence came forward to prove that the biblical accounts were true. *The Shroud of Turin*, by Ian Wilson, wasn't the end; it was the beginning.

Believers could be found in all academic disciplines: McDowell, Packer, Geisler, Price, Missler, and Stoner. Their disciplines included particle physics, statistics, mathematics, archaeology, philosophy, law, historiography, geology, and medicine, as well as from all other scientific, engineering, and social sciences. They came at the Bible from the fields of apologetics and hermeneutics, from a truly multidisciplinary perspective. My mentor, Dr. Ernest Becker, had sought a "unitary science of man" for his entire life. He died before understanding that there *was* one, but it was transcendent and outside the dimension of time and space. The universe was encoded between the covers of the Holy Bible, and verified in twentieth and twenty-first century science. No previous epoch of human history had been able to do it, because the people didn't have the financial resources or computing power.

But God's Word doesn't rely on human proof for its authenticity. It verifies itself. Secular-humanist faith and radical Islam, both antithetical constructs that

---

[24] Crosby, Stills, Nash & Young, "Our House," *Deja Vu* (Atlantic, 1970).

[25] Seals and Croft, "Summer Breeze," *Summer Breeze* (Warner Bros., 1972).

[26] Ian Wilson, *The Shroud of Turin* (London, UK: Victor Gollancz, 1978).

are genocidal and socially malignant, have united to attack not only the faith of Christians and Jews, but their very physical existence. As Michael Horowitz has documented, the persecution of Christians is the number one human rights issue of the latter twentieth, and now the twenty-first century.[27]

> *Then they will deliver you up to tribulation and kill you, and you will be hated by all nations for My name's sake.* (Matthew 24:9)

Concurrently, God has knocked the pins out from under their fundamental assumptions. They are, therefore, without excuse. I was without excuse!

The theory of evolution has been destroyed by discoveries in astrophysics, mathematical probability, and the genome project. Fascism is failing. Marxism is failing. In vitro photography has demonstrated the humanity of the foetus and uncovered the horrors of the abortion mill. History, archaeology, particle physics, historiography, and computer-based code-breaking have established the divine authorship of Scripture.

Dad was right all along! I fought him constantly, but Jesus Christ—HaShem Adonai Elohim, Jehoshua ha Messiach—was exactly who He said He was. Dagon, Ashtoreth, Zeus, Kali, Hitler, Marx, Satan, Mohammad, and the goddesses of Western feminists all demanded human sacrifice. Jesus the Christ offered Himself as the sacrifice.

After repeated demonstrations that man was incapable of saving himself—from the Garden of Eden to the Promised Land, from Solomon's temple to the Babylonian exile, from the Persian return to the miraculous return of the Jews, from the four points of the compass in the modern era—it has been shown that man consistently blows it! In true didactic demonstration, God showed man's failure and provided the redemption Himself. Then He scripted the verifiable story in a love letter written in blood, from the sacrifice in the Garden of Eden, which covered the nakedness of Adam and Eve, to the Cross in Jerusalem two thousand years ago.

I fell to my knees. It was true! It was the *only* truth.

Again, paradoxically, God used a Marxist education, an unbelieving wife (whom I loved more than life itself), a secular career whose ideology was hostile to the faith, a Christian boss, a horror flick, and a crisis of success to bring me to the foot of the Cross.

---

[27] Paul Marshal, *Their Blood Cries Out: The Untold Story of the Persecution Against Christians in the Modern World* (Dallas, TX: Word Publishing, 1997). Introduction by Michael Horowitz.

Since that moment, I have looked into the face of love during times of intolerable pain. I have come to realize that He and He alone can know me and love me. I know that when you submit to His will, He blesses you with joy, and blesses you even more with a serious spanking when you get out of control. But like the incorrigible lamb in the flock that keeps running away to be killed by the wolf or mountain lion, the shepherd is forced to break its front legs, splint them, and carry the lamb over his neck until it heals and bonds to the shepherd. The lamb will then no longer leave His side. That incorrigible lamb is me!

Since my close encounter with God, there has been divorce, death, a seriously broken heart, near-kidney failure, emergency hospitalization, three surgeries, the bedside of a dying father, an end to mountain life, Jamaican horror and success, pride, fall, time spent in the Israeli Army, closure to a beloved career, and motorcycles.

Once again, Naphtali is a deer set loose (Genesis 49:21). This time it was eternal, tormenting separation from the God of life that I escaped… into His everlasting arms.

> *For by grace you have been saved through faith, and that not of yourselves; it is the gift of God, not of works, lest anyone should boast.* (Ephesians 2:8–9)

Man's salvation, indeed, came as the result of a violent act by man, but not of his own design and not from the barrel of a gun.

This revolution happened not only to me, but to tens of thousands of youth all over the world. Chuck Smith's outreach to beach bums, hippies, and the student radicals of Southern California led them to become Calvary Chapel pastors and elders. Concurrently, the underground church in China, the Soviet Union, and the Muslim world exploded under the most vicious persecution. It has exploded again with the millennial revivals in Latin America and Africa. From the Sudan to the Sub-Saharan states, modern Islamist crusaders slaughter them with devotional abandon.

This revolution and genocide, traditionally known as revival and persecution, is not of interest to the global managed news networks, but it matters to someone far more significant: One who hears the cries, sees the blood, and will execute justice.

> *"Do not weep. Behold, the Lion of the tribe of Judah, the Root of David, has prevailed to open the scroll and to loose its seven seals." And I looked, and*

behold, in the midst of the throne and of the four living creatures, and in the midst of the elders, stood a Lamb as though it had been slain… (Revelation 5:5–6)

11

Crash and Burn

BE VERY CAREFUL WHAT YOU SAY, AND ESPECIALLY WHAT YOU PRAY FOR. The Lord said that we'll be held accountable for every careless word (Matthew 12:36). The Lord commands us to be anxious for nothing, but when we fear, we're suggesting that His grace is insufficient to carry us through. We have thus challenged Him and He, in turn, may challenge that very fear with a specific test.

At a previous church I attended, a dear young saint, the son of two elders, got struck down with a severe case of chronic fatigue syndrome. In expressing sympathy to him and his dear wife, who were enduring the trauma of adapting to his illness, I said, "I don't think I could go through such an ordeal." Two years later, I was going through a variation of the same condition.

This happened twice in my walk with Christ.

I was busy getting "famous" and "godly," working 130% at my job in community psychiatry, developing new programs and videotapes, doing research, and writing articles. Then came the workshops for first, second, and third-year residents in psychiatry, as well as med students, community college continuing education workshops, and the conference-speaking circuit. After that, in order to avoid the grief of my divorce, I undertook prison, skid row, and urban storefront music ministries. There was no time to consider what had happened to my fourteen-year marriage with Amber.

I said to myself, "I can do all things through Christ who strengthens me." The super-saints and high performers in my profession did it, so I could do it, too—or so I said to myself.

One thing was missing: the unction and empowerment of the Holy Spirit of Jesus Christ.

I remember saying to a friend who was concerned about my pace, "I'm electric…" Well, God was about to pull the plug. To another friend, who expressed caution about my multiple involvements, I said, "I have boundless energy." God was about to set a boundary. At the time I said these things, they echoed in my ears as a challenge to God amidst trepidation and pride. The Holy Spirit as much as whispered in my ear, "Be careful what you say." I didn't listen.

I knew deep down, amidst my pathological and insecure pride, that I was a loser. This success couldn't be real. I also knew that such opportunities didn't come often, especially to me. Doing what I loved and getting accolades and applause was a new experience for me. I liked it, especially in the wake of my failed marriage!

It had to be from God, I felt. I got to demonstrate competence and touch issues of my faith. I was snowed with positive reinforcement. People were being helped and attitudes were changing. New ideas were being adopted, too, and some were my original ideas. I was sought-after and treated with consummate respect. I liked it!

New opportunities presented themselves, and I accepted them. I was doing God's will, right? This was a blessing, right?

But was I seeking His will? Was I running in His power? Was I mounting up on wings like an eagle? I thought so! That's when my devotional life evaporated.

The days were nonetheless full and exciting. I was up early in the morning and out the door to my job. One day, I paddled to work in my kayak in the morning light—across two arms of the Fraser River. I came ashore next to my truck, which I had left parked on a side road along the river. I loaded the kayak into the truck and drove the four remaining blocks to work. I intended to write an article entitled "Paddling to Work in Vancouver."

In the evenings, I would regularly conduct group sessions for the families of people who suffered from schizophrenia. These groups of often neglected, isolated, ignored, and grieving families were incomparably rewarding. I also took on the Provincial Electives teaching program, and after that the Canadian Psychiatric Association Conference in Ottawa, the Open Learning Agency, and on and on. It was intoxicating! Periodically, I would overnight in the mountains or form a kayak group and scare myself to death on the Chilliwack River.

Every day, I was up and running by 6:00 a.m. I had a varied and meaningful job I loved working with committed and cooperative colleagues. The hours were long, and mixed with seeing ring-neck pheasant strutting outside my office window in the evenings. Sometimes I would grab my customized hollow-body electric guitar, which I got for free in an insurance settlement, and head downtown. I would go to Emmanuel Mission on Cordova Street, where a senior Pentecostal saint would deliver fire-and-brimstone messages for the addicted, mentally ill, and homeless. Rats scurried out from under the pulpit riser and the occasional fight broke out. We fed the guys and gals, providing sandwiches and social time afterward as many shuffled off to bars or to find a quiet place in an alley to shoot up.

We were the first to open up on Christmas morning, as folks we knew from the weekly services drifted in with hangovers. Sweet Christmas hymns drifted down the silent streets, sometimes in a light snow. The coffee flowed and the Christmas treats filled traumatized stomachs and eased the pain of pounding headaches.

I would spent many evenings by reading, writing, and researching suicide rates among schizophrenic clients, the effectiveness of family psycho-educational programs, and the clubhouse model of rehabilitation practiced by the Canadian Mental Health Association, our partners.

Into bed I would go, only to arise to another day of routine community care assessments, interviews, clinical crises, and hospitalizations. Sometimes there were kicking-and-screaming certifications with clients who had become dangers to themselves or others by reason of psychosis or severe mood disorders. Other days were spent in routine planning meetings, case conferences, audit committees, or research committees.

At the end of the day or weekend, I would be consumed with recording the events. Then I'd head off to a little suburban storefront church outreach to apartment-based mentally ill, working with addicts and lonely people who didn't adapt well to church services. The music teams often had skilled musicians, where the praise and worship really rocked. I performed vocals and rhythm guitar; others much more skilled than I would fill in so that it sounded good.

I'd be up early the next day and catch an interprovincial flight to a mental health team in the Interior or the Kootenays, teaching all day on providing psycho-educational programs to families suffering with schizophrenia. There were long periods of routine work, but it was all very satisfying—lots of office politics, interdepartmental politics, provincial politics, and labour relations issues. There were occasions of addicted employees, marital breakdowns, therapeutic relationship indiscretions, and constant change. It was rewarding to see psychiatric patients who would otherwise be locked up in Riverview thriving in the community. This warmed me amidst the stress.

We saw beautiful art produced and watched as the hospitalization rate went down and Riverview Hospital emptied. We facilitated employment and social volunteer work. We saw our clients get married and find permanent and part-time employment. We saw them have children and put on parties. We had Christmas carol singalongs and summer music events in local parks. Our clients and their families would leave our Christmas parties saying they could hardly wait for the summer barbecue.

We were family and shared the joy of success and the heartache of failure.

But the dark side always weighed on one's psyche. There were attempted suicides (some successful), the threats of violence, concern for child neglect or abuse, and the ever-present weight of medico-legal responsibility. Professional and employment standards of practice sometimes contradicted one another, and new acts, regulations, policies, and procedures constantly came to bear.

Sometimes, at one o'clock in the morning, I would point my Ford pickup truck toward Chilliwack Lake and arrive in rain or snow or a full-moon night to open up a cold building, turn on the gas, light a wood fire, and fall exhausted into bed with the sound of the river in my ears. God's whisper in the pines quieted my soul.

Sometimes I would sleep ten hours, then twelve hours at a time. I would wake and go back for another eight and spend sixteen hours asleep. I began to feel sick most of the time. The long sleeps left me waking very tired. I would get every cold and flu that came into our office. The colds became bronchitis, and the bronchitis would require a course of antibiotics—then two, then three.

I started to cut back. I'd say goodbye to a Christian ministry I had planned to work with, then two, then I'd cancel a conference engagement. Pretty soon I was cutting out Open Learning Agency, then community college, then all teaching and speaking engagements.

It was time to drop the writ. My condition was starting to affect my work. I couldn't think, my stress tolerance dropped off, and I felt sick most of the time. After a medical workup and a sleep study, I received the final diagnosis: chronic fatigue. I announced this to my director, who announced to the team that I was taking a medical leave.

This was a stunning, watershed moment. My identity was so entangled with my work that leaving presented a massive blow to my overinflated ego. For all my friends and colleagues, I heard a justified "I told you so!"

Two years later, the building was evacuated of all its workers by the union and Workers Compensation Board. Lawsuits resulted because four people collapsed after me. I had spent more time in the building than anyone else, so it made sense that I was the first casualty. It was declared a "sick building" and the entire team moved out.

Chilliwack Lake

12

Mountain Life

IT WAS THE FULFILMENT OF A DREAM THAT CAME OUT OF THE "CRASH." THE six months I spent off work introduced me to renewed solitude, abandoned from youth. Amidst the God-inspired ego-buster of ill health, I made my Phase One moves. When things changed dramatically at work—my boss was about to retire, I had abdicated my star status, and an organizational re-structuring was afoot—Phase Two kicked in. I was forced to take time to hear His voice.

While on long-term disability, I shut down my city apartment and crammed my life into a five-hundred-square-foot dwelling and two outbuildings I had built. While recovering from chronic fatigue, however, I was plagued with doubts over whether or not I would ever get well or return to my beloved profession. I had forced the Lord to shake my self-confidence.

Be careful what you pray for, as His answer may surprise you. God's fingerprints were all over these unexpected developments, but that insight was yet to come.

Amidst the cold rains of November, while feeling sick, I packed my belongings and transported them in several trips up to the two-thousand-foot level of the Chilliwack River valley, one mile from the wild and technically bottomless Chilliwack Lake.

In order to stow all my stuff, I had to improve, shelve, and furnish the woodshed and workshop. I prepared to turn them into liveable rooms. This served as vocational rehab, but I was still sleeping sixteen hours a day and awaking tired. The result was that I was often significantly depressed.

As the cold rains turned to sleet, hail, and then snow, I watched my world turn from green, grey, and the pale pastel colours of autumn to white over evergreen. Soon the mountain goats would return from the seven-thousand-foot peaks down to the five-thousand-foot cliffs directly above me. However, I wouldn't see them until April because of their perfect winter camouflage.

The accumulated snow slowly climbed to the level of the deck and I'd put on my cross-country skis and glide directly off the back step. Eventually I'd have to step *up* onto the snow as it sought to overtake my dwelling.

Occasionally, some cottagers would come up to the cabins in the area for the weekend and drop in for coffee or tea. I often didn't feel like receiving guests, but country hospitality demanded an open door.

I had some fascinating neighbours: executives from CP Air (pilots and administrators), teachers from University College of the Fraser Valley, a female physician, small business people, and nurses. We would ski together and visit for meals and baking, flaming Christmas plum pudding and the occasional turkey or roast dinner.

My only company most weekdays was the crackle of the scanner picking up police, forest service, conservation, and correctional service frequencies. It kept me apprised of trouble in the valley before emergency vehicles arrived. However, my place was in the relatively steep canyon outflow of Chilliwack Lake, which was known to be even a police radio dead zone. Centre Creek Correctional Facility for Juveniles was only three miles west, however, and they needed ploughed roads for emergency vehicles, and radio contact for security.

A library lined the living room walls and the colonial rocker sat by the window in a little shelved alcove across from the woodstove. After a cold walk on frozen snow, or a cross-country ski on new snow, I'd hang out the stuff to dry, grab my Bible (or another book from the shelf), stoke the stove with fir, pine, or cedar I'd bucked and split myself, and rock… and rock… and rock.

Reading and meditating, while glancing up periodically to see the Stellar Jays or Whisky Jacks, helped heal my exhausted body and restore my soul. These aggressive birds would cause little avalanches in the jack pines as they fought over the seed in the feeder. The sound of the river grew more muffled as the snow deepened, and the occasional big, healthy coyote would amble by my kitchen window. The ever-present mule deer and robust raccoon families were regular friends. All I saw of the cougar were tracks. They were seeking a rendezvous with raccoons. The brown and black bears snored comfortably in their dens deep beneath the warm, white blanket.

God used the sound of the river, the cold wind in the pines, the symphony of cloud, and light in the mountains to lift the burden off my heart, and off my shoulders. It took a long time.

My eyes often snapped wide open in the cold stillness to ponder the fact that no one was waiting for me. No one would know if I fell ill or got injured, until it was too late. There was no phone, no radio contact, and frequently it would take three or four hours to dig out the truck. It was sobering to realize what it meant to be me—the consequence of being a rock, an island, a lone soldier.

***

The constant physical demands of staying warm, getting crystal water from the spring-fed pools at Post Creek, and shovelling paths to the outbuildings and driveway were highly therapeutic. Also, the memories of having this delightful retreat for twelve years flooded my mind. Some of those memories were profoundly joyful, others crushingly painful. Once the energy I *did* have was fully assigned, I'd fall exhausted into bed in the sullen wilds of a Cascade Mountain winter.

What was to become twenty-one years of ownership (Amber and I had taken possession the same Sunday that Mount St. Helens erupted) would fill a three-hundred-page book. A lot of water had flowed under the upper Chilliwack River bridge since this little piece of paradise had become mine. A fifteen-year marriage had come and gone, a speaking engagement and tour of Europe, and multiple trips back to the Maritimes. I would go back with my brothers to see our dying mother, then again fourteen years later to bury our father and liquidate the homestead. I ultimately spent seven years in Jamaica with the Mennonite Central Committee, only to return briefly to this beloved home of mine, on furlough. Before returning from Jamaica (with only twenty-five percent kidney function), I'd sell it from Kingston and never see it again.

My sign-up log, from all those who had borrowed the place in my absence, remains one of my most treasured possessions. The idea came from Uncle Artie and Aunt Doy, who had a cottage on the St. John River upstream from Fredericton. That cottage was filled with memories from my youth and when I would return on furlough from Jamaica as an adult. When I visited, Aunt Doy would bring out that log of memories, and in it I'd see my little-boy handwriting, notes from when I could barely write. It was a time capsule. A treasure chest of Post Creek memories remains to this day, and I draw them out to warm my heart—and occasionally break it, as the circumstances require.

> Where the fish swim up and down
> The sparkling waterfall,
> Where the thunder rolls
> And the lonely puma calls.[28]
> —Gordon Lightfoot

One such stunning memory came on a fall night when I was roofing the east and west decks. The cold rain was changing to sleet, but I had set up a generator to power the drills and drivers I needed to set the washer-bolts holding down the corrugated sheet-metal roofing. I was lost in the task, and in trying not to fall off the roof.

I was so absorbed that I didn't notice when the precipitation stopped. The mast lighting covered the whole roof, so I was blissfully unaware that a rare condition was taking place; to this day, no one else I've told about it has seen it.

When I shut off the generator at 2:00 a.m. in order to collapse into bed, I was stunned by an atmospheric phenomenon. A full moon had climbed up from behind the mountains, bathing the valley in light. The fogbank along the river, however, remained a hundred feet deep. In the deep-forest darkness, the moon turned the air pure white. So the otherwise dark air was light in the prism of every water droplet, and the trees were black. It took me a few moments to ascertain what was so unusual and wonderful. It was like being in a photographic negative. The moon was a bright ball, floating in a milky, ethereal sea where trees and outlines of mountains were black, foreboding shapes.

Transfixed, I walked out to the road to get some perspective. After wandering in this surrealistic dream world for about half an hour, I collapsed into bed in the dry, wood-heat of my mountain home, never to see such a thing again.

World of Translucent Gold

On a quiet January day of constant snowfall, when all sounds are absorbed in the powdery silence, I came out from reading and devotions to encounter five inches of the driest, coldest snow I had ever seen in the coastal rain forest. The sun was setting down the valley toward the Pacific. The squirrels kept dumping the snow from the branches of the jack pines as they leapt from branch to branch, trying

---

[28] Gordon Lightfoot, "Sixteen Miles," *Lightfoot* (United Artists, 1965).

to chase away the Stellar Jays from the feeders. It was magnificent in its godly beauty.

The white world then turned yellow-gold in the setting sun. The vertical rock cliffs were ebony-in-gold, framed like faces in a picture frame. It was so magnificent. I thought of the biblical descriptions of New Jerusalem and its translucent gold. I dropped to my knees in my driveway in praise to the God who values such incomparable beauty, and then in His grace fashions the eye to perceive it. Tears froze to my cheeks.

In orchestral metamorphosis, the gold world turned pink and ever paler as the light waned. I waited with bated breath for the icy-cold white light of the moon to flood the valley.

When I came inside, the candlelight and wood panelling, coals on the fire, and frosted glasses welcomed me back to a world I had a part in fashioning, having left a world that only God could fashion.

> The lamp is burning low upon my table top.
> The snow is softly falling.
> The air is still in the silence of my room.
> I hear your voice softly calling.[29]
> —Gordon Lightfoot

---

[29] Gordon Lightfoot, "Song for a Winter's Night," *The Way I Feel* (United Artists, 1967).

Construction Site

From my veranda, I enjoyed the peace and comfort of falling snow or torrential rain without going outside. I could stoke my pipe and think of the comfort the pipe had represented to my dad. I could inhale the aroma of scotch whisky tobacco, listen to the crackle, and see the glow in the pipe bowl as snow gently fell against the warm colours of my living room.

Using my limited carpentry skills to design and build decks on the west and east side of my home gave me such joy. It was so different from the practice of psychiatry. I would draw in the pipe tobacco and look up into the rafters, remembering the struggle of securing joists, posts, and sheeting, working alone. It hadn't come easy, but the satisfaction had been worth it.

I got a short window of weather in November, loaded my truck with materials at the local lumberyard, and headed up into the mountains. Up before first light, I took in some coffee and breakfast and set up my three-thousand-watt generator.

I set posts and beams, then the joist-hangars, dropped the rafters in place, vertical and horizontal, squared them and then secured them. Cross-brace rafters then nailed down the sheeting. The tar paper provided the layer of protection against moisture and I lay the sheeting in place. Up and down the ladder, load after load of corrugated sheeting and bolts… then I'd head down for coffee and a meal. I'd light up the pipe and rock, look out the window, and survey the progress. Then it was time to put on dry clothing and rain-gear before again heading up the ladder onto the slippery roof.

It began to snow! I had drilled bolt holes into on the crowns of the corrugation and gotten out the big drill set to bolt them down, but the snow soon covered the holes. In the next four hours, I managed to get all the roofing down—and then it *really* snowed.

I turned off the generator and got into bed, cold but satisfied that the roof was secure in case the wind came up, threatening to tear off the sheets. Not only that, but I'd managed to do it without falling off the roof!

The next morning, I awoke to a winter wonderland. I felt so satisfied as I looked up into those rafters and had a coffee on the deck, in a lawn chair, with the choreography of wildlife, cloud, and light passing before my eyes. Blessed be the name of the Lord.

Rescue

My place was just off the Chilliwack Lake Road and I was often present there. Smoke would come out of the chimney and my truck would sit in the driveway.

I was quite amazed at how brain-dead some city people could be when they came into the mountains, but then I had to remember all the brain-dead risks I had taken that had put my wife and me in danger.

While on a Christmas holiday about ten years ago, a man took his wife and child up the Skagit Valley toward Ross Lake on a very cold, snowy night, ostensibly just for a drive. They had no winter clothing, no emergency provisions, and no extra gas. When the car got stranded and ran out of gas trying to stay warm, the man set out for help. None was to come, since it was Christmas. They all froze to death—he on the side of the road in street clothes, and she and the child in the car.

One Saturday evening in January, I was having supper when I heard a knock on the door. Standing and shivering in the freezing cold was a twenty-something Indo-Canadian kid in street shoes and street clothing, with only a light jacket on. I got him inside by the fire, wrapped him in a blanket, and gave him wool socks to replace the soaked, black dress socks he was wearing. He was quite agitated and said that he'd gotten his car stuck up on the Chilliwack Lake Road. His girlfriend was in the car with the engine running and he was afraid the car would run out of gas. He was inconsolable.

I lent him a pair of my gum boots with felt liners, then grabbed my knee-high Sorels, socks, ski jacket, toque, and gloves. We jumped in the truck and headed toward Chilliwack Lake. At the provincial park gate, he pointed straight toward the lake road: it was unploughed with only snowmobile tracks on the surface. This was bad!

Because my truck wasn't a four-by-four, I had put large pre-fab patio slabs in the box (for weight and traction) and had chains if I needed them. I uttered a few expletives about why he would drive down an unploughed road in a sedan, and he demonstrated appropriate shame and embarrassment. Fortunately, he hadn't gotten too far.

Around the first curve sat a muscle car, still pumping up a huge cloud of carbon monoxide. I had to be careful that I didn't get stuck as well, because we were a mile from my place. He jumped out of the truck and ran to the car, opening the door. I followed, and saw inside a gorgeous young girl with long black hair in a party dress and high heels. She had been crying but was quite composed under the circumstances.

She looked terrific in the mid-length skirt with my knee-high snow boots, ski jacket, toque, and thick work gloves. The car still had a quarter-tank of gas, so I got him to shut off the engine and we climbed into the cab of my warm truck.

Once she began to warm up, I gingerly backed out to where the road had been ploughed a few days earlier. I put on the chains and ran a long and heavy polypropylene rope to the rear of the souped-up Firebird. Only by God's magnificent grace did we manage it, but we got him pulled around onto the skimobile tracks. He followed my instructions perfectly.

We drove back to my place and I put some more gas in his car from my generator supply. Soon they were on their way. I followed him to the Centre Creek Corrections Camp, where the blacktop had been ploughed. I offered to convoy to Sardis, but he declined and told me they would be okay from there.

A few weeks later, he dropped in on me, returned the clothing, and expressed sincere gratitude. It was an excellent outcome to a potentially tragic event. Various forms of this rescue were repeated frequently from my place, with minor variances, but there were no more beautiful girls in party dresses.

The Twenty-Six-Ounce Cardiac

An RCMP cruiser pulled up to my driveway late one Saturday morning and the young constable told me that he'd gotten a report that a fisherman had suffered a heart attack up at Lindeman Lake. He asked if I could guide him, and if I had any emergency equipment. The ambulance had been called, but their response time would be at least an hour due to heavy call volume. Lindeman was the magnificent alpine lake north of my place, out of which Post Creek flowed. It was a forty-five-minute walk up a relatively steep trail.

I locked up my place and drove with the officer to the trailhead, where a hiker met us and guided us to where he had discovered a sixty- to seventy-year-old gentleman lying on the ground with spinning rod and tackle box beside him. There was a light skit of snow on the ground. He was conscious, somewhat disoriented, and couldn't walk. The one empty and one half-empty whisky bottles scattered around him pointed to the precipitating factor. He adamantly denied that he had been drinking.

Using the rope and axe I had brought, we built a rough stretcher and began walking the guy out, down the winding and steep trail. The old man's gratitude and civility at being rescued from possible hypothermia gave way to irritable, foul-mouthed resistance when we reached the log bridge over Post Creek. It was too narrow to get him across, unless we put the stretcher up onto our shoulders. He ranted and railed… until we hoisted him to our shoulders and he looked down and saw the ten-foot drop into the raging stream below. He quickly sobered up and said, in a fit of foxhole religiosity, "Oh Lord, boys, don't drop me!"

Well, the three of us sweated and depleted ourselves for nearly two hours getting him down the mountain. An ambulance waited at the trailhead near the campsites. When the old gentleman saw the paramedics, he swore, threw his legs over the side of the stretcher, and began to stagger off toward the lake again.

"Oh, that's old Fred," one of the ambulance attendants said. "He's the town drunk."

When the attendants told the old man that he'd have to be taken in for tests, he began to fight them. The exhausted young police officer had had enough by this point, so he cuffed Fred, tucked his head into the squad car, and drove off as the ambulance followed, with the medics laughing knowingly; they had been through this many times before, just not this far up into the hills.

I walked the quarter-mile home and fell into bed, exhausted.

13

Magnificent Peril

Flood

CHRIS WAS A YOUNG MARRIED KID FROM TORONTO, HUSBAND OF A Christian friend's daughter. He hadn't gone hiking in the mountains before, and my main hiking buddy Don thought we should take him out for a walk.

It was November and the weather had been cool and bright for about a week after heavy, cold precipitation that dumped about four feet of snow in the Coastal Range Mountains.

The temperature was beginning to warm up and the forecast was for rain, so we decided to take him on a walk so his first trip didn't end up taking place in the wet, hypothermia-inducing snow. Our target was the upper, upper Chilliwack River.

We took my old '72 Chevy Nova. In a light, spitting rain, we drove up the potholed, winding gravel road along Chilliwack Lake to Sapper Park at the southern end of the lake, just three miles from the U.S. border.

The trip was to be a cakewalk. Though soggy and potentially unpleasant, dealing with the coastal rainforest was a necessary experience if you were to live in B.C.

The three of us packed up and headed down the trail toward the ford where the Copper Ridge trail of Mount Baker State Park in the U.S. met the Upper Chilliwack River trail. It was beautiful. The weather was warm for November, and the upper Chilliwack River was crystal-clear emerald. The jungle was lush, the sounds from the river melodic, and the signs of the salmon spawn still evident in the river.

Before we got to Bear Creek Park (an apt appellation, given that we saw three black bears and a mother with cub during our hike), we set a camp. It was a beautiful spot, eight feet above the river at a curve where we could get our water easily from a big pool. The camp was on a rise, so drainage wouldn't be a problem if the torrential rainforest downpours overtook us. We were in a stand of cottonwoods with goodly distance from the jungle undergrowth of Devil's Club, Skunk Cabbage, and fern. We were also just off the trail, in the event that anyone else was idiotic enough to go packing in this weather. Needless to say, we never saw another soul.

I have only ever backpacked with an ethafoam mattress, a mountain goose-down "mummy bag," a rope, polysheet, groundsheet, and tie-downs. This was lighter than a tent, and if properly constructed would suffice both in summer and winter. It solved the condensation problem by allowing lots of air movement. I simply tied the rope between two trees and draped the poly over it. With creative anchoring, this made a tent. We set a comfortable camp, started a fire, and got water. The aroma of coffee emanated from our bedroom doors as we wowed Chris with fireside tales. As the showers swept through more frequently, we retired in the very early darkness of fall.

The jungle canopy kept us from the heavy rains except when wind gusted up the valley; then we were doused with the reservoir rain in the high trees. We went to sleep from exhaustion with the somnolent splatter of rain on our poly flysheets.

During the night, we heard distant rumbling and I thought we might be on a flight path for commercial jets. But I was to learn we weren't! Quite frequently, we heard distant gunshots, and I thought it strange that hunters would be shooting on a night of heavy rain.

Occasionally during the night, we felt the ground shake and didn't know how to interpret that, but it couldn't be of much consequence. I wasn't even trying to connect the dots.

Don didn't sleep well at night in the bush, or at best he had a fitful sleep. The rain could be torrential at times, enough to wake me up. I checked to make sure my sleeping bag wasn't getting wet before drifting off again.

As a soggy, dim, dark, and dank morning broke, I heard Don shout an expletive and call for me to look at the river. I propped myself up on my elbow in the sleeping bag and looked out just as a large tree moved by our camp at high speed. I scrambled out of the bag and threw on some clothes. To my horror, I saw that the river had risen six or seven feet overnight. It was no longer crystal clear but muddy, and if it rose any further, it would take out our campsite.

I barked out orders to break camp immediately. We stuffed our gear into our packs and unceremoniously sprinted out of camp as a small stream began to flow down what had been the trail along the river.

Fortunately, over the next quarter-mile the trail climbed a few yards before levelling off. On our right shoulder, however, was a nightmare of thorns, tangled vines, thick jungle growth, and steep, heavily wooded hillsides. The river was rapidly expanding and there was no place to retreat to. We hadn't brought a machete or other bush-slashing equipment.

The torrential rain let up for a brief time as we force-marched north toward the lake. Then the inevitable happened. We had delicately crossed two side streams feeding the torrent before we came to a fifteen-foot-wide raging stream that converged with the main river. There were no logs to cross; they had all been blown out by the flood, and we were only a hundred feet from the Chilliwack River. If we tried to swim and were grabbed by the current, we would be in the main river, catapulting downstream with the trees.

Finally, I connected the dots. The warm rains had washed out the high-elevation snowpack all at once. The roars we had heard were debris dams being formed and then blown-out in the mountain cataracts. I had seen what could happen a few years earlier on Radium Creek on the north side of the river. A warm washout of an earlier snowpack had caused Radium Lake to rise ten feet very quickly; the debris had choked the outflow, causing a massive pressure build-up, until it finally blew out and swept everything down the steep mountain canyon. Afterward, it looked like a bit of Mount St. Helens. Trees of two-foot diameters had been snapped off like matchsticks. The undulating flow bounced from side to side of the gorge, scouring the banks and undermining further trees, creating further mudslides. The torrent then carried boulders, gravel, trees and branches, where Radium Creek met and fanned out into the Chilliwack River. Unimaginable power!

Now we were caught in a version of that.

Seeing that this wide stream flowed out of a bog, we assumed that if we went far enough upstream, we would be able to cross a log or a beaver dam. What we didn't know was that this was a bottleneck and that we would end up in a huge bog the farther upstream we ventured. I had a map but no compass, because we had intended to stay on a trail all weekend. I could see the bog on the map, but I didn't know how far it would take to navigate around.

We started up the stream. The intensity of the torrent began to diminish, but the banks became increasingly boggy and we ended up having to skirt it by wider and wider distances.

This area at the south end of Chilliwack Lake was old growth, with 150-foot firs mixed with hemlock and cedar. It included one of B.C.'s largest trees, a double-cedar with a butt of over fifteen feet. It stood right beside the trail, about a mile in from the lake. The further we got into the bog, the steeper the mountainsides and the thicker the undergrowth. Huge deadfalls crossed one another to a height of sometimes ten to fifteen feet. It was a nightmare!

We had a meeting. I proposed crossing the bog in the event we could find a trail on the other side, on higher ground. My recommendation was adopted—but I turned out to be wrong!

The bog was essentially composed of interwoven floating logs, moss, lichens, grass, and roots. There were small puddles and ponds, with water-logged trees and branches and the occasional channel flowing through it. We slogged along, sinking knee-deep most of the time, and occasionally waist-deep. When we attempted to walk atop the imbedded logs, we frequently fell off.

Eventually, we got across to the steep hillside that rose opposite us. By this time, the sun was directly overhead under heavy cloud cover and it was impossible to determine direction.

The nightmare then shifted into more frightening phase. Big trees don't usually break off; they end up in a rhythmic, circular sway in harmony with a strong wind, and then uproot themselves. That's what had happened on this hillside, and they had fallen on one another. We ended up climbing high on the deadfalls. Because of the rain, we were at risk of sliding off and breaking a leg or arm. *That* would have been serious, since we were already in danger of hypothermia. A bone break could have meant shock setting in quickly.

I realized I had made a mistake when Don took a fall and cracked his tailbone. He was in unremitting pain. Also, our gear was getting torn on the branches and we weren't making any time at all up the steep mountainside. I was seriously afraid of night overtaking us.

We stopped, rested, and had a meeting. I admitted my mistake and we decided to return across the bog, if necessary roping our way across the narrowest stream crossing. Chris was a Christian, and it appeared that he was the only one (Don was agnostic), because I was in breach of Proverbs 3:5–6. The kid very wisely said, "Let's pray." The agnostic was perceptive enough to restrain protest.

I prayed beseechingly because I was the trip leader, and supposedly a mature Christian, yet I was blowing it to the point where I was putting us all in danger.

I later told this story to my New Brunswick family across a restaurant table, and they all looked down in embarrassment because I had become either a compulsive liar or wacko mystic. It was too much for non-believers to take.

After we prayed, we began our slog back across the morass. It seemed we were sinking deeper, but that was good for Don because the creeping cold was literally freezing his injured tailbone. We no longer knew if we were heading in the right direction, but it seemed right because our back was to the mountainside on which we had stalled.

Unbelievably, astoundingly, astonishingly, I saw a brief glint on a mound of moss next to a bog deadfall. The reflected light suggested something made of metal or glass. It could have been a beer bottle as far as I knew, but my curiosity was piqued. When I approached it, I couldn't believe my eyes. It was a partially submerged compass! I was breathless. Even Don was impressed, calling it a remarkable coincidence. Chris and I got down on our knees on a nearby log and gave thanks and praise.

Most people don't realize that a map is useless in the absence of visual landmarks, or without a compass. Out came the map; I took a bearing which directed us about thirty degrees to the west, but I still wasn't settled, because we were going to end up back where we had started with the same old problem.

As we stepped out of the bog onto solid ground, I kept our bearing generally westward. Within ten minutes, we hit a path that took us to the main river trail which hadn't yet been washed out. Without the compass, I never would have found it.

Upstream, we found a tree for an anchor and belayed (roped) one another across the stream. My relief and gratitude to the Lord for honouring us with a miracle was beyond measure. I couldn't help but sing hymns of thanks on the way out.

However, we weren't out of the woods yet. We didn't know how many other raging torrents we would have to cross. The river was rising and the side streams were getting more aggressive. There was even concern about where I had parked the car. Would it have been washed away?

The light waned. The sun had gone behind the mountains, and evening was soon upon us. We had no industrial-quality torches, because we hadn't expected an emergency. Thus, we had to make tracks. The other crossings were mercifully uneventful, except for one.

About three-quarters of a mile from the end of the trail, we encountered a relatively slow-moving but wide stream through the sand beds at the moraine where the river entered the lake.

We belayed Chris across first. The water was muddy and moving quite powerfully, but not in a raging torrent. He managed to get through it about hip deep and scramble up the other bank. Now we had a rope anchored on the other bank. I don't know how it happened, but somehow Chris had skirted a big hole. Don, on the other hand, stepped right into it and ended up swimming with his pack. He couldn't gather enough breath in desperate gasps in the snow-fed water, but regrettably Chris and I broke up in gales of laughter while Chris pulled Don up the other bank.

From this point on, there were only two anxieties. We heard the sound of engines off in the distance and interpreted it either as rescue equipment or a sign that the road had washed our car into the lake and the road was being reconstructed. The lake road hugged the steep cliffs of the south-eastern shore, and there are numerous vertical cascades running through culverts under the road. Any one of these could have been washed out; either that or the road could have been broken by a rockslide.

The meandering trail through the delta was a welcome relief, and the sound of the tractor or backhoe got louder and louder. We came off the trail and onto the road. A hundred yards away sat my old 1972 Chevy. What a heart-warming sight! Chris and I couldn't help but break into further fits of gratitude.

The battle wasn't yet over. There were no washouts, but rocks the size of armchairs had blocked the road in two places. We managed to roll them out of the way and then clumped through the front door of my mountain home a short time later, shedding our wet gear. I cranked the gas range, opened the oven door, and began a wood fire. Don cracked a bottle of wine he had stowed in the car as we changed into warm clothes.

For a while, we didn't speak. We just soaked in the stove heat, sipping the wine that warmed us on the insides. We meditated on what could have happened if the river had overtaken our camp in the middle of the night before we'd had the chance to properly stow our gear. We pondered the possibility that someone could have broken a leg in the fallen timber, forcing us to spend a night in the sodden bush as the river rose around us. We pondered that our car might have sunk, or the road been covered. We pondered the great mercy and long-suffering kindness of God.

We dumped the wet gear unceremoniously around my living room and decks, then jumped in the car for the trip to Chilliwack where Bozzini's Steak and Pasta awaited our arrival. We consumed all the ribs, steak, and pasta our stomachs could consume, and a bottle of Cabernet Sauvignon—for medicinal purposes, of course.

Loneliness

For a long time, I dreamed of a life like the one I had in Post Creek, in a wild valley away from telecommunications and social demands, the sound of a wild river constantly in my ears. The radio frequencies faded in and out, and the snow squalls blew in and adorned the landscape with multicolour crystals before disappearing. Clouds swept up the valley, engulfing the world like a swirling flood. The river receded to a trickle, then grew in the fall or spring rains, swelling to a muddy cataclysm. It swelled from its icy constraints and glazed banks. The seven-thousand-foot giants surrounding me were majestically clothed in their wardrobe of rich forest green, ethereal mists, deep white furs, and smoky glow of cyclical fires. The cold rains turned to sleet, then to hail, then to snow, then to frozen death amidst high winds. Vivaldi's four seasons accompanied this world.

The hummingbirds arrived when there was still three feet of snow with an icy crust on top. The perennial Whiskey Jacks, Steller Jays, and flickers scrounged under the watchful eyes of big raptors. Bald eagles and red-tail hawks prowled the days, and owls prowled at night. Under them, the raccoons, squirrels, pack rats, chipmunks, and mice scrapped and scurried and squeaked and chewed.

In the quiet solitude and cover of the timber and valley growth, black and brown bears hunted alongside the occasional travelling grizzly, cougar, lynx, and bobcat. The big deer roamed the forest—elk, black tail, and mule deer. The symphony of air and water, wind and wildlife sang interwoven melodies as salmon appeared from the shores of Japan and the East China Sea—life, death, and life again.

As the alder, mountain ash, and aspen turned to their warm fall colours, reflecting golden and orange light onto the green rainforest floor, the entire world converged on the river. The ragged and heroic salmon pooled as their strength diminished, laying their eggs. The ritual of life was magnificent, the male fertilizing the eggs as death overtook them. The eagles and seagulls, bears and raccoons, and all small rodents descended on the river all congregating on this magnificent river of death and life… a perfect metaphor for the redemption story.

High in the meadows, the mountain goat sensed the change and their hair thickened, with nature holding its breath on motionless, brilliant fall days, awaiting the coming ferocity of winter. The bears gorged on salmon and the last berries before seeking warm, sleepy dens. The deer dug through new-fallen snow to the tender roots below. Here was breathless anticipation of the ferocious blast to come.

Orchestral winds and woodwind pines, the drums of rockslides and snowslides and mating grouse, the bugle of bull elk and the night bay of wolves enacted an incontestable theme: the majesty of God and his redemption of life from death.

In the cold morning air, at the sounds of life outside my window, my eyes snapped wide open. I was alone. No one else could share this beauty. No one was thinking about me or waiting for me. The life-and-death struggle outside my window had no concern or interaction with my thoughts or emotions or being.

My mind was drawn to the astonishing words of Eric Ryback in his book, *Ultimate Journey: Canada to Mexico Down the Continental Divide*.[30] After his younger brother abandoned the trip, Eric reported that his major challenge amidst the stunning beauty of the Washington, Oregon, and California wildernesses, amidst the most arduous of physical challenges in his young life, was loneliness and depression.

In the painful tragedy of Chris McCandless' life and death, we hear echoes of the same sentiment. Weakened by plant-poisoning and starvation, he scribbled, "Happiness only real when shared." Then, his dying message: "I have had a happy life and thank the Lord. Goodbye and may God bless all."[31]

Then Lightfoot's plaintiff call:

If I could know within my heart
That you were lonely, too,
I would be happy just to hold the hands I love…[32]
—Gordon Lightfoot

Koko and the Deer

Koko was such a big part of my life. He shared some of my most remarkable mountain moments, but one at Post Creek still causes me PTSD symptoms.

Directly across the road from my house were two A-frames. Behind them, in the bush, was a cabin that belonged to a friend of ours. His cabin had a large deck on the south side that got afternoon sun. Koko and I were out exploring one day and he literally pointed toward Jeff's cabin; the hair came up all the way from his shoulders to his tail. He growled threateningly and ran around the cabin. I

---

[30] Eric Ryback, *Ultimate Journey: Canada to Mexico Down the Continental Divide* (San Francisco, CA: Chronicle Books, 1973).

[31] Jon Krakauer, Into the Wild (New York, NY: Anchor Books, 1996).

[32] Gordon Lightfoot, "Song for a Winter's Night," *The Way I Feel* (United Artists, 1967).

heard a *ker-blump* off the boards on the deck and he went barking through the bush. I then saw a brown flash pass through the thick pine overgrowth. Koko was obviously herding the deer toward the road and I wanted to see it. I was having an episode of acute stupidity, not thinking that what had just happened didn't make any sense.

As I rushed to flank the animal and Koko pursued, out of the bush, just a hundred yards ahead of me and onto the road loped a large juvenile brown bear. He wasn't running, and he wasn't amused. That was a bad sign, since Koko was a ferocious "bear dog." Koko understood the situation and totally uncharacteristically came to me on my first call. The bear looked at me holding Koko by the collar, and sauntered across the road into the high timber. Though young, he was not afraid. Again, a bad sign!

I connected the dots. The bear had been sunning himself on Jeff's deck when Koko and I came upon him. Deer don't sun themselves on decks, twit! It was a beautiful sight—and memorable, because the bear was kind enough not to charge.

Mountain Goat

Mountain goats were among the most exciting features of my mountain home. They inhabited the cliffs directly to the north and probably only three-quarters of a mile away as the crow flies. A magnificent seasonal feature, they would become visible on the cliffs only as the heavy snow retreated, and not long afterward they would begin to fawn their kids.

The mountain goat isn't a true goat at all. They are closer to the antelope. These beautiful shaggy creatures adorned the impossible cliff face opposite me and almost seemed to eat the rocks, but in fact they were finding grasses, mosses, and lichens in every crevasse and along every tiny ledge.

On the knobs of these cliffs would grow stunted juniper and fir trees that in some places represented little forests of just twenty or thirty inches in depth. The billies would tuck their front hooves under their shaggy beards and preside over justice in the valley. The herds were as large as nine, but sometime during April half the herd would disappear, only to reappear days later. Soon the kids would become visible and the nannies and billies would keep the kids against the cliff; the greatest risk to the kids wasn't big cats, bears, and wolves, but eagles swooping down and knocking them off the cliffs to later retrieve.

The interrelationship among family members was amazing. On one occasion, I saw two billies actually jousting on the cliff face. It was unbelievable.

One year, I climbed up there in hopes of finding tufts of hair, or perhaps a horn, on the spot where they had jousted. Without rope protection, I was barely able to hang onto the cliff. Much to my disappointment, there was absolutely no goat-sign, but strangely enough I did find a three-point deer antler. I pondered the scenario that had brought the little antler to this knob of rock.

As the snows passed over the top of the five-thousand-foot peaks, so did the goats. They disappeared into the meadows immediately below the highest ranges. I was always sad to see them go, knowing it would be eight months before I would see them again. It was somehow comforting to come out on my deck and look up at the rock face and see five or six white dots grazing back and forth on the cliff, or chewing the cud in meditation over the magnificent view.

The Cougar

I'd see its tracks. Hunters in the area said that when they were deer-hunting, they would literally see a tail disappear fifty feet from them, never hear a sound, and certainly never see the big cat. Cougars are amazing. I would see their tracks in the snow, but never the animal.

When the adults drove the juveniles off their territories, the young came looking for easy prey. That's when it got dangerous for raccoons, rabbits, dogs, cats, and small children.

Every few years, my neighbours would see one. When I was living up there alone, I would clip bear spray on my belt and at dusk go quietly along the river trail (or along Post Creek) in hopes of seeing one. The closest I ever got was when a cougar screamed at me and by pack buddies at Hannegan Pass near Mount Baker. It was a haunting, otherworldly sound.

When I took a trip to visit my friend Errol and his wife in Victoria, that very weekend my neighbour saw a raccoon back up oddly against a tree just off my front step. In an instant, a big cat had it. There was no fight.

In a moment of temporary insanity, my neighbour opened his back door and went out on his porch to get a better look. The cat looked at him, put back its ears, and hissed threateningly. He and his wife, who was trying to dissuade him from going out, beat a hasty retreat and slammed the door. The cat grabbed its prey and disappeared toward the river.

14

Contrasts

Running the Canyon

I could barely sleep that night. My friend Mark Creer, a truly amazing young man, was the son of a kayaking legend in the Vancouver area. When he asked me to join a crew running the Chilliwack Canyon, I felt there could never be a safer time. I was also too embarrassed to decline.

A relatively strong intermediate paddler, I'd had a dozen or so "clutch-rolls," but very few "swims."[33] There was no end to the harassment you got from your crew when this happened. A minimum white-water kayak crew was comprised of three boats—one to go after the swimmer and one to go after the boat. It was hard work getting swimmer and boat to the shore, especially if you were dodging hydraulic holes and log jams, all the while being at risk of getting knocked over yourself.

In white water, you often don't know how disaster strikes. Suddenly, the world turns green and there's thunder in your ears. Then you're in the middle of a washing machine, and the water is ice cold. You had just better roll up.

I only had one bad swim at the Campsite rapids just below Tamihi, but I was with the best crew you could hope for. Peter Buchmeuller, who with his father ran Walter's Ski Shack in North Vancouver, had been provincial slalom champion. Then there was Mike Neckar, of Nimbus Kayak fame, a downriver provincial champion and coach. There were other assorted provincial team members and strong paddlers, so I was in good company.

---

[33] Clutch-roll: when you're knocked over unexpectedly in white water, but successfully roll back up (Eskimo-roll). Swim: when you get knocked over in rough water; if you don't roll up, you and those who try to rescue you will have a rough quarter-mile or so.

I was spending a lot of time on the river at that time in my life, much to Amber's dismay, which meant I was paddling quite well. I bought a life insurance policy and told her I was worth much more alive than dead. I expect there were many times when she would have liked to collect the life insurance face value.

The strong team actually became a momentary detriment when Mike, whose belly was so big that his teammates said he didn't need a spray skirt, came blasting into an eddy I was sitting in with his big downriver boat. You can get your ribs broken if you're speared by someone driving hard into your eddy (when you're facing upstream in the current behind an obstruction, usually near the shore). That's how you slow your progress downriver; you lean the kayak hard upstream as you drive the bow into the current, then snap around upstream. You sit in the eddy to rest and look over your shoulder to read the river below and pick your path.

Well, the eddy I was sitting in wasn't really an eddy; it was the lower end of a massive hydraulic hole which was careening over a fourteen-foot rock, like water over a dam. Those were the most dangerous because the current moved straight down and often curled back under the rock before it flushed out at the bottom. This hole was about six feet deep. Bad news! The upstream current was so strong that I had to back-paddle vigorously to not be sucked into the falls.

When Mike blasted in from the top, I was left with no choice but to try to exit above him by driving the bow of my boat into the downstream current to the left of the submerged rock. As I did so, the hole pulled the stern of the kayak straight down to the bottom of the river. There I was, like a log held under a waterfall, bouncing up and down in the undulations of the current. My helmet kept hitting a rock on the bottom of the river; it was more unnerving than injurious.

With this crew of macho paddlers, my pride determined that I not swim. That was a mistake. I didn't have the expert skills and strength to propel the kayak out of the hole, which required real finesse. So there I was, hanging upside down with the hull of the kayak three feet below the surface, bouncing up and down in the current, my helmet colliding rhythmically with a rock. Not good!

I kept trying to roll, thinking I was failing. Peter watched from an eddy further out in the river. He could see my blue helmet come up just below the surface, so my roll had been successful, but I was still submerged. After two or three attempts, I was exhausted. I finally decided to bail out, but when I pulled the loop on my spray skirt, my neoprene wetsuit pants stuck to the ethafoam blocks that served as knee-pads just under the kayak's deck.

Out of breath, out of strength, and having pulled the spray skirt off the cowl, I thought this was it. I used my last reserve of energy to flail wildly with my straightened legs to get out from under the deck of the boat, not knowing if the current would pull me back under the rock. By the grace of our Lord Jesus Christ, I flushed out the bottom nearly immediately and my mouth came to the surface just as I was seeing blue spots. My hungry lungs gasped in the cool, fresh air.

There was another rapid below Campsite which used to be called the Sawmill. It wasn't so bad as Tamihi or Campsite, but it would still wear out my paddling crew. It's a good thing we had a big team because, in the panic, I let go of my paddle—the unforgivable sin. That means somebody has to chase after you, another person has to go after the boat, and another after the paddle. I didn't care.

My head popped to the surface. As I gasped for breath, hyperventilating, there was absolutely no strength left in my arms. They just lay on the surface in front of my face, floating on the buoyancy of the wet suit as I drifted down the chop into the next drop. As the water drained from my helmet, a grab loop came into focus about two inches from my nose. It belonged to the bow of Peter's kayak.

The only strength I had was to raise my little finger and hook it through the loop. I closed my fist, hard. I was totally wasted.

That was enough, and he pulled me into a little eddy on the north bank. I just lay there. After twenty minutes, I walked down the shore to where the other guys had pulled out my boat and paddle. I finished the run to Pointa Vista.

Cold, exhausted, and more than a little shaken, I sat on a log at the shuttle vehicle. Mike and Peter laughed at me, condescending to tell me that for a moment they had been worried they were going to have to get out the rescue rope. That comment was my *rite de passage*—my badge of honour.

The next week, I was asked by a female Christian friend if I had been in any trouble at about 3:00 p.m. Saturday afternoon. I told her that indeed I had been, and she explained how she had felt an urgency to pray for me at that exact time. Bless His holy name!

But I digress. The canyon was the section of the river from the upper Chilliwack bridge down to the Slesse Creek Fish Hatchery. It was very fast, with a major vertical drop and very few places to come ashore. Someone had died on that section just two years earlier. The paddler had been an Olympic swim contender.

There was a particular hydraulic hole on that stretch that you had to avoid at all costs. It was large and required careful technical manoeuvres upriver to get around. You could make no mistakes upstream, because the river was so narrow and fast.

Mark was a terrific athlete, paddler, leader, and all-around nice guy. He had been selected for a leg of the Sir Francis Drake Expedition in 1981–84, sponsored by Prince Charles to circumnavigate the globe on a replica of the *Golden Hind*. You had to have Navy-level fitness and personality to make it. His dad, Brian, had been the patriarch kayak teacher of the 60s and 70s. Mark later became a fireman.

A large group gathered at the upper bridge to make the run. Friends had invited friends, so there were people who shouldn't have been on the river. I was very tense and had slept poorly. I didn't want to either swim or die on my first (and likely last) run of the Chilliwack Canyon.

To compound my anxiety, Mark asked if I would sweep. I said, "Are you crazy?" The sweep was the paddler that followed the group and was the last chance to rescue someone should the others get carried downstream of a paddler in trouble. Mark just laughed and dismissed my protestations, saying I was the strongest man to perform sweep. He grabbed the bow of my kayak, pulled it into the river, and paddled off to lead the group.

In the group was a Parisian girl, a weak intermediate paddler, but her boyfriend promised to take care of her. The canyon was tight and technical; you had to get your path right and plan it well ahead to keep out of trouble. I couldn't hear the crew leader directing the paddlers—"Eddy out there on the right, then ferry down to that next rock in the middle and paddle downstream past the end of that hole you can see on the left hand side…"—but I could see their path.

It ended up being a pretty good day. The weak paddlers swam a few times and I managed to serve my sweep function and pick up gear. I didn't swim myself. We skirted the big holes and negotiated a few doglegs. The water wasn't so high as to be terrifying, so it became fun.

The last drops to the fish hatchery were steep, fast, and narrow. I dropped back to make sure I didn't overtake one of my charges. I could see the hatchery dam coming up on the left side. We had been told not to go near that wall but to hit the eddies just above, then ferry across and run the last roller-coaster as straight as we could.

As I pulled out of my eddy and turned downstream, I saw a commotion along the dam. A couple of paddlers had drifted by and got caught in the drop down to the pool.

I caught a high eddy and sprung out of my boat to see the French girl's kayak on its side, deck upstream, and her legs pressed into the boat by the incredible water pressure. One paddler was holding her head out of the water as another tried to free the kayak. River water, moving at twenty-five miles per hour at a weight of 8.35 pounds per gallon times the square footage of surface area it was exerting pressure on could literally create tons of pressure.

While she was held above water, Mark and Stan found a large branch caught in the dam debris and extracted it. They managed to pry the boat up a few inches, which took a few hundred pounds of pressure off the upper deck of her kayak, allowing her to free her legs.

Then we had to find a way to get the boat out. After forty-five minutes of engineering, we got it lose. She was far too spooked to attempt the last drop, so someone took her boat down and she walked up to the road. After we all gathered, she kissed us in appreciation. That was really nice, because she was cute!

After a run and a war story such as that one, you stood by the river in the gold-orange light of late-afternoon summer sun, then peeled yourself out of the soggy wetsuit and felt the warmth soak into your body. On would come the warm, dry clothes. You could smell the evergreen. Your eyes would sweep up to the mountain meadows. You'd see the perpetual contortions of the wild river. You'd listen to the thunder and hear the wind in the high timber. All tension abated as you watched the spray on the haystack waves glisten in the remaining sunlight. In the afterglow, you'd remember that the wild river hadn't conquered you, but neither had you conquered her. It had been a stalemate. Every muscle had been stretched to its limit, and others injured in the process. There was fatigue. There was pain. It was all intoxicating.

I unceremoniously threw my gear into the truck, with the kayak protruding from the back as everyone headed home. The familiar gravel road filled my windshield for twenty-five minutes. I opened my mountain home to the evening air, praising God that my prayers for safety had been answered, punctuated by a close call.

Night at Lindeman Lake

I was spiritually and psychologically depleted. It was December and I had to break the dead zone I was in, so I decided to fast and pray, taking my Bible up to Lindeman Lake to spend the night in solitude with the Lord. Lindeman sat just west of the north end of Chilliwack Lake, with a spectacular view of Webb's Peak from its northern shore.

The temperatures were running ten degrees below freezing and there had been a three-inch snowfall. It was quiet. I pointed my truck eastward on Highway 1 and up to Post Creek. I warmed up my place, then gathered my gear, trying to beat the darkness to the lake.

I took my goose-down mountain mummy bag, a foamy, poly sheet, rope, tie-downs, water containers, and a snowmobile suit, just in case it was ferociously cold. It was! No stove, no food… just water.

Needless to say, there was no one there. Lindeman Lake is a jewel of a mountain lake. It was a brisk, steep thirty-minute walk up a cascading Post Creek, but in winter it could take an hour.

When the weather was clear, I could see the snow-capped Webb's Peak reflected in Lindeman's crystal waters; the little lake sat in a steep canyon with crumbling shark-tooth peaks to the east and a knife-edge ridge leading to Goetz Peak on its west side.

Just before Amber and I had taken possession of Post Creek, a Cessna-172 with RCMP officers aboard had made a wrong turn in low-ceiling off the Chilliwack River valley into that steep canyon. They'd flown right into the eastern talus slide, trying to make a turn to gain altitude. All had been killed.

Post Creek flowed out of the lake into a cascading torrent that disappeared underground and then reappeared above a beautiful waterfall which dropped into a deep, cold pool surrounded by high timber.

I got to the lake at dusk and walked to the middle of the western lakeshore in a stand of high firs. I threw out a groundsheet, unrolled the foamy on top, pulled my mummy out of its bag, and began gathering fresh water from the lake.

Once camp was set, I stripped down and changed into long johns. I pulled on the snowmobile suit and hung out the sweaty underclothing to be "dry-cleaned" in the morning; I'd take the cardboard-stiff garment and beat it until all the ice fell out. I scouted out the camp area, gathering everything I'd need near the head of the bag. I placed my water bottle and boots in garbage bags at the foot of the sleeping bag, otherwise in the morning my boots would be frozen solid with undrinkable water.

Night fell over the mostly frozen lake, its surface comprised of inch-deep dark blue ice. Exhausted and miserable from fasting, I threw the skidoo suit over the peak-rope of my tent and crawled in for prayer, meditation, and sleep.

I fell asleep almost immediately as a stellar light show filled the sky. I could touch the stars with my fingers. The moon caught the tips of the ridge, but before long I was in a deep coma. It was only 6:00 p.m.

After a couple of hours, I thought I must be hallucinating. I was in the centre of floodlights, blinded even through my bag. I poked an eye through the mummy bag. As my eyes adjusted, I realized that the moon had come overhead, turning the entire snow-robed world into brilliant reflected light. It was dead silent except for the creaking of lake.

I got out of my warm bag, threw on the snowmobile suit and mitts, put on my Sorel boots, and walked out to see this paradise.

Lindeman Lake was so varied, with steep, ragged cliffs that crashed down into the lake leaving crushed talus slopes. The heavily wooded areas were unmolested, thick timber creeping up the western slopes. A marsh lay at the north end of the lake, with sandy beaches and stands of cottonwood, ash, aspen, and maple.

Everywhere I looked were buttresses, moraines, cascades, ridges, peaks, and wooded hillsides. All were bathed in brilliant light with reliefs of black and grey—not to mention the glassy blue lake.

I walked along the lake, trying to find the trail through the talus underneath the snow. I had come to be alone with God, to speak with Him personally. He spoke to me tenderly in this opera of wonder. I was quickly overwhelmed by all the sensory input. I couldn't absorb all the beauty!

I staggered back to my camp, stripped off the snowsuit, and climbed into bed again. I drifted off into a heavenly reverie of sights and sounds.

What I was unprepared for was the symphony of percussion, with coyotes yipping and howling not far away. It was so cold that the lake froze quickly. From one end of the lake to the other, I heard searing bursts of rifle fire, followed by shells going by at high speeds and the *khrump* of depth charges going off at the far end of the lake.

Eerie, out-of-this-world sounds filled the air. I can only describe it as sounding like the laser guns of *Star Wars*, firing in a hot skirmish. The rumbling depth charges would go off as energy was released from expanding ice, following by up to ten minutes of silence.

These space-age techno sounds came as a shock. I had never heard them before. The only explanation was that they were being reflected off the steep canyon walls. It was wonderful.

Despite the epic drama being played out in sound and light, I slept.

The next morning was deathly cold. The lake was frozen four inches deep and crisscrossed with fractures. The ice was clear blue and I could see all the way to the bottom of the lake twenty-five feet below. Webb's Peak reflected in the ice. The cliffs were frozen and the world was still, except for winter birds scratching, scrounging, and otherwise making their emotions and familial communications well-heard.

I walked and slid on the beautiful glass, casting my eyes on this frozen white world. I was weak from the fast and once again in communion with God.

The mountains will bring peace to the people, and the little hills, by righteousness. (Psalm 72:3)

You are more glorious and excellent than the mountains of prey. (Psalm 76:4)

Before the mountains were brought forth, or ever You had formed the earth and the world, even from everlasting to everlasting, You are God. (Psalm 90:2–3)

Fire and hail, snow and clouds; stormy wind, fulfilling His word; mountains and all hills; fruitful trees and all cedars; beasts and all cattle… (Psalm 148:8–10)

For He says to the snow, "Fall on the earth"; likewise to the gentle rain and the heavy rain of His strength. He seals the hand of every man, that all men may know His work. (Job 37:6–7)

Have you entered the treasury of snow, or have you seen the treasury of hail, which I have reserved for the time of trouble, for the day of battle and war? (Job 38:22–23)

He gives snow like wool; He scatters the frost like ashes; He casts out His hail like morsels; who can stand before His cold? He sends out His word and melts them; He causes His wind to blow, and the waters flow. (Psalm 147:16–18)

He restores my soul… (Psalm 23:3)

The Rocker and the Fire

In the year 2000, I came home on furlough from the prisons and gunfights of Jamaica and only had a few days to escape to the mountains. I also had speaking engagements for the Mennonite Central Committee, church and Bible study presentations, as well as many friends and family to see. After that, I'd be off to the East Coast.

I went to see my friends who had been taking care of my place and using my ninety-year-old aunt's mint-1966 Ramble American. The car had been in my dad's estate and I had driven it from Cape Spear, Newfoundland to Post Creek. I picked up the car and drove it up the road just as I had done in 1995. I turned into the driveway, clumped up the stairs onto the front deck, and turned the key of my house. It wasn't locked!

Everything was just as I had left it, except that my missionary friend Jeri Labelle, who loved the place as much as I did, had put up white, lacy curtains and cleaned the place from one end to the other. Jeri was a short-term missionary to the Amazon, and then long-term in Mexican orphanages, where she remains to this day. Before she went on her mission, she would bring her dog up and stay for weeks. The prose she left in my Post Creek logbook was precious. The Lord truly used this natural wonder to build her up. She'd had a hard life and used the place to minister to others.

Anyway, there had been no intrusion. The Lord must have set one of those flaming angels at the door. On my bookshelf were my binoculars, my antler-handled skinning knife, my eagle feather, and spike-horn buck antler… just as I had left them.

I quickly began to heat the place up; I turned on the propane range, opened the oven door for quick heat, then built a fire in the little cast-iron box stove I had installed in 1980.

I had just come from violence and degradation like one can scarcely imagine. In Jamaica, I'd been in eight car accidents, been mugged at gunpoint and knifepoint, survived two national riots, been expelled from prison, watched a prisoner die from multiple ice-pick wounds, and held a man in my arms who had been stabbed eighteen times.

All of that evaporated! In this perfect silence, perfect peace, time stood still. It was as though I hadn't walked out five years earlier. In the hush, I was afraid to breathe. Time had, indeed, stood still here. It was a time warp, a capsule, a mystic grotto.

Once the condensation cleared from the windows, the massive kettle boiled and I made coffee. I then put my provisions in the fridge, whose motor had just kicked in, and sat down in the rocker by the stove.

The collage of stabbings, oppression, gunfire, corruption, and degradation in which I had been immersed for the past two and a half years waned as the sway of the pines healed my ragged soul. The familiar and distinctive aromas of fir, pine, and cedar intoxicated my olfactory. The somnolent crackle and bang of wood in the stove, and the orange glow of the coals and flame around the box, melted my frozen emotions. The strength drained out of me as the hills of Psalm 121 filled me. My head dropped back against the headboard of the oak rocker. In no time, I was dead asleep.

Twenty minutes later, I snapped awake, so surprised at where I was that I thought momentarily that it might be a dream.

I placed another two sticks in the fire, warmed up the coffee, and started to think about supper. I walked over to the countertop and saw all the cast-iron pots and pans hanging on hooks above the range. I fried up the boiled potatoes I had bought, then threw in onions and bacon and beans from the oven. A dear Christian sister had insisted I take some homemade brown bread, so the kitchen and living room smelled like life again. Another dear friend had sent me with leftovers from a turkey dinner, complete with dressing and gravy. They waited in the fridge for tomorrow's lunch. I placed a smaller log on the fire, then sat down at the kitchen table in front of the lonely hummingbird feeder just outside the window.

After gorging on this delicious cowboy meal, I threw the dishes in the sink and retreated once again to the rocker. The light was beginning to disappear and the familiar reflections on the glass showed the rough-hewn cedar bookshelf I had made one weekend; it sat above the fold-down divan that had slept so many of my friends. The divan was covered with a warm throw, knitted by my wife Amber in herringbone browns, golds, oranges, and whites. She had been so beautiful and so skilled. In the window, the flame of the aromatic pine candle reflected the light of the world.

As I walked in the cold night, the familiar sentinels seemed to ask, "Where have you been?" These mountains, these elders had seen me come and go; they'd seen my beautiful wife come and go. They had harboured mountain goats as they gave birth to their young, as well as the deer, the bears, and the nests of raptors. They were old and close friends who spoke of the might of God, moving at His bidding.

I saw lights in some of the cabins and smelled the smoke from their wood fires, saw people's construction projects in stone and wood and cement foundation. I made my way down to the river, over the bridge where I got my water from the Post Creek pool. I heard the roar of the upper canyon, the place where Amber and I, and our little dog, accidentally boxed-in three deer at the place where the river trail met the main road. The deer had bounded and milled around in concentric circles before bouncing off into the bush.

I glanced up the draw where Goetz Peak brooded in a blanket of snow next to Williams Peak and its Matterhorn-like profile. My head swam with the memories of standing on their crests.

Memories. Rich and sweet, euphoric and painful.

Then I ventured back into the warm blast of my living room, taking off my boots and slipping in with the fluffy moccasins. Logs crackled on the fire as I headed back to the rocking chair. I just rocked and rocked, looking and listening and drinking in the aroma of the burning wood, allowing the stillness to soak into my weary bones—into my soul. My heart hadn't been so still since I'd left my mountain home.

> Harsh nights and candlelights, woodfires a-blazin'
> Soft lips and fingertips resting in my soul
> Treasuring, remembering, the promise of spring,
> Pussywillows, cattails, soft winds and roses.[34]
> —Gordon Lightfoot

---

[34] Gordon Lightfoot, "Pussywillows, Cattails," *Did She Mention My Name* (United Artists, 1968).

15

Transition

Final Vignettes

I BOUGHT THIS MOUNTAIN PARADISE TO BE NEAR THE RIVER FOR PADDLING. It was our mortgage, recreational, and investment portfolios all rolled into one. For hundreds of years, it had been at the crossroads of First Nations commerce, where the interior nations met the coastal mainland nations and the Vancouver Island nations. Chief Khalserton Seepass, the **Perez de** Cuellar of the local aboriginal bands, wrote a book which was introduced to me by an Austrian anthropologist and psychiatrist. Chief Seepass' grandson visited my next-door neighbour regularly and we once exchanged gifts. Arrowheads littered the north-end beach of the lake, which was a major seasonal fishing camp.

A trail which linked the interior bands with the coastal families led to Post Creek from Manning Park. Don and I hiked that trail and got caught in the first snowfall of November just north of Greendrop Lake. We had to dig ourselves out of the snow in the morning of the third day, after having been soaked the morning of the second day, and climb over ice-glazed talus slopes at dusk.

In 1986, my buddy Ian and his prairie-farmer brother-in-law hiked a trail from Mount Baker called Cooper Ridge. It took us over five days and led to the headwaters of Chilliwack Lake.

Williams Peak was a beautiful climb and I did an as-the-crow-flies route with Peter, a German-Canadian paddling buddy. Also, with a kid from my neighbourhood in East Vancouver, I tackled Webb's Peak and MacDonald's Peak, where we camped next to a babbling crystal spring in the alpine meadow amidst the blooming heather. Magnificent.

I hiked Goetz Peak solo right from my front door. I stupidly headed straight up the goat cliffs and along the ridge that led to the mountain's shoulder. I had no idea what lay ahead in terms of terrain, except that the topographical map suggested it was steep. I walked the gravelled ramps down the backside to the utterly hidden alpine meadow lakes above and behind Greendrop Lake. That was an utterly mystical night.

I went alone because I could find no one to accompany me, and it promised to be a perfect September weekend. I had a major panic at one point because I must have been on a mineral deposit and my compass suggested I was in the wrong valley; if it were so, I wouldn't get out by Monday. I would thus end up in the Skagit rather than the Chilliwack Valley, about fifty miles from my car.

On Monday, a Japanese documentary film crew was coming to cover my family psycho-educational group at Richmond Mental Health. Missing it would have been a gross insult to this very formal and dignified delegation of Japanese journalists. They were covering community psychiatric services in Canada after an airline pilot had suffered a psychotic break in 1982 and crashed a JAL DC-8 airliner into Tokyo Bay. The pilot's sister was in the entourage and the documentary later appeared in Japan on prime-time television news.

One time, a catastrophic flood wiped out the Tamihi Bridge, forcing us upper-valley inhabitants to follow the north side of the river in order to get out. Then there was the time a fully loaded logging truck turned over on its side at the Tamihi bridge curve; if a car had been passing, it would have been crushed. I had crossed the bridge just moments before.

I seem to always be right where "stuff happens." Our paddling group once found the body of a drowned prison inmate who had tried to swim the river just minutes earlier. When we found him, the paddlers gave CPR until the ambulance arrived. Then there were the prisoner escapes from the Centre Creek, Ford Mountain, and Thurston Correctional facilities, as well as routine break-ins to our cabins. Amber and I also got stranded at Post Creek once due to a massive snowstorm. This was in the days before the main road was ploughed. Needless to say, we missed some work time and happily stoked up the woodstove, watching the massive flakes bury our world.

When I came home on furlough from Jamaica in 1998, I only had three days in my little mountain paradise. On the second day, the cabin across the road burned to the ground in a spectacular fire. It had been a beautiful partial log and rough-cut lumber house complete with out-buildings, and there were strong indications of arson. Neither the volunteer fire department nor the police even bothered to attend.

An ex-military guy I became friends with at church ended up in Oakalla and Ford Mountain prisons. These were old charges from his heavy-drinking days and I visited him both at Oakalla and Ford. He let me know that they needed church services at Ford. Because my mountain home was just up the road, God gave me a team and we played music and delivered a message. My friend came to Christ, and after release he took over the ministry and carried it for fifteen years, until after I returned from Jamaica. It was more than a small miracle that I ended up speaking at the prison where, by God's grace, I had been allowed to start a ministry so many years earlier.

I love hummingbirds. The de facto mayor of Post Creek and his wife used to put out feeders down at the east end of my group of cabins. He was a pistol-packin' retired heavy-equipment operator from the forest industry and they spent their winters in Arizona in a mobile home. They let me know how to attract large numbers of hummingbirds, so from March until they moved up into the alpine meadows in June, Amber and I fed them right outside our kitchen windows. What wonderful creatures! It was unimaginable that these tiny, fragile birds that weighed the same as a dime and produced eggs the size of a pea could fly all the way to Mexico every year and return while it was still freezing.

On summer evenings, as the last rays of sunset waned, I saw a little male Ruby Throat hummingbird sitting in a pine tree, his incandescent bib catching the last of the light and leaving a dot of neon reflection in the darkness.

The family groups would fight and squabble over the feeder. The aggressive males would stand guard for a while, which I would see from my vantage point from the kitchen window. One time, the pistol-packing mayor's wife saw one on the perch of her kitchen feeder, and it wasn't moving. As she looked more closely, she saw that it had accidentally speared a yellow jacket and the hornet's fluids and carcass had glued its beak shut. It couldn't feed. The feeder was on a hinge, so she slowly brought it into the window frame. The little hummingbird didn't try to fly away. She took it in her hand, pulled the yellow jacket off its beak, and gently washed it, and placed it back on the perch. She hinged the feeder back outside the window and the little angel rested, then fed on the sugar water and flew away. It was a miracle rescue, confirming the remarkable intelligence of these little creatures.

One time in summer, a little hummingbird came inside my house and was exhausting itself trying to escape back through a closed window. I captured it in my hand; with its little head between my index and second finger, my hand closed over its wings. I felt its incredibly rapid heartbeat. It didn't struggle as I looked into its eyes and walked outside onto the deck. I opened my hand and it flew away to a nearby pine tree, resting after what must have been a terrifying ordeal. I was so moved that the Lord had allowed me to hold such a tiny miracle in my hand.

The Watch

The master bedroom was empty. My dad's watch rested on the bedside table and the day calendar was frozen on June 21. The hospital bed was gone, the one I'd sat beside on the high stool and whose side rail I'd leaned over as we looked together over the forty miles of the St. John River, watching the sun go down in silence… but we both knew.

Thirteen years ago, our mom had been treated on this very spot, but she hadn't been privileged to die here. A medical emergency had taken her away from her view by the window and she'd never returned to the room she so loved. Dad had decided that it was to be different for him. His instructions were clear: "Do not hospitalize. Do not resuscitate."

This bedroom, appointed by our mom in soft pinks and lavender and magenta, was bright, breezy, and comfortable. The room had a postcard view that she had watched through every season of the twenty-eight years the Lord gave her there. The matching antique wash basin and pitcher, the white French provincial furniture, and silk flowers set it apart from any other room in the house. This room was her signature.

It wasn't Dad's style, but he came to love its elegance and put his own mark on it. For the past two months, it had served as a living room, a meeting room, a guest room, an emergency room, and now a dying room.

Sitting eye-to-eye with him on the high kitchen stool while he read the paper, he and I discussed what living was about after his eighty-six years of experience at it. We listened to the news on his little AM transistor radio, and as it became more difficult for him to process it, he asked me what the news stories were about. But the world outside this room had become a less relevant place for both him and me.

After the pipe was smoked, the sponge cake and sauce were eaten, the tea was sipped, and the pills were taken, the drapes were closed on the last glow of a central New Brunswick landscape. He would soon sleep.

"It took Mom ten months to die," he would say, and it was so difficult to respond. "Therese told me it took your uncle Don three months to die." After that, silence.

All I could say was, "I know, Dad. It's in God's hands, isn't it?"

He would agree and quote Philippians 2:13: *"For it is God which worketh in you both to will and to do of his good pleasure"* (KJV). This had been his scriptural motto for thirty years.

Then I would cry and go out of the room, only to pace and return to fluff his pillow and get his hand lotion. The tears streamed down my face, but he was unable to recognize or process it, and that was merciful.

The whole room smelled like him. Imagine an old man who smelled good… and familiar… and sweet. The room had the smell of pipe tobacco; by this time, he could only use one arm, so together we would stoke the pipe, tamp it, then light it. He tamped it again and we relit it just as puffs of smoke filled the room with the familiar aroma of forty years of my life. The tobacco glowed in the bowl and darkened as he breathed. The rich scent filled every corner and crevice. "The tobacco gives me a lift," he would say. "It is a comfort. You know, you must get some nicotine from the tobacco, even if you don't inhale."

His arm would reach out and grip the railing of the hospital bed. He would anchor himself there as he looked over that magnificent landscape as if looking into the future.

Now the room was empty, hollow. There was no more sweet aroma, but still a presence. No more talk of the way it used to be. No more hugs and kisses. No more six o'clock news. No more rustle of the newspaper as the pages fell to the floor. No more ringing of the cowbell to call me. No more "Good morning" from the foot of the bed. No more aroma of hand lotion from rubbing down his pressure spots and elbows. No more shaves and the smell of shaving cream and aftershave. No more dinners consumed in the joy of an old man with few pleasures left. The golfing was gone, the shopping was gone, the reading was gone, the TV was gone, the car was gone, and the independence was gone. Now *he* was gone.

The excruciating pain he suffered was hard to take while the nurses tried to get the order for morphine—the groaning breaths, the writhing in pain, and then the injection. The painful moans would be stilled, replaced by a regular gurgle which grew heavier and heavier. We would try to comfort him, to hold him. Psalms were read, hymns were sung, prayers were elicited, and final blessings and long-unspoken appreciations were put to words… for a lifetime. For an eternity.

The room became a medical consultation and emergency room with stethoscopes, syringes, blood pressure cuffs, and serious, anxious looks. In it were the beautiful, totally engaged community nurse. I remember the doctor's

Newfoundland accent and grey hair on a boyish face, and his beard. Details on a landscape of pain.

The doctor spoke in clear terms that the end was near, and that it appeared Dad had suffered a heart attack. We walked the tightrope between Dad's comfort level and the analgesics undermining his already low blood pressure. Comfort was the priority, so we arrived at a medical plan. My brother Allan had to return to Seattle after a long vigil. Brother Bob, his dear wife, and his two adult children—Kathy-Jo and Kim—remained. They slept in shifts and I kept watch. I watched in prayer, and watched in praise, and watched in the Word.

The room became a battleground between the seen and unseen worlds. Each breath was fought through fluid as the waters slowly overtook him. Outside the room, a ferocious thunderstorm raged. Rain lashed the windows, seeking entry. Flashes of lightning illuminated trees frozen in contorted poses. It all seemed such a metaphor for the battle within.

After four hours of heroic struggle, Dad received the 4:00 a.m. injection. The pain arrested and slowly, ever so slowly, the battle eased. I call Bob and Joey and Kim and Kathy-Jo. Slowly, the gurgling stopped. The breath grew shallow. The pauses grew longer… and finally, no more struggle and no more breath.

Sobs and shaking and silence. Look. Listen. Convulsive sobbing.

It's happened. Not really… can it really be…? He looked like he was sleeping. He was warm… he was Dad!

Wails and convulsing.

The room was filled with sorrow as we embraced. *Isn't it all still the same? Can't we go to sleep and wake to find everything has gone back to normal?*

No. Nothing would be the same… ever!

The horizon became visible in the blue dawn, revealing an old man lying perfectly still in his own room. His arm didn't reach for the rail anymore. His arm didn't bring the teacup to his lips. The pipe was cold and silent.

A station wagon glided down the wooded lane into the yard of the house on top of the hill. Two young men in dark suits emerged. The river was faint and blue in the distance. The birds were beginning to greet the morning, in the mists after the storm. There were sobs and pacing, crying out as a son went back again and again to listen for a breath… to look, to see a movement, to feel, to touch!

Those beloved, bent fingers were motionless as the two young men from the station wagon entered the room. The nurse received them, having completed her work.

A son wailed and sobbed and circled the house on the hilltop in the tattered mists of a June morning. The nurse went to him, and he rested from the pain in her arms, arms that know the Lord and how to comfort.

The station wagon disappeared down the lane. The old man had left his room for the final time as the morning light poured through the window and reflected off the watch that lay on the bedside table.

16

Jamaica Psychosis —the Revolution in Practice

WHEN I WAS ACCEPTED BY THE MENNONITE CENTRAL COMMITTEE (MCC) for assignment in 1995, I had two choices: a mountain village in Pernambuco, Brazil, working with a Catholic priest serving mentally handicapped kids in residential care, or Montego Bay, Jamaica, working with a grassroots NGO for the homeless mentally ill.

I had no facility with languages, so I chose the mostly English-speaking Jamaica.[35] Plus, the Jamaican assignment was related to psychiatry, rather than the developmentally delayed, with which I had no experience.

The political party in power at that time was the People's National Party, a democratic socialist party carrying the mantle of Prime Minister Michael Manley. In the 1980 election, a de facto civil war broke out because Manley was pro-Castro and a proponent of the Non-Aligned Movement, though Castro's alignment with the Soviet Union was crystal clear.[36] Manley was to soften his position later in life. While in Jamaica, I saw Fidel Castro speak in Montego Bay, as well as Robert Mugabe (from Zimbabwe) in the city's soccer stadium.

As I began my preparation to work in Jamaica, I was led to literature that not even the MCC country representatives had read. Among the books was *Born Fi' Dead*, by Laurie Gunst.[37] Though an unapologetic left-wing spin on the situation, it vividly described the endemic violence that defined Jamaican society both at home and in the Jamaican diaspora. Thus, I expected to return to Canada in a body

---

[35] In fact, the unofficial spoken language is Patois.

[36] Manley's diplomatic posture was far left and officially labeled anti-imperialist. "It threatened American hegemony in the region, given Castro's mandate, which was to export his revolution to Latin America" (from "Revolution for Export," *Time Magazine*, Monday, August 22, 1960 [http://www.time.com/time/magazine/article/0,9171,869815,00.html]).

[37] Laurie Gunst, *Born Fi' Dead* (New York, NY: Henry Holt & Company, 1995).

bag, even though the dangers were in being a Jamaican, not in being an expat. But a body bag was okay with me, because I hadn't really planned for my retirement.

I shut down a life, closed up my beautiful mountain home, and saw it disappear through the rear-view mirror of my pickup truck, fully expecting never to see it again.

The experience was both heart-breaking and intoxicating. As I pulled onto the Chilliwack Lake Road, heading west, I saw the canyon and the sky above. Vanishing were the peace and quiet, the rocker and the stove, the Whiskey Jacks and the hummingbirds, the deer and the coyotes. A blood-soaked Caribbean island paradise was to replace it.

CUMI people

After a two-week orientation in the middle of Pennsylvania Amish country, with about sixty other recruits who were to scatter to every corner of the world, some incredible things happened. War broke out in the "peace seminar." To settle the heated racial dispute between a black administrator and a white civil rights activist professor, a small-statured Afro-American man from Harlem insisted on washing a white brother's feet. This beautiful, mild-mannered, and biblically solid brother demonstrated Christ in a racially charged conflict, bringing peace where the professor, the activist, and the mediator could not. Further, his godliness sent us all on our way around the world with eyes filled with tears, convicted to the core.

That white brother's feet were my feet. Against my tearful protests, he did this loving act. Then I returned the ordinance. Within a year, he was dead.

We flew over the Florida panhandle and overflew Cuba before taxiing onto the blistering tarmac of Kingston International Airport. The ground crew literally danced their duties around the aircraft.

I landed in Kingston amidst a dengue fever epidemic, and I slathered myself in insect repellent, much to the amusement of the country reps, until I couldn't stand it anymore.

The orientation was exhausting. We toured all the projects on the island, even meeting the MCC justice director, who was visiting Jamaica. We toured the prisons and discovered that the prisons were full of the mentally ill. Their presence was the one issue that the Corrections administration, inmate reps, and correctional officers' union agreed upon: the psychiatric patients shouldn't be there. This was to prove prophetic, in that after three years in Montego Bay, the incarcerated mentally ill came to be our number one human rights concern. With my twenty years of experience in psychiatry, I was just the man to do it.

The chaplain—the very prominent Rev. Renford Maddix—begged the country rep to let me stay and counsel in the prison, but I already had my assignment in Montego Bay at the Committee for the Upliftment of the Mentally Ill (CUMI). The name itself had God's fingerprints on it, though the founders were completely unaware of it. The accidental acronym actually meant "arise." Imagine!

> *Then He took the child by the hand, and said to her, "Talitha, cumi," which is translated, "Little girl, I say to you, arise."* (Mark 5:41)

We got caught in a torrential rain in Montego Bay, getting soaked to the skin, which actually felt good, because we were so hot. Coupled with a later experience in Kingston, when I attended a church in one of the garrison[38] communities at night during a torrential downpour while wading shin-deep in muddy, backed-up sewer water, I began to realize the excitement that was in store.

I was dropped off in Montego Bay after being introduced to my partners and temporary accommodation. Here I was, in an unfamiliar nation, an unfamiliar city known for crime, hearing an unfamiliar language, forced to depend upon an unfamiliar transport system, and there were no other MCC-affiliated workers in the area. It was kind of a lonely feeling.

On my first day at work, the courier I was accompanying was attacked. We were being followed back to the centre after the courier picked up some petty

---

[38] In Jamaica, the term "garrison" refers to gang-controlled communities, with "dons" (such as in the *Godfather* movies) that rule with an iron fist. In the Jamaican press, they are euphemistically referred to as "community leaders."

cash and introduced me to our business supporters. I was walking ahead of him when I heard him scream. A tall Afro-Jamaican had grabbed him from behind, immobilized him, and went straight for the cash. I wheeled around, ran toward them, grabbed the guy by the arms, and screamed bloody murder. The attacker had never seen anything like this—an old, white-haired white man grabbing him and screaming in his ear! He spun around to get out of my grip and raised his right arm. That's when I saw a flash and immediately thought, *A knife!* At that point, he was extremely vulnerable to a hard right upper-cut to the jaw. It would have knocked him unconscious. It was not a knife, though, and I didn't hit him.

Later, I thought of the headlines: "Canadian Christian aid worker with the 'peace church' (Mennonites) assaults Jamaican national on first day of work in community psychiatry." Not good! To my CUMI partners, I would have been a hero. Amidst the slow-motion action, the Holy Spirit got hold of this hot-headed, impulsive, reactive disciple and held me back. The assailant ran off.

When we got back to the centre, I was still treated like a hero amidst gales of laughter. They pictured Colonel Sanders (who I looked like, to Jamaicans) in a white shirt and tie, wrestling with a black youth on the street. The petty cash had been saved.

Thus began a three-year voyage of discovery where my naïve middle-class North American leftist ideology was confronted with the harsh realities of the real world. At the time, Jamaica was the number one trans-shipment point for Columbian cocaine headed for Florida and the U.S. eastern seaboard.

This magnificent island paradise had been bathed in blood since before European contact, as the Carib, Tainos, and Arawak peoples had long fought for their lands and identities.[39] Then came the Spanish colonial genocides, the horrors of the lucrative slave trade, slave rebellions, independence, the Cold War, the drug wars, and now impending jihad.

Jamaica had repeatedly been the "centre of the universe" in that its sugar, rum, and coffee production financed a significant proportion of the British colonial empire, just as Hispaniola financed the French colonial empire. Sugar, rum, and coffee alone netted three and a half million sterling per annum in the 1830s.[40] Jamaican planters were the envy of not only the British aristocracy but

---

[39] Kim Johnson, "Taino: The Story of the 'Caribs and Arawaks,'" *Race and History*, November 13, 2013 (http://www.raceandhistory.com/Taino/).

[40] Robert Montgomery Martin, *Statistics of the Colonies of the British Empire in the West Indies, South America, North America, Asia, Austral-Asia, Africa and Europe* (London, UK: Wm H Allen & Co, 1839).

also the monarchy. The expression "rich as a Jamaican planter" meant "more wealthy than the old, blue-blooded money of England."

They allegedly used their wealth to buy up the "rotten burroughs" of the landed aristocracy, thus acquiring seats in parliament, then using the British Navy to enforce and control an elevated price for sugar. In his book *Caribbean*, James A. Michener floats the hypothesis that the Jamaican planters were responsible for the American Revolution, one of the single most important events in human history.[41]

Thus, little Jamaica built the British Empire and set up its competitor (the U.S.) by forcing the Thirteen Colonies into independence, engendering the creation of a society that has been the most free, democratic, and technologically advanced in history. Jamaica then became a pawn in the Soviet Union's imperialistic aspirations in the Americas, becoming a key feature of the world's second largest business: the illicit drug trade.

In the 1970s and 80s, Cuba went to the Soviet Bloc, and Granada was invaded by U.S. forces after its pro-Soviet Marxist-Leninist coup. In 1974, Jamaican Prime Minister Manley seriously threatened the U.S. with another revolution when he stated, "I will walk to the top of the mountain with Fidel Castro…"[42] The Jamaican party system came to reflect the larger international conflict, with the Jamaica Labour Party of Edward Seaga positioning itself as pro-business and pro-American against Manley's PNP, which was a member of the Socialist International.

It is rumoured that in the bloodbath of the 1980 election, the people of Jamaica voted out their beloved Manley to save his life. Many were convinced that if Manley was re-elected, Fidel Castro would have him assassinated, blame it on the Americans, and take over the reins of the Jamaican government. The thesis goes that they voted in Edward Seaga to neutralize the threat.

By the time I got there in 1995, the People's National Party had been in power for six years, and they remained in power until 2007 (totalling nearly eighteen years). The annual rate of return through money market brokers was 43.9% per annum, for a relatively small deposit. Business couldn't capitalize, because each month they had to make the payment on a debt, they ended up owing more than the previous month.

I couldn't understand Jamaica until the CBC, on my 1998 furlough, aired a long segment on the global drug trade. The guests were Dr. Michael

---

[41] James A. Michener, *Caribbean* (New York, NY: Random House, 1989).

[42] David Howard, *Kingston: A Cultural and Literary History* (Oxford, UK: Signal Books, 2005), 162.

Chossudovsky, renowned professor emeritus and economist from the University of Ottawa, and Michael Levine, a much-decorated twenty-five-year veteran, author, and ex-deep-cover agent for the DEA. My subsequent study of the economics of the trade clarified everything.

The international drug trade had globalized far ahead of national and international governments and law enforcement, and their business provided an almost inexhaustible supply of funding, which meant they could out-gun and out-tech any policing agencies, which were restricted by rules of engagement, ever-shrinking budgets, and high levels of accountability. Infiltration, corruption, and violence flowed wherever the trade flowed, and Jamaica was a key link in the chain.

The violence was endemic. Using comparative analysis, it couldn't be explained by slavery, poverty, class warfare, or ideological or religious conflict. Jamaica is not poor! It has a lot of poor people because of corruption and an imbalanced distribution of wealth. It has twelve major foreign-currency-generating enterprises on an island 150 miles by fifty miles in size. Its soil is rich, its people beautiful and resourceful, and it has an ideal climate and perfect geographical location for tourism. Why were there five murders per day and a killing by police every second day in a population of one and a half million? It made no sense.

The island had a unique romance about it, and Bob Marley was popular beyond measure. The Rastafarians were the darlings of North American and European religious faddists and dope-smokers.

The CBC piece explained the drug trade's crucial part in the Cold War and how Ronald Reagan had made the prudential judgment that to win the Cold War, he had to abandon the drug war. Courageously, Chossudovsky and Levine explained that the official anti-drug war was largely smoke and mirrors, and hugely expensive. They demonstrated the lack of political will to take the measures necessary to stop it and that our ideological enemies were using it to defeat us. The solution was simple but politically unpalatable to our statist and libertarian cultures.

Thus, political parties and individuals interacted with the drug lords. The cartels would first "buy" specific police personnel (offering the carrot or the stick, gold or lead), and then the judiciary. One million dollars is petty cash to the trade. The "offer you can't refuse" might go like this: "Either you get a tax-free million or your daughter gets raped. Any questions?"

As a result of my intense study, Jamaica suddenly made sense. Then I went into the prisons to work. I would be changed forever.

My third revolution in mind was in process. I was becoming a political conservative.

The Shootout[43]

It all began near the small, open-air ghetto cocaine market in Liguanea called the Standpipe.

Four gunmen in a white, late-model Toyota four-door sedan approached a woman who was unlocking her gate as her car idled. As they approached her, she ran for the front door of her house. The thieves approached the car, but then a police jeep turned onto the street and observed the crime in progress. The young men jumped into their Toyota, abandoning the attempted carjacking, and passed the police at high speed. The police pulled a U-turn and assumed hot-pursuit straight up Widcombe Avenue into the hills of the MacAuleys Heights.

Where Widcombe passed the last of its dense residential housing, it hit a tight S- curve through a dry but steep cobblestone gully. Since the police were so close to the fleeing Toyota, decelerating for the curve brought them into range of the gunmen, who opened fire. The police returned fire, blowing the glass out of the rear window of the Toyota. The gunmen accelerated through the gully with the police still in hot pursuit. Sparks flew as the vehicle bottomed out in the gulley.

The criminals were obviously unfamiliar with the area but knew enough to think that Widcombe was a dead-end. They turned up the steep switchback of Doorly Avenue, hitting the next "Y" in the road and another dead-end. They turned down the hill on Lineman Avenue, passing through another sharp S-curve. After only a hundred yards, they faced Ripoll Close to the right, or what would have been a clear exit down the hill to the left.

But at this intersection there was a construction site with piles of blocks and sand at the corner, making it appear as a dead-end. They screamed around the corner to the right… a decision that proved fatal for two of the men.

Within another 150 feet, they were in the Ripoll Close cul-de-sac. There was no exit—only a cliff straight ahead, a huge iron gate to the right, and a steep-sloping driveway to the left. They went left in a screeching four-wheel slide only to find another cliff-top iron railing and dead-end. Somehow they got the car turned uphill just as the police jeep crested the driveway. The doors exploded open as three police personnel with M-16s positioned themselves for a firefight.

---

[43] Originally published in *Jamaica Comments*, November 2000.

Concurrently, the Toyota's doors exploded outward as the gunmen sought escape. The driver was shot dead through the front window. The first man out the driver-side rear door took a bullet in the shoulder but bolted over the railing, across the lawn below (in front of my basement suite), and over the chain-link fence into the construction site.

In the confusion, another gunman firing a .357 Magnum got over the railing and away into the bush without getting hit. The fourth man delayed in the back seat. Finally, as he bolted, he was cut down in a hail of M-16 fire from the police above. One shell penetrated the steel tubular railing as though it was a tree branch. It rang like a bell for six seconds. He collapsed on the driveway above the stairs that had allowed the escape of his two companions.

Fifteen police cars converged on the cul-de-sac. It was midnight Friday night. The police scoured the bush for the other two men as a pool of blood grew to fifty square feet in the driveway. The neighbours gathered.

The gardener reported that the downed man had twenty-two entry wounds in his chest and abdomen. The stench of gunpowder seeped into the upstairs floors, impregnating the drapes, carpet, and furniture fabrics. My landlord stood on the balcony with his nine-millimetre automatic pistol drawn. His wife was rocking and shaking in the bedroom. Everybody's ears rang as the police investigated the scene. Shell casings covered the driveway. Three firearms were found, including a nine-millimetre automatic pistol.

The man who got away uninjured was apprehended in the gully later that night. The man who got shot cleaned himself up and went into Kingston Public Hospital for treatment, claiming a mugging. He got treated and departed before the police arrived. He remained at large.

Where was I during all this?

On an impulse, after a day of teaching at Runaway Bay Correctional Centre on the north coast, I booked into a hotel in Ocho Rios. While death and mayhem took place in my driveway, I slept blissfully as sailboats rocked in the marina.

One man carries a gunshot wound and is a fugitive. Another man languishes in the nightmare jails of Kingston. Mothers and girlfriends and daughters and sons grieve and mourn the loss of their wild loved ones. The police try to recover from the memories of the firefight, including the risks to their own lives.

And me? I wonder how I would have reacted had I been there. But mainly I reflect on the fact that God is good and merciful and highly protective. Blessed be His holy name!

17

Haiti

HAITI CONTAINED ONE OF THE MCC'S LATIN AMERICAN-CARIBBEAN offices in 1997. The UN was there after the Clinton Administration sponsored the installation of Jean Bertrand Aristide into the presidency, thus ousting the Duvalier family. The country had been a bloodbath and was now merely in chaos.

After every three-year term of service, MCC workers would be allowed an all-expense-paid trip to view other projects in their region. Haiti was one of ours. A young Mennonite couple with kids from the U.S. working in the town of Highgate, St. Mary pulled out of their project and arrived at the Kingston Airport, tickets in hand, just as I did, only to find out that there was an American Airlines pilots strike and we weren't going anywhere.

Air Jamaica took up the slack, however, and soon we were on a flight to Miami with connections into Port-au-Prince. In Miami, I came a hair's breadth from missing the flight and Doug Graber (father of the MCC Highgate family) literally had to hold the cabin door open until I arrived. As we made our approach to Haiti, we got a taste of the desert Haiti had become due to manmade defoliation.

I had met Doug's beautiful Mennonite family from the U.S. Midwest. Doug and Nancy Graber had three little blond girls and a boy. We became fast friends over the initial period of our assignments and were to vacation together and support one another in our struggles. In Highgate, their little home had a neighbour's chicken coop right against the bedroom wall. Every morning from 3:30 a.m., the rooster would crow every ten to fifteen minutes. It got to the point where they didn't even hear it, but me? Had I a shotgun, I would have created an international incident and the rooster would have been nothing but a cloud of feathers.

In Haiti, the apparent chaos and degradation slapped me in the face the moment we landed. The dust, dirt, grinding poverty, and dilapidated or absent infrastructure were manifest in a sea of heroic effort by the delightful Haitian people and those from the so-called international community who would rescue them.

On the streets, I could see the living, breathing source of the radical defoliation: coal-carriers. All along the streets and in markets were links in the coalmining chain—those who cut down the trees and burned them in chips that in turn became the coal that fuelled the kitchens, those who distributed it to the vendors, and those who sold it on the street.

The Dominican Republic managed to prevent defoliation by subsidizing propane and natural gas. The result is that when you fly over the border, you see forests on the Dominican side and desert on the Haitian side.

As we bounced through the streets of Port-au-Prince (more like potholed dirt paths than streets), we saw the car-axle-and-tire carts pulled by men, their flatbeds laden with products for the narrow inner-city streets. The country reps told us that the life expectancy of a man from the time he picked up the cart-shaves was three years. Unimaginable.

Rural Storage Depot, Haiti

We drove through the dusty, filthy, crowded streets in our Land Rover, bouncing through potholes and weaving through the various obstructions. We then drove into the walled and secure MCC residence, closing and locking the gate behind us. We saw shards of glass mortared into the tops of the walls to prevent pillage and rape. A home invasion, theft, and attempted rape had happened just months before we arrived and had been foiled by a miracle of God's grace. Life in Haiti was tenuous for the nationals and merely dangerous for expats.

Dan and Wilma Weins, a beautiful couple from the Canadian prairies, welcomed us royally. They became quite famous in Canada by developing a community share system for farmers which took the peaks and troughs out of the agricultural produce cycle and had the town share in the boom and bust.

A large table was set at the MCC house, full of the bounty Haiti was able to produce. After giving thanks, a call came over the radio-phone.

The message was unclear, but it appeared that Pierre, the agricultural project manager for a placement in Vieillard, had been returning from Prince in his flatbed Toyota and collided with a transport truck on the national highway. Traffic was backed up in both directions for miles and it appeared that somebody had taken him to the Catholic hospital in St. Marc.

"I've got to go," Dan said and called their Haitian helper Janvier to attend with him. The Haitian didn't drive, so I said I would go and we headed out over the spooky, crime-ridden streets toward the only paved highway in Haiti. "Paved" is a relative term, because the roads hadn't been maintained since the Papa Doc Duvalier days and the average speed at which one calculated their ETA was thirty miles per hour.

There was another very interesting feature of the National highway: bandits! They took over the highway after 11:00 p.m. From that moment onward, anything moving would be robbed, hijacked, stripped of parts, and left derelict in a matter of minutes. We had to find Pierre before 11:00 p.m. It was already dark.

About an hour and a half out of the city, we met the traffic backup. It was stopped almost dead. Dan jumped out of the Land Rover, ran a mile or so to the wreck, and found the mangled wreck of the Toyota, a tanker truck lying on its side nearby. Dan decided that he had to get to the hospital in St. Marc to see if Pierre had survived or not, and then to inform Pierre's young family, who were going crazy with worry. He left me with instructions to park on the roadside until 10:00 p.m., when hopefully the gridlock would clear, and make a run for St. Marc before the hijacker-imposed curfew. Dan then caught a ride to St. Marc on a tap-tap, the brightly coloured trucks that acted as public transport; they usually had twenty to thirty people crammed into them.

I was exhausted from having worked most of the night before we left Jamaica, so I fell asleep in the Land Rover.

At 10:00, Janvier woke me and we started off again, this time in the pitch black. There were no streetlights, so we bobbed and weaved, trying to find patches of highway surface to drive on; going off the main route could have brought dire consequences. Mercifully, we soon saw the lights of St. Marc and got into town at about ten or fifteen minutes to 11:00. There were no words to describe the relief I experienced.

We drove into the compound of the St. Nicholas Hospital and parked the Land Rover. We met Dan at the gate and proceeded to try to find Pierre. In the centre of the courtyard, surrounded by wards of sleeping patients, was an open-air gazebo structure with operating tables in it. We surmised that this was the casualty unit, because there were bloody bandages in a wastebasket surrounded by a cloud of flies. On the gurneys were blood-covered sheets. As we surveyed the wreckage, a woman came out and urinated into the drainage trench. Dan had momentarily disappeared and returned to us in a few minutes to report that he had found Pierre.

Another windowless ward served as Recovery. Inside, we found six hospital beds with casted, bandaged, and sleeping post-op patients who weren't ambulatory. There was no staff, no IV bags or bottles, no water, and no visible access to bathroom facilities. None of these patients had as much as a glass of water on a bedside table.

Pierre was casted from foot to hip, with plenty of abrasions and contusions, but he was very happy to see us. The cast he received was only temporary. He then gave us the details of the accident. We were so relieved that he was still alive, and Pierre was relieved that we had rescued him from this rough casualty hospital to actual treatment at Haiti's only complete hospital facility: Dr. Albert Schweitzer Hospital in Deschapelles.

Pierre informed us that this facility was short of doctors and nursing staff, and that food and comforts had to come from the family. In the morning, as we took Pierre out of the facility, there was a queue of family members carrying food and supplies at the gate. Lord help the patients who had no family to provide and minister to them.

That night, we found a room in the village and spent the night on uncomfortable cots. The air was hot and sticky, and we only got two hours of sleep, because at 4:00 a.m. the trucks started moving again on the national highway. They seemed to be coming straight through our hotel room, using compression brakes on a hill just above us. Every few minutes, I dreamt of a tractor trailer rolling over my cot.

The next morning, we began our trek to the hospital in Deschapelles. With the temporary cast immobilizing Pierre from hip to ankle, we had a significant challenge fitting him into the Land Rover. He was only minimally stable and the roads were little more than a gauntlet of huge potholes created by the intermittent torrential rains and heavy traffic.

We travelled through the magnificent Artibonite River valley, marked by failed international development projects and killing fields. Duvalier's paramilitary terror squads had allegedly drove these roads, spraying field workers and farmers with machine-gun fire during the "troubles." Every few kilometres, we would come upon a voodoo houngan hut with its flagpoles and brightly coloured ensigns. Word had it that Haitians were afraid of Jamaicans for their violence, and Jamaicans were afraid of Haitians for their voodoo practices.

When we arrived at the hospital, there were massive numbers of people seeking treatment, with family members petitioning for them. We were to wait several hours, and finally Pierre came up for treatment. Each of us had a role in the division of labour, and mine was to go into the treatment room with him.

The doctor had no assistant, so I had the experience of applying my first cast. Pierre was in obvious distress as the old cast was cut off. Of greater concern was the fact that as the new one was being applied and the African doctor asked him if it was okay, Pierre said it was; I could see on his face that it wasn't. I said, "Pierre, don't be stoic. You'll regret it." He just winced and said it was okay. We immobilized him in a large, heavy plaster cast.

Then came the rough ride into the hill village, where Pierre's Haitian wife and kids awaited him.

The entire village greeted him in celebration. As beverages were distributed, the family gathered to watch him receive his little girls into his arms. Beverages were distributed. He learned to navigate the small dwelling with his crutches and hip cast, and we momentarily joined village life.

That night was possibly the most miserable night I have ever spent in my life. Dan and I were consigned to a small, thatch-roofed wooden shack. It was a sweltering ninety degrees Fahrenheit and the wooden shutters over the windows had to be closed due to the risk of invasion. Mice ran through the thatch and rafters, and small insects moved through the straw tick mattress Dan and I shared. It was a night of sweating, itching, and vigilance, trying to keep the mice from running over my body—or worse, stopping. I can't have slept more than two hours waiting for the sun to come up.

The next day, my medical concerns for Pierre became a reality. He awoke in significant pain. His leg began to swell inside the cast, because it had been immobilized in a position that put pressure on the injury. He once again had to go back to the hospital. This time, he went in the family vehicle, with his wife driving. We headed back to Port-au-Prince.

We reached the outskirts about an hour after dark, just as the dim lanterns lit the tiny shacks which served as houses and small vending outlets. The Land Rover was of the suburban variety, with side windows and a latched door in the rear. It was designed to seat five, with a cargo compartment at the rear. In the dim light, we could see Haitians running alongside and jumping onto the side running boards, trying to unlatch the doors to gain entry and take what they could. A man jumped onto our rear bumper and was pulling at the latch of the rear-door cargo compartment at the same time as people tried to gain entry from both sides. Dan unceremoniously headed for the nearest large pothole. He bounced in and out of the largest potholes until everyone was dislodged.

That night at the MCC house, the sound of NATO helicopters orbiting overhead made sleep difficult. The next morning, we learned that when it hovered directly overhead, that meant marauders were trying to get over the walls and into the compound.

Over the next several days, we toured MCC projects. We clung to the outside of the brightly coloured tap-taps and jumped on motorcycle taxis at monumental risk to our lives. One project was located in a school at the waterfront slums. It had open sewage in the run-off canals. Its poorly nourished children got their only decent meal per day at the school. Then we saw the rural agricultural project in the Artibonite valley where Pierre had been trying to reintroduce the use of oxen to farming so as to reduce people's dependence on complex agricultural equipment. We were also introduced to high-yield varietal crops in rich soil areas along with the introduction of new marketing and distribution methods.

As it is all over the world, the development projects were plagued by corruption, exploitation, and risk of entitlement. In the verdant Artibonite valley, we saw irrigation canals overgrown with weeds that killed the water's oxygen content. We were told that the canals were developed and the local population paid to keep them clear of weeds. When the money for aquatic weed cleaning had run out, the workers didn't return because they were no longer being paid.

They returned to their traditional farming and vending. The weeds had filled the canals and the project had died.

The MCC had health programs dealing with a parasitic condition which resembled elephantiasis in the far north of the country. They also handled extremely creative social and economic development initiatives that were absolutely cutting edge. In 1995, I was told that the MCC ranked second on the *Forbes Magazine* list of accountable and efficient development- and-relief NGOs. That was a remarkable tribute to a hard-working organization that demanded the best from its people. Its work in Haiti was demanding and dangerous, yet the MCC stayed the course.

A contingent of United Nations forces kept the peace while we were there, and Jean Bertrand Aristide had been installed by an American-led coalition. But Haiti was a tragic place which seemed to defy social, political, and economic advancement. From the bizarre and gross atrocities of the post-independence days to the sellout by Napoleon Bonaparte, to the succession of tragedies through Toussaint Louverture and Jean-Jacques Dessalines, it seemed Haiti was cursed. Those who emigrated to North America and Western Europe often returned in hopes of using their education and experience to ease Haiti's suffering and give hope to its youth. They often gave up and returned home in despair. As the saying went, "Every time I leave Haiti, I say to myself, 'It can't get any worse,' and every time I return, it has."

Getting on the plane to Jamaica ten days later required enduring a four-hour line-up. There were thirty or forty people behind me with tickets on the same flight. When I walked up the mobile staircase and through the aircraft cabin door, it closed two or three passengers behind me, leaving the rest behind. That was a metaphor for Haiti—a snaking queue of people waiting patiently to get out, but only a few actually did.

Blue Mountain Rhapsody[44]

Thy mercy, O Lord, is in the heavens; and thy faithfulness reacheth unto the clouds. Thy righteousness is like the great mountains; thy judgments are a great deep: O Lord, thou preservest man and beast. (Psalm 36:5–6, KJV)

Just back from two months of heaven in Canada, and not all that happy about returning to Kingston, my landlady wanted to paint my bedroom chartreuse. I

---
[44] Originally published in *Jamaica Comments*, September 2001.

tore the bedroom/office apart and dumped it into the living room, put my pack on my back, and caught a taxi to the coffee farming village of Mavis Bank. My dear friend Nelson drove until the taxi began to bottom out on the streambed road above the Yallus River crossing. He was going nuts over the idea of leaving an old white-haired white man in the middle of the bush with a forty-pound pack on his back. I literally had to chase him away. I told him to come back to the river bridge in three days. It was two o'clock in the afternoon and very hot as I did violence to my fifty-five-year-old legs, not having had a pack on my back in five and a half years.

A little boy who must have come from a nearby house in the bush joined me halfway up to Hagley Gap. He warned me about the duppies (indigenous Jamaican ghost/demons) if I spent the night in the mountains. He explained that I better lash the tent door tight so the duppie wouldn't get me, because if I "come out da tent him a chase yu and kill yu." I asked him what the duppie looked like, and he said it was "smady wid no head." (Translation: somebody without a head.)

He left me at Hagley Gap and wandered off quite convinced that "mi a go dead mon." (Translation: "I'm a dead man.")

I caught a Land Rover to Whitfield Lodge, forty-five minutes over a streambed road, and began my walk up the mountainside. Farmers and farm workers were filing out of the coffee groves. Enterprising farmers who had diversified their crops marketed their ganja. The last European hikers met me at about 6:00 p.m., on their way down the mountain. They looked miserable. I had the mountain to myself for the next two days.

They were the best two days I had in the five and a half years I spent in Jamaica. Much more significant experiences were to come. I hiked through the intoxicatingly aromatic coffee plantations. As the sun set, birds of limitless variety called to one another across the vast valleys. A howling wind, cool and refreshing, came up as I entered the jungle. As it got dark, the sky cleared, moonlight casting mottled shadows into the forest.

Pini-walley (fireflies) danced in the dark bamboo tunnel. At 7:00 p.m., I reached Portland Gap, threw my MCC bedspread on top of a poly sheet, ate supper, put on every item of clothing in my pack, and fell asleep inside a minute. That night, I wore a T-shirt, collar shirt, full-length winter underwear, and flannel shirt with canvas outer layer, army pants, wool socks, and a cap with gloves. Nonetheless, I was still chilled.

The next morning, my pain-ravaged body unfolded from my tangled bedding to an overcast, ferociously windy morning with flashes of sunlight. Surrounded by flowers, I had a leisurely breakfast that tasted better than eggs benedict, put on my pack again (screaming in pain), and started toward the peak.

I became a botany student on that trip. In the Blue Mountains, there were over five hundred flowering plant varieties, with 240 of them unique to Jamaica. At Portland Gap alone, one sees cigar bush, begonias, frangipani, yellow pouie, red and purple fucia, heliconia, white antherium, monkey tail, and countless evergreen-like trees that would be ornamental in North America. The forests were full of herbaceous plants and epiphytes, eight-foot tree ferns, bromeliads, and remarkable lichens and mosses, including the hanging unsea. There were sixty-five varieties of orchid in the Blue Mountains.

Quits and tanagers, thrush, warblers, mockingbirds, woodpeckers, and hummingbirds flitted through forests of yucca, bamboo, soapwood, and clethra. Turkey buzzards and small hawks hunted from overhead.

At noon, I arrived on the peak, catching alternate glimpses of both coasts. I looked for Cuba through the haze, which incidentally was composed of sand carried all the way across the ocean from the Sahara Desert). I unfurled my MCC bedspread on the veranda of the derelict shelter and was asleep in about twenty seconds, the wind trying to blow away everything I owned. What a wonderful sleep! I realized that the last sixteen hours had been the only hours of complete silence I had experienced in all my time in Jamaica. They were delicious!

A drenching fog came in while I slept. When I awoke, it had soaked all the clothes I had been trying to air out. The jerk bacon plantain chips tasted like filet mignon. I got up, screaming in pain when the weight of the pack hit my exhausted legs. I started down at 3:00 p.m. amidst a delightfully breezy evening. I arrived at Whitfield Lodge by moonlight, escorted by fireflies.

I took a quick shower and was asleep *before* I hit the bed.

The next morning was spent having delightful conversation with the lodge caretakers. There was freshly ground Blue Mountain coffee in the dining room of the two-hundred-year-old lodge. I made a long entry in my mountain journal. This time, the pack didn't hurt and my legs felt powerful.

It was a gorgeous day of coffee-scented breezes, friendly people, donkeys, farm workers, Christmas tree planters, honey gatherers, and clean and neat little houses. A dreadlocked Rastafarian advised me to take the footpath to Mavis Bank rather than the taxi road, claiming it was much shorter.

Leaving the villages, I switchbacked steeply down a mountain buttress into the Yallus valley, and then followed the river road up to the bridge. It was a beautiful walk through varied topography and vegetation. The view was spectacular all the way down, and I didn't meet a single person on the trail.

You would never know there were environmental problems in this idyllic setting unless you were well-read on the topic. Except for the obvious erosion visible on some of the lower, steep-sloped coffee plantations, the landscape appeared robust. But it had been reported that Jamaica had the highest deforestation rate of any of the Caribbean islands. The potential consequences were frightening when I visualized my flight into Port-au-Prince, where tropical forest had been degraded into desert.

I saw what looked like ponderosa pine stands. Rumour had it that the Canadian government had conducted a project for planting the pine to slow the deforestation but that the trees weren't well-adapted to the ecosystem and somehow dried out the soil. However, they grew well and were used for lumber.

As for aesthetics, well, Jamaica was very economically developed—not at all third-world if one was in the drug trade. Development brought with it wax juice containers, plastic bottles, and wrapping. Further, Jamaican's weren't yet sensitive to litter, so the top of the mountain could be pretty unpleasant for a North American if there hadn't been a recent clean-up crew to clear the debris.

I reached the bridge at 1:00 p.m., right on time, and started the walk up the main road to the village.

A truck full of farm workers stopped for me. I tried to decline a ride, but I was afraid it would be insulting, so I nearly killed myself climbing up over the five-foot rear gate of the truck, tumbling into the back with my pack on. When I arrived in town, no one spoke to me. I sat on the veranda of a store and drank the best Coke that had ever been bottled in the Western world.

Punctual to the minute, Nelson was profoundly relieved when he saw me. He told how he'd fretted for two nights about whether some animal would eat me or some "bad man" would kill me on the trail. Fortunately, he had prayed and left it to the Lord, just as I had asked him. In the meantime, he'd told everyone about this mad customer of his who had walked off alone into the Blue Mountains. He said that he'd known I was all right because when he slept, "mi na see yu face." (Translation: "If he had seen my face, I was in serious trouble.") That meant God had taken care of me. The Lord Jesus had indeed taken care of me, leaving me with one of the most precious memories of my entire life.

18

Cuba

ANOTHER IMPULSIVE DECISION: I CAME BACK FROM TEN DAYS IN THE sleepy tourist town of Negril and decided to take a walk down Gloucester Avenue in Montego Bay, then maybe swim at Doctor's Cave. The vacation in Negril was much-needed after nine months of working with the homeless mentally ill.

Before I went to Negril, one of our clients had been doused in gasoline and set on fire, while another had been splashed in the face with battery acid. One time on our street pick-ups, with police escort, I ended up getting into the back of a packed ambulance with eight homeless folks. A virtual riot had taken place with the good citizenry of Montego Bay, with us grabbing every homeless person—addicts, poor, elderly, and mentally ill—and throwing them into the back of the ambulance. I was worried about fights breaking out and someone getting injured, so I climbed into the ambulance with them.

Well, the air inside was a musky stench. I was packed in with raving kids, the elderly, and one seriously mentally ill guy who was obviously stressed at being confined. He eyed me suspiciously. Then I heard the side door of the tiny van click; the driver had locked me in with a key and there was no interior latch. The cab had a steel barrier and meshed windows, so I was totally imprisoned with eight seriously aroused Afro-Jamaicans. They couldn't figure out what an old white man in a shirt and tie was doing in there with them. Fear etched every face.

The thirty-year-old psychotic man was dressed in a loincloth rag with strings all around his body. The strings were ornamented with pieces of coloured cloth and beads. He was missing an eye and was scarred all over his face and upper body from an acid attack. He looked like he had escaped from the cartoon series "B.C." I watched him reach into a pocket sewn into his loincloth and grab something, throwing it in my face. I managed to get my hand up, but waited for the fiery eruption only to discover that it was… laundry soap. The man must have attributed the smell inside the ambulance to me, deciding that I needed my laundry done.[45]

But I digress. Back to Gloucester Avenue. On my stroll through Montego Bay, I stepped inside the Cuban tourist bureau office and asked, academically, about what a trip to Cuba would cost. The answer: "$375 U.S., including airfare, hotel, breakfast, and tour of Havana." Great!

"When do you go next?" I asked.

"In two hours," the agent said.

"I'm on it."

I took a taxi up to my house, grabbed my passport, cash, and credit cards, and headed off to the airport.

The Cubana aircraft, owned and operated by the Cuban government, was an old rear-entry YAK (Yakoviev) 49, with engines configured like a DC-9 but double jet engines on both sides. As we approached, it appeared that the cabin was on fire. Smoke tumbled down the passenger stairs. I saw passengers disappearing into the smoke, however, so it must have been ganja. It wasn't ganja; it was refrigeration fog.

When I went aboard, all I could see were the heads of the other passengers, and they disappeared as they sat down. This was Soviet technology at its best.

During the U.S. embargo, Jamaica was the bridge for Miami Cubans to reach their families in Castro's Cuba. At the time, the Manley administration had warm relationships with Cuba. Thus, aboard the plane were many Miami Cubans and business people from all over Latin America who were doing business in Cuba.

When I had arrived in Jamaica, I'd been all starry-eyed about Cuba, as I'd been taught by the North American media and most of my professors. Fidel was a friend of our former Prime Minister Pierre Trudeau, along with his wife Margaret. The Trudeaus used to snorkel and scuba-dive with Fidel on his favourite secure reefs.

When I met my first real-world Cubans, many of whom became my best friends in Jamaica, I learned about the grim realities of life in the "worker's paradise." Now I was off to see it for myself.

Aboard this wonder of Soviet technology, the threadbare seats were ornamented by seatbelts that didn't work. Then we learned that the air

---

[45] My fear was not unfounded. Monkey acid is so common a weapon in Jamaica that the Canadian High Commission put up signs preventing people from carrying it around.

conditioning that had produced the refrigeration fog had just two settings: on and off. "On" meant you froze, so they handed out blankets, and "off" meant the sweat rolled down your forehead. We all chose—on democratic vote, of course—to freeze, and the blankets weren't warm enough.

Beside me sat a serious Indo-Belize businessman who was doing business in Cuba. He was an engineer in environmental industries, and he invited me to his home in Havana. He gave me a phone number and address.

When we landed in Santiago de Cuba, the pilot managed a gentle landing, but as the nose-wheel touched down, I kept waiting for the thrust-reversers to kick in. I waited and waited… and waited. No thrust reversers. We were landing on the brakes. Yikes! Landing in Havana, I was nervous already at the thought of worn disk pads, or even drum shoes on this liner.

As we came in, I had even more cause for alarm. All along the landing strip lay the wreckage of retired Soviet airliners of all different makes and models. Pirated for parts, they now languished under the Caribbean sun, tilted and askew with missing doors and landing gear, engines, and wing parts. Maybe our particular YAK was wearing a pair of their brake shoes.

Much to my relief, we stopped short of the end of the runway and taxied to the terminal, where I was assured of a shuttle to my hotel. It never arrived. When I started asking around the small reception room, a couple of comrades zoomed in on me and were very helpful. They called the hotel and arranged transport which arrived after I had been injected with a full dose of the "party line."

The hotel was clean and had everything I needed. It all worked, except for occasional water pressure and temperature problems. It was a 1970s era design in the late 1990s. People were friendly and helpful, without the guilt or pressure of a midlevel Jamaican hotel.

I loved it! It was such a change from Jamaica, where the hostility and threat were visceral on the street. The Cubans were well-educated and appreciative of European art, letters, and science. However, you could sense the demoralization. They didn't resent my relative wealth, as the people did in Jamaica, nor did they see me as a lamb to be fleeced. There were no visible homeless people, mentally ill, or addiction on the streets.

I arose to a nice breakfast in the dining room. Then the bus rolled up for the tour. We got a tour of the good side of the city—the industry and technological centres, the new European hotels along the beach (Spain was investing heartily). We then moved on to the castles above Havana Harbour (Castillo de los Tres Reyes), and their native art centres. They were spectacular. We then headed off to one of the central marketplaces near the harbour, with delightful promenades and musicians and families finding entertainment and relaxation.

I got the requisite Cuban cigar (though I don't smoke) and a tiny bottle of rum (though I don't drink), percussion instruments (claves from Rosewood marked "Havana"), and a few other small mementos. I then went looking for my Belize businessman and his family.

There are camels in Havana, but not of the Middle Eastern variety. They were tractor trailers with rough seating, a sheet-metal cab, and windows pulled by a diesel cab. They were humped toward the pallet in the front, and again over the back wheels, which was where the term "camel" came from. When I got aboard, one man spoke some English and recruited the entire bus to seeing that I got where I was supposed to go. He was a Cuban veteran from Angola and introduced me to another Cuban veteran of Afghanistan. These were lovely but defeated people.

The North Americans and Western Europeans still here had sanitized the Cuban regime and turned a brutal Stalinist dictator into a folk hero. They have never cared about persecution of the Christian populations throughout the world, because they were themselves fundamentally bigoted against Christians. Thus, when Fidel and Che committed atrocities, they were systematically ignored. While I was there, the plight of the rural population was allegedly so drastic that the villages had to keep bonfires burning perpetually for fear of running out of matches. Basic personal products were in short supply while Fidel has amassed a fortune on the backs of his people. He was allegedly one of the world's richest men—a true communist!

What could have been the economic dynamo of the Caribbean had ended up a shabby Stalinist dictatorship. Cubans value education, identify with European culture, and appreciate the United States of America. The Pan-African and Rastafarian culture considered it to be a sort of Babylon, preaching a culturally devastating entitlement mentality and mystical belief system that included identifying ganja as the "herb of wisdom." Most Jamaicans abroad don't buy this; they're identified as excellent, qualified, and hard workers. In Jamaica itself, however, the boys sit on walls, tumble the girls, and wait for the barrel to come in from their family in America, Britain, and Canada. Not so in Cuba.

When the camel let me off at the street I had requested, all my fellow passengers waved goodbye to me. I began to walk down the streets of a dilapidated European-style neighbourhood. Nobody graced the streets, though I heard classical music emanating from a second-story apartment. The sound was very poor quality, coming from an old mono amplifier, but the music was spectacular. An old man in an undershirt sat thoroughly enraptured by the strains.

A tired old '55 Chevy drove by.

This poverty amidst an intelligent, hard-working, and resourceful population was inexcusable given the fact that the equivalent of eight million dollars a day had come into Havana in subsidies and aid from the Soviet Union for twenty-five years. That should have made it the most prosperous nation in the Caribbean. But the deal was that the Soviets would pay an exorbitant price for Cuban sugar, as well as arm it and supply technology. In return, Fidel would export revolution to Latin America and the Caribbean. While the money was flowing, Castro supporters said, "What embargo?" When their patrons collapsed in 1989, they bellyached that the U.S. embargo was hurting their people. Of course, the remaining North Americans and Europeans joined the chorus.

I couldn't find the Belize businessman's address, but I found a suite with an open door. I called out loudly and got no answer. I decided to take the risk of walking in, and was met by a shocked middle-aged man who spoke absolutely no English. I showed him my scrap of paper with an address and showed him the map I had obtained at the hotel.

He smiled knowingly, and then graciously offered me a beverage. I declined, because all we could do was endure a pregnant silence. He then took me down the street to my Belize acquaintance. I was welcomed by an Afro-Indo-Hispanic Cuban family.

The cultural and linguistic boundaries were tough, but we all tried to navigate the shoals. It wasn't relaxing, though, and there was something about this businessman I didn't trust. I couldn't get a fix on him. On the plane, I had told him about the Christ but had a sense that he was stressed and guarded, all the while trying to appear relaxed and in control. Beverages and snacks followed. Some of the family members could speak elementary English, while his English was very good.

After polite and appreciative goodbyes, he accompanied me back to the camel stop. I retraced my path to my hotel after dark. Unlike Jamaica, I never felt a moment's fear. That may have been the last time I felt that way, since MCC workers serving with me in Jamaica got mugged and hassled in the coming years and saw evidence of poverty on the streets. Cuba was changing.

At my hotel during Sunday breakfast, I met a very interesting couple. She was a Harvard ornithologist studying black-billed parrot populations in the Cockpit country above Trelawney. I thought of her as the "parrot lady." She and her mate were very interested in what I was doing in Montego Bay. After rich conversation detailing life in a bird blind in the mosquito-ridden Cockpit, we departed.

The measure of Fidel's political brilliance was represented in how he managed the challenge of Che Guevara and Carlos Cienfuegos. Both were more popular than he, especially as the revolution ossified into an undemocratic party apparatus. After Carlos disappeared in an off-shore plane crash, and no trace was found, the dissidents said, "Cuba has airplane-eating sharks."

Che was sent on a losing guerrilla operation in Bolivia. All revolutionary doctrine pointed to the fact that Bolivia wasn't fertile soil for a rural-based guerrilla operation, but he went anyway. Allegedly, Fidel's own intelligence service tipped off the Bolivian military as to where he was and they "smoked" him. It was Cuban expats who told me that.

In another brilliant turn, Fidel splashed Che's death photo over the whole world and on every building in Cuba, making him a martyr to "American aggression" and turning his memory into an asset for Fidel's own control system. This was communist *realpolitik* at its best.

Despite all this, while I was there, little or no military or police presence was evident, but it was reported that total control was maintained by the "block committees." My Cuban friends and the dissident literature reported how even bags of groceries were checked at the door; if so much as a tomato was found that was not from government stores, it was confiscated and an entry made in the "block file," which was then shared with the government. A worker's paradise, indeed. This gentle, intelligent, moral, and dignified people languished in non-productivity because of the fundamental flaws in socialist economics and the control obsession of Communism.[46]

At the airport, I realized that I had run out of Cuban pesos as well as U.S. dollars, and there was a significant departure tax. While talking again with the "parrot lady," I was forced to explain my humiliating predicament. She and her partner were happy to accept a cheque from me, and I gave them my business card from both MCC and CUMI, so I couldn't escape if the cheque bounced. No problem for them!

I had enough Jamaican cash to get me from the airport home on Sunday evening. On Monday morning, I was back at the day centre, working with psychotic Jamaican street people. However, given my impulsive judgment in running off to Cuba on the spur of the moment and running out of money, I felt right at home among them.

---

[46] See F.A. von Hayek and William Bartley, *The Fatal Conceit: The Errors of Socialism* (Chicago, IL: University of Chicago Press, 1991).

19

Curacao

AFTER BEING MUGGED AT GUNPOINT BY A FOURTEEN-YEAR-OLD KID IN rags riding a BMX bicycle on the Kingston waterfront, those around me told me I needed a rest. My dear, beautiful Afro-American friend Shelia said, "I knew you were going to get yourself killed." She saved my life, I think, because I was stupid enough to be planning how to get the gun away from the kid while she cried out to Jesus, fell on her knees, and started to pray. I had been through seven minor car accidents by that time (while in buses and taxis), two national riots, held a prisoner in my arms who had been stabbed eighteen times, and saw another client dying of ice-pick wounds on the prison fence in a Spanish town prison. I was beginning to look a little worn.

My beloved country reps insisted that I take a two-week vacation—"like, right now!" At that time, I didn't realize, nor did they, that my kidney function was seriously compromised and my stressed appearance was a symptom. I reluctantly agreed to the vacation, because to me it seemed a measure of failure to be *told* to take a vacation! My budget allowed a discounted week in Curacao, and none of the other MCC workers had been there.

Part of the Netherland Antilles, the ABC Islands—Aruba, Bonaire, and Curacao—are located off the coast of Venezuela. As usual, I had no idea what I was getting myself into.

I boarded a brand-new MD-80. It was clean, smooth, tight, and nearly *empty*. It was like being flown in a private jet. There were only four or five other people aboard the airliner. Being totally exhausted, I slept for most of the flight.

When we landed at the Curacao International Airport, it, too, was almost empty. For such a romantic Caribbean tourist destination, I was shocked that it was underutilized. It must have been mid-week and off-season.

Upon landing, the drive into Willemstad showed a desert island complete with sand dunes, pillar cacti, and oil refineries. I was to discover that these wonderful islands refined Venezuelan oil; tankers moved in and out of its magnificent bottle-shaped harbour constantly. The place was magical.

Across the canal from me was a floating market where small Venezuelan fishing boats rafted up along the docks and sold fresh fruit, vegetables, and fish.

My discounted deal included a stay at the new Howard Johnson Hotel, right on the Otrabanda side of the canal entering the harbour which split the city of Willemstad into Punta and Otrabanda. The price was only fifty dollars per night, and I was soon to discover why. I had arrived late, and at eight o'clock the next morning, the jackhammers started on the floor above. The hotel was so new that they were finishing the final stages of construction.

I complained assertively and was summarily moved to a canal view with a balcony overlooking a magnificent square that wrapped around the canal entrance and into the open sea to the west.

I slept and slept and slept. When I finally emerged to tour the city, I was enraptured. This was a little Dutch city on a tropical desert island.

The ABC Islands had maintained an administrative connection with Holland, which meant advanced infrastructure, economic development, industry, social and health services, and civil rights in active practice (as opposed to only "on the books"). The tourism industry had allegedly been dying until a Canadian consultant was assigned the task of developing and marketing this wonderland. Ever since, tourism had taken off.

The city of Willemstad was an amazingly successful mixture of industry, commerce, residential accommodation, and tourism. While shopping on a narrow Dutch street on the Punta side, looking at Rolex watches, diamonds, and crystal, I looked up to see the mast of an oil tanker, the size of a city, moving lazily into the harbour. Such a shocking visual!

I tried to catch the ferry to Aruba, not knowing I would need my passport. Thus, I was refused boarding and instead headed off to the maritime museum. It portrayed the most amazing history of navigation, war, transport of cargo, and exploration I had ever seen. Up a small alley, I found the Kura Hulanda Museum, which documented the slave era, which was horrific and overwhelming but depicted the economics and mechanics of the trade which dominated the colonial era of competition between the Dutch, Spanish, Portuguese, French, and British. It well-characterized the quadrangle of trade as ships picked up slaves in West Africa, sold them for rum and sugar products in the Caribbean, then headed for the Canadian Maritimes to acquire the necessary salt fish (cod) to feed the slaves on the next voyage. They then dropped off the sugar and rum in Europe to finance the next trip.

When the mechanical footbridge connecting both sides of the city was open to allow shipping, little ferries crossed the canal ahead of, around, and behind the large ships that entered the dry docks and loading wharfs. As I returned from shopping and trying to book a trip to Maracaibo, I boarded a little ferry, and to my amazement saw a recognizable profile I had never seen in real life before: the sail of a Dutch Navy submarine. I rushed off the ferry, expecting to hit a gate preventing access to the dock, but there was none. I walked straight up to a Dutch Navy submarine to find a sailor standing at attention on deck. I saluted him and he showed no response. Military personnel wouldn't salute civilians, only their own commanders. Looking further down the dock, I saw a large U.S. Coast Guard frigate. This was after 9/11, yet I could walk right up to the gangplank. The harbour must have featured amazing optical or electronic surveillance to let civilians get so close, especially with Hugo Chavez having shown enthusiastic support for Iran.

It turned out that this week marked the tall ship race from Jamaica to Curacao. The ships were lined up along the docks, many with crew on board, and the tours were magnificent. These had been the technological spaceships of their time—complex wonders of engineering and the product of millennia of mariner experience—using every conceivable mechanism of physics to harness the wind for the purpose of speed, war, cargo, and comfort at sea. They had magnificent woodwork, metalwork, rigging, masts, pulley systems, chemistry of preservatives, and varnish. Caulking paint and solvent dealt with ice, sun damage, salt, ultraviolet rays, rock and barnacle, cannon balls, and fire.

Part of my package included a shuttle to the beach at Caracas Bay, since there were no beaches close to town. It was a thirty-minute drive southeast to this lovely bay surrounded by cliffs. There, I saw a sandy beach and moorage for tall ships.

On the cliff side of the beach rested a cute little cottage and a blonde woolly-haired Dutchman of about thirty who taught scuba. He had a spectacular offer for an introductory lesson and I asked when it would start. He told me it would be an hour, so I signed up. There I was, with two Dutch Navy sailor kids, taking land lessons. Before I knew it, we were gearing up to go underwater. Was I crazy?

When I arrived in Jamaica, I'd had no interest in snorkelling. That is, until one Sunday when I crawled out on one of the rock headlands that protected beaches from storms. I was in a meditative mood on the Lord's Day and looked down into a pool under one of the huge rocks. It blew my mind. The fish down there were psychedelic in colour.

On my next trip to Kingston, I got snorkelling gear from the MCC and went into the water at Doctor's Cave. When I got out to the coral reefs, I couldn't believe my eyes. I kept following the reefs and diving under the ledges to see what was hiding underneath. One year later, I had identified sixty-five fish varieties and twenty-five coral, shellfish, and worm varieties. That day, I burned myself to a crisp. I forgot to go ashore and forgot about sunburn, for I had become intoxicated by the stunning alien world below the sea. The water was warm yet cooling and the experience was one of overwhelming euphoria.

After two years of snorkelling, I had to swim with the fish. I fantasized about looking at the sun through a school of fish—and now I was about to do it.

The scuba instructor was fantastic. The kids had no fear, but when I strapped on that extremely heavy lead belt and left the shore for the abyss, I was scared to death. All I could hear was the thunderous breathing and bubbles in my ears, knowing that all that kept me alive was that tank, regulator, and mouthpiece. I also knew that if I shot to the surface in a panic, even from as shallow as ten feet, I could get the bends.

As we ran through the buddy breathing (passing the oxygen mouthpiece from your mouth to your diving buddy and back) and removing the mouthpiece, I told the instructor to wait until I was ready. I slowed down the kids who got it quicker, but finally we abandoned the surface and headed out toward a sunken tugboat that had been "holed" on the cliffs and sunk in about thirty feet of water.

I was paired up with the instructor. When I asked him what I should do if I gagged into my mouthpiece at depth, his simple answer was, "Don't do that!"

As we swam into the depths, I lost all fear. The experience was such a rush that I could barely control myself. The Navy kids were much more cautious and reserved, but at this point our psychological roles had reversed. I took off ahead of the instructor, chased a school of sergeant majors, and got into a school of sea trout. I tried frantically to touch them, but they were untouchable. I chased flat fish along the bottom and butterfly fish and angel fish, all stunning angels of the deep. We observed schools of squid and spotted eagle rays. At last, rather than just looking down on their world, I was looking up into theirs. I was a part of it.

Then I saw the beautiful wreck of the tugboat. It probably dated to the 1950s, and it was intact. It still had mast and boom and an open cargo hatch on the aft deck. I headed for it! I was in such a state of hyper-exertion that the instructor grabbed my fin and pulled me to his face, signalling me to slow down. If I hurried, I could get hyper-oxygenated. He also signalled that we were a buddy system, and that I had responsibilities to watch out for him even though he was an instructor. I contained my euphoria superficially and carried on as a responsible diver.

I don't think I'd ever had such a thrill. The tug, listing on its starboard side, had an open hatch and I swam partially into it. I was afraid that I would snag something, but I wanted to get right inside the hold. We then went to the edge of a massive wall that disappeared forever into the abyss. We descended to our requisite sixty feet, all the while checking our watches, depth gauge, and oxygen levels. Peering into the end of the world and seeing all the little creatures going about their lives was intoxicating

A different ecosystem existed on the wall of the abyss. Small moray eels stared out from their caves, exhaling demonstrably; they occasionally came toward us because they saw their face in our masks. Sea anemone waved lazily or violently, as the currents imposed. Fire coral, elk horn coral sea grasses, and blackfish moved up and down with the wave action and tried to feed while avoiding predators. The entire world seemed to dance.

When we came out of the water and onto the warm beach, the Navy kids looked embarrassed. The instructor said privately to me, "In all my years of teaching, I've never seen anyone take to the water with such enthusiasm. Come on over on Monday, when the crowd is gone, and I'll take you on a free dive."

On Monday, I found him all alone in the cottage, no other students or visitors in sight. It was a beautiful day as we suited up and went for another spectacular dive. I was even more relaxed now, intoxicated but controlled.

Two tall ships were moored at a large, deep dock that protruded into the bay. When we went under the docks, the sunlight angled through the hundred-foot wooden pilings like a forest of Douglas firs, and yet there were sea creatures everywhere rather than Stellar Jays and chickadees. Then the big black, deep keels of the ships, like inverted whales, moved monstrously and rhythmically with the planking and dowelling visible. We swam underneath the leviathan dorsal fin, then off to the abyss again, swimming lazily downward.

It's always cold there, even in the Caribbean, and even in summer. When you begin the walk out of the water, carrying your tank and regulator, fins and belt, the sun soaks into your cold skin, muscle, and bone. Then you step onto the warm sand to see the palm trees and great masts of the ships sway in opposition.

My mind and body were blown. It was one of the most sensual and spiritual experiences of my life. We washed off the equipment and showered the salt off our skin. I shook hands and said goodbye to the woolly-haired Dutch scuba instructor, thanking him profusely.

I had missed the last shuttle bus back, so I started walking the lonely way into town. Unlike Jamaica, there was no threatening atmosphere. The local Afro-Caribbean people spoke a combination of Dutch and Creole (Papiamento), so we couldn't converse, but they showed me where I could meet a late city bus a few miles down the road. After the sun set, the lights of this magnificent city became more dense. I walked into the lobby of my hotel, caught the elevator, and collapsed into bed amidst a physical and mental state I had never before experienced.

The next day, I walked over the footbridge to the angle-docked floating market. The enterprising boat captains had sailed in from Venezuela and backed their fishing boats into the dock, where they sold fish and other products off their tented sterns. It was incredibly charming. The Hispanic crews hocked their wares to Dutch-Creole Willemstadians, as well as tourists from Europe and North America. All this happened just a few hundred feet away from some of the most elite gold, diamond, and jewellery merchants in the world.

The sense of safety, organization, and rule-of-law I felt in Curacao relaxed me. This beautiful, high-tech, advanced industrial economy had given me the rest I so badly needed.

Full Circle

IT WASN'T UNTIL I STARTED DESCRIBING THE ASSIGNMENT TO OUR MCC colleagues at the head office in Akron, Pennsylvania that I realized the elegant completeness that the Lord had created in my three assignments over seven years: CUMI, Corrections, and the Independent Jamaica Council for Human Rights (IJCHR).

It was complete in its balance of traumas and joys, love and hate, death and life, successes and failure, and beauty and horror, all tied up in a bow which included an exhausting media blitz in the final week and six days in hospital upon my return to North America. I was complete in the grace and mercy of Christ Jesus, except for the catharsis and sharing of the storytelling yet to come!

Jamaica Department of Corrections orientation started out with a tour of District Prison, with Howard Zehr, the MCC's criminal justice director. We were invited in by the chaplain after some scathing Amnesty International criticism had been levelled at Department of Correctional Services as a result of alleged extrajudicial killings of inmates by warders. It was then that we discovered that inmates, staff, and administration were concerned about the number of mentally ill in the prison; they were dying in corners of the institutions when no one even knew they were sick. We floated a job description to MCC that I was to fill three years later. No appropriate candidates applied.

Then came CUMI. In December 1995, I walked up to the day centre on Brandon Hill, drenched in my own sweat and dressed in flannel pants, blue blazer, and tie. After all, I had been told that Jamaicans valued professional dress. I had missed the point. A couple of times, I walked around in loafers as torrential rain turned Union Street into a river. I arrived in soaking blue blazer and tie, dripping with tropical rain.

CUMI turned out to be a gem in Jamaican society—financially accountable, forthright, non-partisan, no-nonsense, clinically astute, forward thinking, vigorous advocates for the rights of their clients, and courageous beyond measure. But they had no statistics on how much service they were delivering, and no client management information system. We were given a computer that the hospital said didn't work; it was gathering dust in their Department of Psychiatry. We traded it for an overload of injectable chlorpromazine, an emergency medicine we seldom used. The computer didn't work—until we plugged it in, and CUMI entered the information age.

In the three years I was there, I wrote newspaper articles for public education that actually worked. When the population stopped abusing the mentally ill, government officials took over. Thus, after I left, the Montego Bay street people scandal broke.

It was an intoxicating time of data collection, promotion, fundraising, clinical social work, night shelter coverage, spectacular labour relations disputes, break-ins, AIDS patients, stone fights, miracle resurrections, conflicts with hospitals, proposals for mental health system reforms, police actions, and tender interactions with clients, colleagues, and supporters.

When CUMI went before hostile opponents at the Commission of Enquiry into the street people scandal, I had generated caseload statistics, diagnostic breakdowns, and performance indicators in three-dimensional coloured graphs that not even the hospital could match. Its credibility in front of the Commission grew exponentially. Praise the Lord.

Next, I headed off to prison. Having nearly killed myself trying to finish up all the documents at CUMI, I arrived in Kingston with bronchitis. At first, I had to be up at 4:00 each morning to walk the hill and catch a ride to the corrections facility at Matilda's Corner, a forty-minute walk. Getting used to the hopelessness, chaos, brutality, and corruption of the maximum security institutions made for a rough couple of months. It was also difficult learning to tow the party line.

Once again, taking on a huge caseload was unacceptable as a development goal. No one would be able to sustain it after I'd left. From the start, I produced caseload lists and some analysis of my own caseloads. Thus I discovered that I wasn't seeing enough seriously mentally ill people. Where were they? That was MCC's reason for being there in the first place.

A computer provided by John Vanderkruk, an MCC volunteer at Jamaica Bible College in Mandeville, proved invaluable. I also enlisted a SALTER (Serving and Learning Together) worker one day per week to load the psychiatrist's "fit to plead" list, and what came out of it shocked us all. The number of mentally ill in the prison was vastly larger than any of us knew, and we were finding it harder to get court dates for these unsentenced men.

Then the really rough ride began. In October 1999, the medical team[47] peer-counselling course was implicated (then vindicated) in the largest prison break in the history of the Jamaica Department of Correctional Services (DCS). Our own collected spreadsheet data cleared the medical team of culpability; this was the first computerized data on psychiatric patients in DCS facilities in its history. The department didn't want to know about all these madmen in prison, so they didn't respond. We got one man out who had been in prison five years without a sentence, but his case was consigned to the tabloid newspaper. The middle-class press wouldn't touch it.

Then the prison commissioner laid off over half his correctional officers in a labour dispute, bringing in the army. Security and medical service delivery were almost totally disrupted. Only the medical team spoke out, and only the medical team got "hammered." Then came the systematic beating of over three hundred men in district prison, including one death and several incidents of maiming, followed by lockdown and an attempted cover-up.

Once again, the medical team got hammered. Two of the team's most vocal advocates departed—one physician, who had witnessed the beatings, and one dentist. Over my term, four of our clients were murdered, one virtually in front of my eyes while two soldiers stood by passively. A media confrontation with the DCS commissioner ensued.

Next came the Ivan Barrows case, but again the department didn't want to know about it. Barrows had been in prison for twenty-nine years, unsentenced, for breaking a window. This case received international media attention through a skilled Jamaican investigative journalist. The government was seriously embarrassed. We never brought these issues to public attention unless invited to, and never without the department being given maximum time to respond. But there was much politics involved in the issue. Without interview, without investigation, without formal acknowledgment, I was barred from the maximum security institutions. Praise the Lord.

With the blessing of our partner, the coordinator of the medical team, I was freed to process and analyse these large lists of mentally ill. There was no

---

[47] I was assigned to the DCS medical team on approval of the department's commissioner, under the supervision of a young Christian psychiatrist by the name of Dr. George Leveridge. He had a new graduate social worker from the University of the West Indies program, who I worked with to provide psychiatric case management services under Dr. Leveridge's direction.

electronic data collection and no management information system in the prisons, and there were men without files and files without men and corruption at every level. Soldiers of the crime dons allegedly were released on the names of mentally ill men who were then assigned the names of criminals who were serving long sentences. They were henceforth lost in the system.

I then had some quality time to supervise the social work student placements from the University of the West Indies. I was able to reach the mentally ill men through the students and have them start programs while the academic and clinical quality of the placements improved significantly. My medical team colleagues handled the onsite supervision.

Concurrently, in collaboration with my Kingston church (Mona Heights Chapel), I got an ex-architectural student (a mentally ill man) off the streets; he had languished there for fifteen years, and we saw a delightful soul resurrected.

I was asked to write social commentary and scriptural analyses for Christian Radio, do topical pieces from the pulpit of my church, as well as be on the roster for adult Bible class. My connection with the church was vital and vigorous, and they were hungry for social issues involvement. The church essentially adopted the mentally ill in the prison, giving them the first home-cooked Christmas meals they'd had in DCS history. It was remarkably touching to see these middle-class, dignified Jamaicans mingling with and loving rag-clad and dirty inmates in a deplorable and dilapidated prison. To the larger Jamaican society, these mentally ill inmates were considered untouchables.

By the grace of God, Mona Heights Chapel agreed to underwrite Ivan Barrows' care and located a placement for him near Mandeville. Ivan was released in March 2001 with above-the-fold front-page newspaper coverage.

The Independent Jamaica Council for Human Rights agreed to seek compensation for him. This meant that a little old madman from prison became a household name, represented by the most respected constitutional lawyer in the English-speaking Caribbean. History was being made. In the wake of Ivan's release, three other long-term incarcerated prisoners were released, with constant public pressure exerted through the media.

The problem was always placement for these men. Their lives had been ruined, and their family and community contacts lost. Their work reputations and opportunities had vanished and they were stigmatized for being madmen, criminals, and diseased.[48]

---

[48] The assumption was that they had been sexually abused in prison and were now infected with HIV/AIDS. In prison riots, these "batty men," as they were called, were murdered and burned in the courtyards by other inmates who thought they were stopping the spread of AIDS.

Working to get them released was one thing, and it could take years, but improving their quality of life in prison was another. Proposals were formulated by the medical team for a forensic psychiatric unit (within the institutions), staffed with nurses and designed for the few seriously dangerous psychotics in prison. There were also a large number of mentally ill men who were sentenced for their crimes, as well as those who had become psychotic while in prison.

Thus, by God's grace, MCC's Bill and Marianne Thiessen, from British Columbia, offered their services for three months. Bill had senior administration, human resources, construction, and football coaching experience, and Marianne was a registered nurse. They represented a gold mine opportunity to affect the quality of life in the institutions with infrastructure improvement, activity programming, assessment, and nursing support to the medical team matron.[49]

The zinc roofing had been blown off the General Penitentiary (GP) Hospital during Hurricane Gilbert in 1988. You could see the sky from inside the condemned hospital. For fourteen years, the hospital flooded after every rainstorm. Inmate labour could be used as occupational therapy. Again, my church agreed to assist with design and materials.

For the mentally ill patients—although they were now being assessed, diagnosed, medicated, legally processed, and seen through emergencies—there were no systematic activity programs. They simply slept their lives away.

Bill, Marianne, and I started a systematic social assessment effort, as well as five weekly activity groups in the three maximum security institutions. Bill even began to work with my church to repair the hospital. He arranged a supply line of clothing and personal care products to the mentally ill from Jamaican charities.

By the time the Thiessens left, some seventy mentally ill inmates had received preliminary social assessment interviews, 150 had been received into the activity groups, and the DCS nursing matron had received the assistance of a fully registered nurse to accompany her in her round of duties. Fifty-two boxes of donated clothing and personal were targeted specifically for the mentally ill in prison. They had heretofore appeared filthy, smelly, barefoot, and attired in ragged clothing. Their appearance added to the grotesque level of stigma and abuse they endured as sexual currency and AIDS-contaminated fluid-handlers. They weren't given any hazmat protection materials.

The roofing project, which had held such hopes, ended up being a sensitive political issue within the institution, and regrettably it could not be initiated. The clothing distribution got co-opted by corrupt inmates and staff and only a

---

[49] Jamaica uses British terms for medical roles, and "matron" was essentially a nursing supervisor-administrator in charge of the paramedical staff, known as "medical orderlies."

small proportion of the clothing reached the mentally ill. The rationale stated: "Madman dem nah need kris cloth." (Translation: "Mentally ill don't need nice clothes.")

Our attempt to control distribution led to retaliation and false accusations. As a result of the seriously abusive treatment we received from the highest levels, we withdrew from Correctional Services.

But the transition was relatively easy into the Independent Jamaica Council for Human Rights, since they legally represented the men I had been seeing in prison. Our Jamaican MCC lawyer needed clinical assistance with the clients, and case management for the families, as we continued to provide the only social work assistance to the released men who were awaiting action on their applications for compensation.

We had a dramatic situation when a mentally ill man was released after twelve years without sentencing for an assault charge. He had no place to go! After our court appearance on his behalf, the Thiessens, my social work student, and I headed up into the hills of St. Elizabeth on the first night of serious flooding. By a miracle of God's hand, we located the family just as darkness fell. He later became unstable because of medication noncompliance and we had to provide case management services out of Kingston, with trips to St. Elizabeth, to assure that he stabilized. Although having finished her term, my social work student continued to assist me through the whole complicated certification procedure.

The biggest bang came at the end. We tried to have the issue of the illegally incarcerated mentally ill addressed in the run-up to the October election, but neither the official opposition nor the government would touch it with a ten-foot pole. Our documentation to Corrections, the Ministry of Justice, and our ex-partners got no response. After the election was won and the government safely ensconced in power, however, the media attention exploded.

In my last week in Jamaica, I was on three primetime talk shows, one late-night talk show, and a public forum sponsored by Jamaicans for Justice (JFJ). That turned into a kind of de facto press conference. In that meeting, a civil society agreement was made between JFJ,[50] IJCHR, and Mensana[51] to keep alive the issue of the imprisoned mentally ill.

IJCHR had a list of approximately sixty "fit to plead" inmates who had spent anywhere from two to thirty years in prison without sentence, ninety percent of whom had no place to go. Thus, the legal problem of their release was only half

---

[50] Jamaicans for Justice, a citizens organization monitoring alleged human rights abuses by the Jamaica Constabulary Force.

[51] A family support group for families of the mentally ill.

the challenge. It was accompanied by a social problem of homelessness, requiring social work and advocacy. IJCHR agreed to convene a public forum to address the issue of placement of the homeless mentally ill. The political ramifications were significant.

Among the intricately interwoven issues were the legal processing of detainees, written law for the mentally ill in prison, compensation for the wrongfully detained, and placement for the long-term incarcerated. We had stumbled on the legal trigger which was required to make it a social policy issue.

I had thus started out with the answer: CUMI, a model program offering cost-effective community rehabilitation which had to be replicated throughout the island if these sixty illegally detained men were to be released. I had started and ended my assignment with the issue of homelessness.

The Lord had taken me full circle.

21

In the Israeli Defence Force

And five of you shall chase an hundred, and an hundred of you shall put ten thousand to flight... (Leviticus 26:8, KJV)

...they shall mount up with wings as eagles; they shall run, and not be weary; and they shall walk, and not faint. (Isaiah 40:31, KJV)

MASHUGINAH GOY.[52] THAT WAS THE NICKNAME GIVEN TO ME BY MY eighty-six-year-old dorm mate, Sam Senior, who was doing what he called his bar mitzvah tour. I loved it. Sam became a fast and dear friend, and I loved him like a brother and a father. He had a terrific sense of humour.

Handsome, smart, and a hard worker with a full head of white hair, he kept us laughing and kibitzing through twenty-eight-degree temperatures under a sheet-metal warehouse roof that had thirty years of accumulated dust in it. He had been a C-47 flight engineer during the Second World War. His employers wouldn't let him retire because he was so good at what he did.

Only Sar-El,[53] the Israeli Defence Force, could bring together a sixty-two-year-old Goy from the West Coast and an eighty-six-year-old Florida Jew in profound brotherhood. There is no military on earth like this military.

Why "Mashuginah"? Well, I took this tour of duty deadly seriously, because I had never expected to get accepted. So, when I was approved, I did *everything* the Sar-El manual suggested, and much, much more. I arrived in worn-in

---

[52] Hebrew for "crazy gentile."

[53] Founded in 1982, Sar-El is the national project for volunteers for Israel, represented in some thirty nations worldwide and founded by IDF General Aharon Davidi in response to the Galilee War (see: http://www.sarelcanada.org/who-we-are).

Special Forces desert combat boots (which were as comfortable as hushpuppies). I had a superb utility belt hung with compact tool sets, a small LED flashlight, leather work gloves, a thermos flask, and an army-fatigue sweatband to keep perspiration from running into my eyes. I had high-quality dust masks for myself and a mountain emergency first-aid kit with a small pharmacy, in waterproof and airtight plastic boxes, that could cure all ills. Over my three weeks with Sar-El, virtually everything I brought with me was used by me or one of our crew at one time or another.

I bought Israeli mementos like "a drunken sailor," to quote Sam Senior. We decided that the Israeli economy would go into recession upon my departure. I took a solo trip to Sderot to spend some money in their damaged economy and express solidarity with those heroes in their forgotten siege. Sderot is the western Negev town in southern Israel, one mile from Gaza, that was ruthlessly rocketed by Hamas once Israel unilaterally withdrew from it in the hope of peace. As many as five Qassam[54] rockets a day fell on this civilian town of twenty-four thousand people, which felt totally abandoned not only by the international community but by its own national government. A significant proportion of the population suffers post-traumatic stress. The Qassams are purely anti-personnel weapons filled with shrapnel that shreds anything within a hundred yards, aimed at hospitals and schools on a town with no military significance.

Once having been there, I would never be the same! It is a beautiful little town of incredible survivors who just dig out, bury their dead, and reconstruct after every attack.

They are Jews!

Qassams came in two days before and two days after my visit.

Mashuginah? I wept at the Russian Compound in Jerusalem when my colleagues sang the "Hatikvah" in Hebrew to the dead Haganah soldiers. Dumbstruck, I wept when in our evening training session we looked at pictures from the last Lebanon War. I was overcome with grief and anger.

When we got working in the warehouse, I would forget to take breaks until I nearly dropped dead. I'd even forget to drink water, because I was having such fun. I would stare at the C-130 Hercules aircraft in the distance and think of the memories they and their crews must have carried from the Yom Kippur War, the

---

[54] Qassams are simple steel artillery rockets produced by Hamas terrorists in Gaza to fire at civilian targets in Israel. The terrorists use the irrigation piping and fertilizer left behind by the Israeli kibbutz farmers that made the desert blossom to kill Israeli civilians in Negev towns, such as Sderot.

Entebbe rescue, and the Ethiopian Airlifts—some of the most daring operations and rescues in Israeli military history… carried on the wings of HaShem!

I was surrounded by gentle, humble, and gracious heroes. For a moment, I was part of it.

We Americanos began having coffee withdrawal at breakfast after about three days. I discovered that if I put instant coffee in a mug and held it under the hot showerhead, it created a kind of latte. Sam tried it but was unimpressed.

Was I Mashuginah? Crazy? Yeah, you bet. And I was delighted to be so.

It was such an undeniable privilege to set foot in the Holy Land for the first time with the purpose of doing service with the Armed Forces, which to their credit have seven of the most spectacular, first-time-ever operations in military history.

Not only was this the base out of which the Entebbe rescue had taken place, in 1976, but the Ethiopian Jewish rescue had launched here. This base had handled the transport and supply of the Yom Kippur Sinai Campaign, and all the Lebanon Wars. Many other classified operations were conducted here as well. Those runways, taxi strips, warehouses, and Air Force staff board rooms had seen unimaginably creative, heroic, and historic acts.

As if that wasn't enough, this tour was also my first witness to God's most stunning miracle—Israel—and not just as a spectator, but as an active participant. Consider the agricultural miracle, the technological miracle, the Aliyah[55] miracle, the vibrancy, the conflict, and the impossible growth of an impossible nation.

My tour of the northern coast saw an amalgamation of the international and Canadian group, which had arrived one week after we did. We got along. Political, economic, military, and biblical history unfurled on the shores of the magnificent Mediterranean, at Caesarea, Mount Carmel, Haifa, Acre, and eventually Rosh ha Nikra on the Lebanon border. Then we spent a night on the Nes Ammim Kibbutz, then Jerusalem the Golden, then Tel Aviv (at Independence Hall and the Rabin Memorial).

Given the church's history of viciously persecuting the Jews, what could I expect, as an outsider who had never before spent time among Jewish people? I was included, praised, teased, and left alone when I needed to be—and I was respected. I came to love everyone on my team. They were the most amazing folks—intelligent, accomplished, real, and affable… to the tenth power. They

---

[55] Aliyah is a Hebrew term used to describe the return of the Jews to Eretz Israel from all over the diaspora (see: http://en.wikipedia.org/wiki/Aliyah).

were businesspeople, professionals, technicians, and tradesmen. We were unified at a spiritual level.

We all shared different theologies and political positions, yet our discussions were good-natured, informative, and exhilarating. Every breakfast and supper was like a university seminar. I asked stupid questions and once nearly broke a kosher law, but I was so well-treated. My already-idealized image of Israelis and Jews was only reinforced.

The military personnel were magnificent. The staff and officers were grateful and treated us with such respect and appreciation. They gave us multiple ceremonies and gifts, and were profuse in their praise. Coming from these gentle giants, it meant so much.

The Madrichot were amazing.[56] They oriented us, shepherded us, and answered our million questions. When we got lost, they worried and scolded us. They made our connections, got us the things we needed, taught us about Israeli society (from first-hand experience), and gave us lovingly devised hand-drawn copies of the content of our information sessions. They arranged for a wide array of fascinating people to come talk to us, including young people who were vibrant, passionate, and diverse in temperament and belief.

There is no army in the world like this army.

The captain in charge of flight operations gave us a tour of a Herc, and then posed with us in photographs. Afterward we were invited to his home for a reception and very personal hospitality.

Pam Lazarus, the program coordinator, had learned the skill of bi-location, in that everywhere I turned there she was with tours and signup sheets, and materials and suggestions. She made herself available, it seemed, twenty-four hours per day, as did the Madrichot. That was very comforting, especially when I took off on my own.

One special perk was the idea that we might be saving some reserve soldier (perhaps even a fighting man or woman) the duty of having to leave his or her family to do unskilled grunt work, rather than rest and/or train for the next war. We were contributing to the economy of this heroic nation. Our experiences, taken to a burgeoning, propaganda-immersed, anti-Semitic world, could serve to dispel the mythology. At some level, we were part of precious *Erutz Israel, Am Israel*.[57]

---

[56] These were young female soldiers with language and diplomatic skills who received commander training and wore a braid. They acted as our officers and served as liaisons between the base command, Sar-El administration, and us Sar-El grunts.

[57] Meaning, in Hebrew, "the land of Israel, the people of Israel."

Sderot

Dear Joseph:[58]

It's great to hear from you and I'm so glad we were roommates at Baca.[59] You and Sam Senior were the best I ever could have hoped for. I was so struck by how well-read you are, and it was so instructive to discuss major issues with you. I know you have a heart for HaShem[60] and I really appreciate that. It was a real honour to serve with you. Maybe Aliyah is in your future?

As for Sderot, yes, I got down there but I couldn't get accommodation until I had already returned to Ashkelon,[61] and by then it was too late. Because of the constant rocketing, none of the tourist accommodations were available, likely due to the risk.

I met a female police officer from Sderot who told me there was no accommodation, and that even the local kibbutz was just a maybe. I think no one wanted responsibility for a visitor who might be injured. So I got the last room on Thursday (no rooms available for Friday) at the Holiday Inn in Ashkelon and headed in on Friday morning. Nefar the Madrichot was going to see if she could make family arrangements for me, but I didn't hear from her until after I had made other arrangements. Sderot is a wonderful little city, clean and well-organized with parks and memorials and mid-sized malls. The policewoman had told me to get off the bus at the police station, and that I could see some unexploded Qassam rockets leaning against a wall there. I did and walked into town. When I stopped at a convenience store, I got patted on the back and greeted warmly.

I had run out of disposable cameras, so I went looking to buy more. As a joke, I also bought six box knives to leave in my warehouse, because the ones the supply officers provided got lost or damaged, and I had taken the blame for it. I took a bubble-pack of them to Linoy and Ephraim (the Madrichot) at the base. They got a good laugh out of my sarcasm. And I modestly contributed to the economy of Sderot.

---

[58] Joseph was a Jewish-American chemist from Boca Raton, Florida. He wanted to accompany me to Sderot, but he had to leave before it could be arranged.

[59] A C-130 Hercules Air Force base, since moved to the Negev.

[60] In Hebrew, this means "the name" (specifically of the God of Abraham, Isaac, and Jacob).

[61] Ashkelon is a major southern port city on the Mediterranean coast of Israel.

The people of Sderot were tense but stoic, and life carried on. There was no sound of laughter or music.

At the mall hardware store, I asked where I could purchase cameras, but no one spoke English. A family followed me out of the store, and they were Oleh[62] from Chicago. The wife and daughter spoke English. They gave me directions to a camera store and I immediately got lost. There was no sign of bomb damage or shelters (all the shelter signs were in Hebrew).

I was told that they got twenty seconds of warning from the air raid sirens before they had to find cover. Many mothers had stopped driving their children around because that didn't give them enough time to assure everyone's safety. Qassams came in two days before and two days after my visit, largely because the IDF had made a minimal strike into Gaza, and the daily attacks had stopped.

Lost, I ran into the family from Chicago again and they took me to a camera shop, where I bought three cameras. I ventured to ask them about the attacks and they took me to a side street I had passed where a section of street hadn't been black-topped. They said that the alarm hadn't gone off and a woman's car had taken a direct hit. The shrapnel the attackers had put in the bomb had shredded the street. The IDF came in, tested for unexploded materials, dug out and filled in the crater, and repaired the street so no one would know it had hit there. The restoration psychology is powerful.

The Chicago woman's brother-in-law and wife spoke no English, but he had a broken thumb in a cast and a bruised and swollen lip and mouth. I asked the woman if it had been from a Qassam. She replied, "No. Just stupidity." We all laughed, including the brother-in-law.

I went to a restaurant and ordered a large meal I didn't need. After repeatedly being told that there was no available accommodation, I went back to the police station bus stop, cognizant that Shabbat was coming and not wanting to get stuck by a preparation shutdown.

Standing at the stop, I saw what I understood to be an orthodox Kibbutznik. In thirty-degree weather, she was dressed all in black with a velvet-looking skirt down to her shoes. She wore a black tam and I assumed that she was waiting for my bus. A modern tourist-type bus came by and her cute little four-year-old boy got off. She hugged and

---

[62] "Oleh" are those Israelis born abroad who later become Israeli citizens.

kissed him with such pleasure, it made me smile. I said to the bus driver, "Ashkelon?" He said no and drove off. I waited over an hour for another bus.

The bus never came, so I tried to make myself understood to a man who looked like the manager of the apartment block across the street. He hailed a taxi with a chain-smoking Turk who gave me a good price to Ashkelon. In the meantime, the Holiday Inn had called to say there was a room in Ashkelon, so I took it.

On the way out, I looked across the western Negev landscape to see a side road with a flatbed tractor trailer barrelling down in a cloud of dust. It had an IDF Merkava main battle tank as its load.

Ashkelon, too, had been a Qassam target over the past year, especially the power plants nearby. But I had the pleasure of warm Mediterranean swims and long, beautiful beaches with surf caressing my ears all night long. Those were my two nights of luxury in the Army. I headed back to Tel Aviv the next day, so I wouldn't be caught late for the Sunday morning muster at the bus station.

The captain of flight operations had us come to his home for a reception. The volunteers were giving their impressions of Sar-El. I remained quiet but was asked by Sam Senior to give a newcomer's perspective. I reported that it was stunning to be able to assist a miracle armed service in a miracle nation that shouldn't exist. Then Michal, the Madrika, broke in and mentioned that I had gone to Sderot, and I was given an applause. Unbelievable!

Anyway, Joseph, that's the story. I know you would have been in Sderot with me had you not had to leave. We might have been able to find accommodation with your Hebrew language skills. But by God's grace, maybe next time.

Blessings my brother,
Shalom, shalom,
Roger

22

Pilgrimage

IT TOOK ME FIVE YEARS TO RECOVER AFTER RETURNING HOME FROM Jamaica in November 2002. First came my hospitalization in Ephrata, Pennsylvania; then I had three months of medical tests in Akron, and reverse culture shock. Afterward, I underwent three surgeries in four years, all in Vancouver. I had two new jobs, one seriously broken heart, and spent three weeks with the IDF in Israel.

After five years away, I made the decision to pilgrimage back to Jamaica. Since so many years of relative silence had passed from my end of the telephone, I expected a cool reception from my friends in Jamaica, with recriminations for my abandonment of the beloved MCC, colleagues, partners, and my clients. But that silence was in keeping with my avoidant personality. While I had been in Jamaica, my family, friends, and church back home had seldom heard from me, either.

On approach to Montego Bay, as we flew past Doctor's Cave, my mind began to swim in a high-speed collage of memories from twelve years earlier, when I had arrived in Jamaica for the first time. I was stunned with how much it felt like coming home, and rightly so, because from the ages of forty-nine to fifty-six, I had "grown up" in Jamaica.

It was so good to have money in my pocket and not have to keep a PMR.[63] I could spend profusely, not negotiate, give big tips, and love Jamaica in a way that I could not have five years earlier.

---

[63] A personal monetary record. PMRs were the bane of every MCC volunteer worker, because they were such a detailed financial accounting system. That said, that may well have been what rated MCC second on the *Forbes Magazine* list of financially accountable charities.

The Montego Bay airport had grown dramatically, and the city itself was stunningly clean compared to when I had lived there. The tropical heat soaked into my bones and dried the West Coast fungus from between my toes, soothing the grief inside my heart.

Some things never change. I retained a taxi that was, of course, hemmed in by parked cars. Then I arrived at the Gloucester Hotel to find that my online reservations had been a scam for Jazz Festival weekend. I was in trouble, but by the grace of God I had arrived early enough that they had a perfect room for me until I could check in at a bed-and-breakfast called "Miss Betty's Chatham Cottages."

I took a swim in the pink and purple glow of post-sunset Montego Bay. In the crystal water, I looked up into the sky, past the royal palms as a few Montegonians swam, talked, and laughed around me.

I found Miss Betty walking on a path between the houses, looking bewildered. She flashed that beautiful and welcoming smile, not having the foggiest idea who I was.

"I seem to have lost my way!" she said. We talked and I hugged her fragile frame, explaining who I was. I got reservations for the next night to cover my full stay in Montego Bay. I returned to the hotel to fall into a delicious sleep in my second floor room above the pool. The sound of the waterfall flowing down the cliff through the hotel caressed my ears.

This was January 24, and in the morning I wrapped my Christmas presents for CUMI.

I surprised everyone there by arriving unannounced. My fears of rejection melted with the unrestrained outpouring of the kind of reserved warmth, exclamations, hugs, and deep sweetness that only Jamaican people could produce. I got an undeserved hero's welcome.

I spent two afternoons on that veranda, and they delightfully provided a guitar for me. We sang the old hymns and folk songs because Lukee[64] could remember them all. A lot of the time, we just sat in silence, listening to the wind through the almond tree above. As in my memories, the cows grazed in the field beside the house, with the pure white cattle egrets standing on their backs.

There aren't enough pages in this book to cover the memories that streamed through my mind of the many who had died since I had left. Their faces appeared

---

[64] The story of Lukee is one of amazing redemption. Lukee lived in madness, on the streets, though he was eventually had a family, gained full-time employment, and even had his own home. He was CUMI's chef and the subject of numerous newspaper articles and TV interviews.

among the living as I sat on that familiar veranda. I had led praise and worship there in the mornings, facilitated skills training sessions, stood my ground in a rock fight, chased a thief down those stairs, and watched the police escort an assailant away with a nine-millimetre pistol pressed to his skull. I had thought I would never see that assailant alive again, but praise the Lord I did. After his release, he went on to rob a church.

That night, I went to visit Victor Wong, the samurai proprietor of the profusely generous Super Save grocery market. He escorted me to the computerized, camera-surveillance command centre of his large store. It was like I had never left. Jamaicans made for such loyal and forgiving friends. I was greeted by his beautiful assistant, and after an hour or more of talking about the state of Jamaica and the world, he ushered me up another set of steel spiral stairs into his beautifully appointed split-level penthouse. From the outside, you would never have known it existed.

He had a Jamaican meal set out for me. Amidst constant bombardment of questions and comments from his monumentally intelligent and inquisitive mind, the sun set over Montego Bay.

I arrived back at Chatham Cottages and had a moonlight swim before retiring to the rattle of the overhead fan and the groan of a semi-functioning air conditioner. Once again, I fell into a delicious sleep.

On the night before I left Montego Bay, I decided to treat myself to a luxurious meal at the Sandals Inn, right beside the Chatham Cottage gate. I walked in and told the maitre d' that I wasn't staying at the hotel but wanted to have a meal anyway. He settled me at a single table by the pool, bordered by royal palms on the street side and genteel second-floor rooms. I luxuriated amidst a four-course meal to the strains of jazz on a grand piano played by a seventy-year-old matriarch of Jamaican jazz. The waiter took me to meet her as I gushed over her creative renditions. She graciously condescended to accept the uneducated accolades, and all the world was in balance. I waited for half an hour for the bill to come, but it never came. Finally, I asked the waiter about it, and he said, "We don't take money here. This is an all-inclusive and you got a free feast." I left the cost of the meal on the table for the staff.

I caught a commercial flight to Kingston. As we came in over Port Royal, I remembered the flying fish, the frigate birds, and the spectacular diving brown pelicans. I also remembered the delightful day I spent on the Lime Keys, when a guy brought two beautiful young women and an eight-foot boa constrictor in a hockey bag onto a narrow long boat. Fortunately, it wasn't until we landed that I learned what was in the equipment bag, which I had noticed had kinetic contents. They were obviously part of an act in the Kingston nightclubs.

My beloved friend Nelson, the taxi man who had saved my life repeatedly, met me at the airport, and the greeting was raucous. He chided me for my lack of communication and gave me pictures of his grandson. He then drove me past the garrison communities whose names I couldn't remember.

It was so good to see Ron and Gussie, my last country reps. The meeting was a reunion of a band of brothers (and sisters), since we had gone through many battles, strategy-and-tactic meetings, presentations, orientations, and tours of the island. We had seen many beloved friends come and go from our island. Their miraculous deliverance from death and disfigurement in a cataclysmic van accident two years earlier was one of the greatest sagas of deliverance in MCC Jamaica history. But both were left with permanent scars. To have this reunion after five years of triumph and torment for all of us was sweet beyond measure.

After two years of protracted grieving, I was euphoric. There weren't enough hours in the day to catch up. We talked, ate, and talked and talked. It was like coming home to Mom and Dad's house. Though it wasn't the MCC house of my memories (I dearly missed that sprawling cottage and its profuse garden), it was Ron and Gussie that constituted "home."

We visited my old landlord and remembered the police vs. carjackers shootout in the driveway. We even revisited the M-16 bullet hole in the stair railing. The landlord, an Afro-Jamaican with an English wife, was gracious and invited us in for cool fruit drinks. He kept a sailboat and talked about the hurricanes and his sailing trips around the island, and to Cuba. We all laughed hysterically at his animated, articulate, and vivid short stories. He was a hugely intelligent and accomplished man and used to collect my rent with a semi-automatic pistol tucked in his belt.

I split my time between the MCC house and my dear friends, the Russells of Mona Heights Chapel. They had been unbelievable saints in my life during the hard prison days. The church itself had been instrumental in the Ivan Barrows story. They had me do an evening Bible and prayer meeting presentation on Israel, and it was a stunning homecoming. What beautiful people! They spiritually fed, encouraged, supported, and networked us all. A person *has* to have a home church when they're in a war zone, and the Lord sent me these durable, intelligent, and accomplished people to bring a naïve Canadian to maturity.

Prison Reunion

I began to call my former colleagues from the prison: Dr. Leveridge (a psychiatrist), Jerine Singh (the medical team social worker), Clement Reid (a paramedical corrections officer), and the men released by Christ's grace. I was met again with a warm, excited, and forgiving spirit that made me feel as though I had never left.

George, the St. Elizabeth farmer who had broken the dam of prisoner releases, just couldn't stop laughing on his cell phone when he heard my voice. He came flying in on the "sufferation express" (privately owned van taxis) from St. Elizabeth, and he was his usual joyous yet dignified self. Without him, none of the prison saga would have unfolded, yet he had been the last to receive his financial settlement. But he had, indeed, been the *first* to be released, a miraculous answer to prayer.

We talked and ate and he came over to the MCC house to meet us. He was with us only a few hours, only to then begin the six-hour trip back, complete with a long walk on a donkey road, to the family homestead. George would have arrived home very late at night. He was a successful and resourceful farmer who had been floridly psychotic when he'd entered prison. On the trip, we also met his lawyer who had represented him, gratis.

Ron and Gussie then organized a tour over two days to meet other miracles in human form. It all came back to me as we travelled the highways and roads toward Clarendon. Towns, people, events, and Patois expressions flooded over me. It felt so good to try massacring the language again.

Mottled light slipped through the canopy at Ivan Barrows' house as we pulled into the driveway. Barrows went by a new name now: Ferdy Nettleford.[65] His family's house was on two intersecting gullies, surrounded by a stream and jungle hillsides. It was a little piece of Jamaican heaven. Cesline, Ferdy's seventy-year-old sister—still attractive, plump, and fully in charge)—greeted us as grand nieces and nephews. We flooded the small veranda with beautiful smiles.

Ferdy was ecstatic to see us and showed us his room, which was bright and mostly filled with a big bed. The free-standing closet looked somewhat dog-eared, with the wood grilling covered with gouges and holes. We were to soon meet the culprit—a house parrot that landed on the grills and sharpened his

---

[65] While psychotic, Ferdy Nettleford had called himself "Ivan Barrows," either as an artifact of psychosis or an attempt to keep his good name. Therefore, for a long time his family couldn't locate him. Because there were no psychiatric social workers in the prison for his first thirty-five years, no one tracked his real name. Once treated for psychosis, he protested, saying, "I am Ferdy Nettleford." But the prison doctors thought "Ferdy" was an artifact of his psychosis, when in fact it was his real name.

beak, making big holes. We all laughed at its demonstration of vandalism. One of Ferdy's daughters, who worked in the airline industry, teased the parrot; it squawked and chided and made short flights but seemed always to come back for more. It was a beautiful bird, raised from a wild chick.

The moment came for a timely departure and we left with an inexpressible sense of satisfaction, joy, and closure. We were so thankful to God that this happy, well-cared-for man had been set free from a miserable, anonymous death in a stinking Jamaican prison for the crime of mental illness.

After a delicious meal of jerk pork on Spar Tree Hill, we moved on to the next leg of the pilgrimage.

As we approached the town of Malverne, I was once again flooded by memories. In my mind, I remembered standing in a Black River courthouse under an angry, pitch-black sky, taking into my custody a man, Jocelyn, who had been in prison for twelve years for assaulting a police officer, because his family had not appeared. We had headed into the hills ahead of an advancing storm—Bill and Marianne Thiessen, Sherine (a social work student), and a floridly psychotic man. I came to learn later that the orderlies, for an indeterminate period, hadn't been giving Jocelyn his antipsychotic medication. I was the only one in the truck cab who had realized what a fix we were in.

Bill had boldly walked into a local restaurant and asked about our client and his family. The proprietor of the restaurant had said that Jocelyn was dead, but Bill announced that he couldn't be dead, because we had him in our truck. Thus, a predictably explosive reunion ensued, and by the grace of God we had Jocelyn into the arms of his cousin and aunt by the time the first raindrops splattered down on the truck.

I snapped back to the present. We had loaded donated furniture for Jocelyn into the box of the truck. Bill and Marianne had left Jamaica the year before, having made the building of Jocelyn's new house a community development project. As with everything, it had turned political and complicated. By the grace of God, the problems had been solved through multiple long-distance phone calls, visits by Bill and Marianne, and creative diplomatic interventions by Ron and Gussie.

We walked down a mountain path past a derelict house that a Rasta-Man had captured and came into a beautiful clearing surrounded by hills and crops. Jocelyn didn't recognize me, either because of my advanced age or the fact that he had been psychotic the last two times I'd seen him. But when Ron identified me, he almost went into a dance of joy. He held my hand and took me on a tour of his immaculate home and planted fields, giving me an update in rapid Patois, only ten percent of which I actually understood.

In a moment of reflection, I once again thought of the Christ-centred miracle of this schizophrenic farmer. Here he was, building, planting, harvesting, and marketing his produce, all on a paediatric dose of a 1960s psychotropic medication. He had been destined to die a miserable death in prison. Allegedly, the charges against him had come as a result of a frightened policeman falling down and cutting his leg on a sharp rock while trying to apprehend an out-of-control "madman" who had just lost his wife.

To Jocelyn's great delight, we unloaded the furniture, some of which had come from the MCC office, and it nicely appointed his simple one-room house. Jocelyn carried the table down the trail on his head, no hands. We then said difficult goodbyes and headed toward Treasure Beach for the night.

It was a satin January evening. I took a swim in the powerful but soothing surf and walked the beach with Ron and Gussie, looking over the massive changes forced on the landscape by the last hurricane. We watched the sun go down in the soft haze, then returned to our bed-and-breakfast rooms and cleaned up for a Jamaican pig-out at Jack Spratts.

The next morning, on what was going to be a hot and clear day, we had breakfast at a small hotel restaurant under an almond tree, fifty feet from the surf. The incomparable aroma of Blue Mountain coffee punctuated the immaculate scene.

Just sitting quietly and rerunning the mental tapes provided a strange time-capsule catharsis. I reflected on it all—the Montego Bay battles with Cornwall Regional Hospital, the constant lit-fuse character of the prison, murder, stabbings, and the intrigue of garrison politics. Ron and Gussie triggered my mind with people, places, terms, and events that had long been compressed and archived in my mental hard drive. I was once again in Spanish Town Prison, caught in the sudden lockdown when government officials the JDF/FBI scooped Vivian Blake in a Bell jet helicopter as another armed surveillance helicopter orbited overhead. We later found out that the whole operation had been a diversion, as Vivian was being loaded onto a Gulfstream executive jet at Kingston International Airport for extradition to the United States.

Then there was the evening I got caught in the Tower Street prison, enraptured by an interview with an inmate who had been carved up like a side of beef in a political torture session. His torso, face, and legs were a road map of inch-wide scars, lacerations that should have been sutured and yet never were. It had represented hours of exquisite torture and horror.

Afterward, I came out to a city shut down in burning roadblocks and the sound of M-16 fire as police tried to drive off thugs who were robbing bus passengers as the rule of law subsided. The sun sparkled on the sea, the palms danced in the breeze as waves caressed the small patch of beach—contradictory perceptions of psychotic proportions.

In Mandeville, I had a second rendezvous with George. He had survived two prison riots and brought Ferdy Nettleford to me. He had been struggling to farm in the St. Elizabeth hills without finances after a five-year incarceration for mental illness. His last crop had been washed out in the hurricane.

George had become a good friend and I had spent a weekend with his family in the mountains, having to walk part of the way in and out on a donkey road. He looked terrific. He was fashionably dressed, with some gold around his neck, and appeared a very happy man. His disbursements had cleared the debts he'd incurred while awaiting his final settlement. An intelligent and remarkably durable man, we talked nonstop for hours, catching up. It was as if I had never left.

George's release had been part of a miracle the Lord had performed. Ron had been there that amazing day at court when we returned him to the arms of his family at Halfway-Tree Courthouse on the eve of the new millennium. Of the five men we had walked out of prison, two were dead now, but at least they had died in freedom rather than having to endure a humiliating prison death. It had broken my heart to hear inmates say, "Please don't let me die in prison."

After our return to Kingston, another reunion took place. A prearranged meeting at Matilda's Corner deli brought together one of the psychiatrists I had worked with, along with a foreign social worker, a medical corrections officer, and an ex-inmate orderly. We laughed like we had laughed when we'd thought we would never get through it all. We ate together and caught up on where everybody was in their lives. We shared war stories from our days working together until the deli closed and I walked back in the darkness, remembering the intoxicating excitement and hyper-vigilance required by a Kingston night.

The people of Mona Heights Chapel represented an irreplaceable piece in the puzzle of these success stories, but time and space do not permit me to go into it.

If anyone symbolized the heroism and stoicism of the Jamaican people and the power of Almighty God to deliver, it was a woman named Lurline who served as the MCC housekeeper for decades. I was spellbound when I heard her tell of her life in the garrison community war zone. If ever a life was a miracle of faith, it was hers. I was awed and humbled by her, considering it an honour to have known her. I deeply miss her.

I never had expected Ron and Gussie to arrange a reunion of all these heroes and heroines of my life.

As Nelson took me back to the airport, I asked him to stop to see the derelict freighter that had blown aground in the isthmus connecting the airport to the mainland during one of the hurricanes. It had been used in the 1998 *Godzilla* movie. It was unrecognizable from when I had left in 2002, yet so much had remained the same.

Apart from the deep sadness of leaving Jamaica again, returning had given me a peace in my soul that had eluded me. I had lived not knowing if my health would return or if the funds would become available, not knowing if I would be welcomed or rejected, not knowing if I would once again see these beloved people.

Now I had seen with my own eyes and knew in my heart that I always had a place with these heroes and saints who had been used by the Christ to generate the most exciting and productive years of my life.

23

Kosovo

IT HAD BEEN A ROUGH RIDE FOR MY DEAR AND COURAGEOUS MISSIONARY family in Ferizaj, Kosovo, who had been inviting me to visit for years. We'd had a wonderful meal and evening at a French restaurant in North Vancouver right on the water, days before they disembarked upon their mission. Bret and Chelsea had one small child, Sarah, and had just learned of a second one on the way as they left for Kosovo.

Their new little boy, Mark, had been born with inadequate lung capacity, so as they set up home and mission with the team in Ferizaj, they ended up having to find proper medical care in Thessaloniki, Greece. The travel, worry about their little boy, and the challenges of beginning Christian witnesses in a Muslim nation bore a weight on their young shoulders.

I joined the Kosovo visit on an extended leave of absence, without pay, from my job with the CRP (community residential programs) at the New Westminster Mental Health Centre. After Kosovo, I would go to Tel Aviv and join my next tour with the Israeli Defence Force.

In 2008, the Kosovo Force (KFOR) saw a significant reduction in violence. The soldiers only carried sidearms, not automatic rifles as before. There was a vibrant economy around Bondsteel, the large U.S. army base near Ferizaj, and there were significant employment opportunities at the base. People were building onto their houses, acquiring land, and opening small businesses. The city thrived, with crowds of jean-clad youth and working adults in the small stores of this European community. The people, largely a mix of Albanian and Serbs, were extremely handsome. But there was much about their cultural appearance that was misleading.

President Bill Clinton had become a national hero ever since instructing NATO to bomb Yugoslavia in 1999, in response to the Serbian crackdown on the independence movement. He breached the NATO mandate in so doing. There was Bill Clinton Boulevard, the Bill Clinton statue in Pristina, and the Bill Clinton honorary degree from the University of Pristina. It was an unusual love for all that was American, as this was a Muslim state. There was a very notable exception to the love for America and Bill Clinton among the remaining Serbian population.

While booking the trip, I had wanted to save the missionaries the long round trip from Pristina to Ferizaj late in the day, so I tried to book a hotel near the airport. Despite the twenty-two nation KFOR troops, I was told there were no hotels near the airport in Kosovo. My agent agreed that it was strange.

I had another worry. I would be flying from Vienna to Kosovo, and afterward back to Vienna and on to Israel. I had to make the same loop back after my next tour with Sar-El and the IDF. It didn't sit well with me to come back into a Muslim country with an Israeli stamp in my passport. My travel agent tried everything she could to reroute me, but there was no affordable option. Thus, I would be coming back to Kosovo, having to go through customs and immigration with Sar-El papers, mementos, and military garb. Not good!

Loaded with a hundred pounds of supplies and gifts for the missionaries, as well as my own luggage, I took off to Toronto, Vienna, and then landed at the airport in Pristina.

Pristina's airport was filled with troops from all over the world, mixed with businesspeople trying to assist in the country's economic development. My reunion with Sarah and little Mark, who I had come to know quite well during Bret and Chelsea's furlough in Vancouver the previous year, was spectacular. They were so happy to see me as we gathered the six huge boxes of supplies and loaded them into the van.

The airport was in an arid bowl surrounded by the Beskid Mountains. We started out along the road, and only a few miles from the airport we came upon a beautiful hotel. It was several stories high, large, and boasted modern architecture. It even had a convenience store and all amenities.

I turned to Bret and said, "What were you talking about? Here's a hotel! I could have stayed here so you wouldn't have to drop me off or pick me up in the middle of the night."

He looked at me sadly. "That's not a hotel. It's a brothel."

Much about the countryside and villages reminded me of Jamaica. Houses were constantly under construction, old men and youth stood idle in the squares and storefronts, goats and chickens ran amok, and kids played football in fields with surrogate balls. The roads had no rules. Narrow alleys winded through the animal-choked towns. Many of the vehicles shouldn't have been on the roads. This was all typical of the so-called "third world."

One aspect, however, made it so different from Jamaica: the presence of mosques. Virtually every town of any size had a brand-new, golden-domed, minaret-endowed, Saudi-funded mosque.

In the Serbian enclaves, the demoralization and hostility was visceral, and with little wonder. Only a poor underclass remained. Anyone who had the means got out and the remnant held to the memories of Christian kings and princes, battles and victories of old. Albanians would drive by and harass people, shouting, "Kill the Serbs, kill the Serbs." They looked at us with hatred and distrust. They thought we were Americans.

President Clinton, while ignoring the Saudi-sponsored genocide of Christians and animists in Sudan (estimated to be over a million people), became very irate about the much smaller Serbian genocide of Albanian Muslims in Reçak and Srebrenitsa, Bosnia. In righteous indignation, and to placate his oil-rich sponsors, he bombed the daylight out of the Serbs, turning the Glasnost-intoxicated pro-American Russians into enemies, setting the stage for the next Muslim terrorist state.

This beautiful missionary family had been missing their father for weeks due to his work in the States. They needed a change of venue, and a rest for Chelsea. We therefore packed up the kids and headed for Skopje, Macedonia.

Along the way, Bret pointed out the "sniping tracks." Allegedly, for a few thousand dollars, rich Russian mafiosi could have acquired a high-tech sniper rifle and had a chance to shoot fleeing men, women, and children along the railroad tracks. That and the tragedy of the killing fields near a farm we visited brought home the horror of that conflict and the grim realities of the Balkans.

While in Ferizaj, an Australian family of new missionary recruits arrived and told us of their walk of faith. They had left everything behind in Australia in order to serve in Kosovo. We entertained them over a meal and heard their story of following the Lord's direction. Like Bret and Chelsea, they were a beautiful young family with early teens all the way down to small children. Here they were, in a conflict-ridden nation, struggling with a new language and challenging conditions, all to serve the Lord. Just like my dear friends, they were starting a new family with a sick child in a war zone.

The Albanian Kosovars were beautiful people—handsome, Caucasian, and western in dress. They even had Western educations, but the culture was radically different from ours. One young adult had been severely beaten by the Imam's men when they heard he had converted to Christianity. Another man told me that he had spent time with a girl he liked, and when her brother found out, the brother told him he would kill him if he did it again. For all intents and purposes they were peers, but in this shame-honour culture, marriage and sexual relations were severely controlled by familial, de facto tribal, religious, and status affiliations. Family honour demanded death to those who crossed the line.

Aftermath of war in Kosovo

We drove far out into the country to visit a farming family who Bret and Chelsea and the other missionaries aided. The lush, peaceful valley and open fields gave the lie to the fact that only years ago it had been strewn with the dead and dying bodies of Albanian families after a genocidal attack by the Serbs.

Upon the heels of the devastation of the war, the family's barn had burnt down and they hadn't been able to afford to rebuild. This had meant the loss of their animals, and therefore their income. Bret and Chelsea collected supplies and delivered it to this family, which consisted of an Oma and Opa (grandparents) and two very attractive adult daughters with children up to seven years of age. We were treated to rural hospitality with round after round of Turkish coffee and snacks. I kept making the mistake of emptying my glass, which protocol demanded they then refill. We had a long conversation, with Bret as interpreter. I was treated as an honoured guest, humbled by the graciousness of these people who had been through a personal holocaust and yet held me in high regard.

There was an old-world charm to the farmhouse with woodstove and couches. It was sparse yet warm; the women dutifully served men who barked orders, but these lovely young women were dressed in Western garb and were very magnetic. Oma, with her cane, was given apposite respect and deference, and we were appropriately honoured by the introductions. The women laid out snacks and Sarah and Mark were treated like royal children, though they had their place. They played with the Albanian kids and ran around the yard. As we prepared to leave, we posed together for photos in the front yard, by the garden.

The mission organization arranged a sports day in the Sar Mountains National Park. These delightful, affectionate youth seemed to love our presence. We played American football, sang praise and worship songs in Albanian and English, ate heartily, and then climbed the hill above the park.

We went for coffee in the park restaurant, and around the table I was introduced to a teenage hero and miracle of reconciliation. This handsome young kid, Ali, had converted from Islam, which usually meant expulsion from one's family and possible revenge from other family members for blaspheming Islam and bringing shame on the family.

Ali had given his testimony of meeting Jesus as his Saviour while at a showing of a Christian movie. The Imam's men came in, singled him out, and beat him severely, threatening his life. The other believers weren't able to prevent the violence without using violence themselves, so they shielded him as best they could, which probably prevented life-threatening injury.

Ali was a construction worker. While working on a home in the village one day, he saw the Imam walk into the house. Then he realized that this house was the Imam's brother's home. He prayed.

In subsequent visits to the house, the Imam caught a glimpse of him and seemed to struggle to recognize him. Ali decided not to hide, but instead keep working. Eventually, the Imam approached him and began inquiring as to why he had accepted the Jewish Messiah. Ali explained and showed himself to be forgiving about the abuse and mature in the faith, despite his youth. The Imam was impressed and told him that it had been his assistant's idea to send in the thugs. Ali continued to work on the house until it was finished. This can only be explained by the direct intervention of the Holy Spirit.

After our time together, we drove home in the evening light, exhausted and euphoric. With Ali's story in my mind, I had been touched by the magnificence of God.

But the peace was misleading. These were the Balkans—the spark to the Great War, the source of monumental atrocities in World War II, and central to global Soviet aspirations during the Cold War. Today, in an era of jihadist aspirations for the Islamic caliphate, in the twilight of American influence, this place was a football in international politics.

Just a few blocks down a curving alley, we encountered what appeared to be bombed-out homes, marking a field littered with garbage. These had been Serbian homes, and they'd been destroyed by Albanian Kosovar sledgehammers. They remained a disturbing remnant of the genocidal war, a scar reminding the community of what had happened.

Mark was an extremely high-energy little boy, a miracle given his medically troubled infancy. Thus, Bret and Chelsea assigned me the job of tiring him out. Virtually every day that he wasn't run ragged by other children, he would ride his little bicycle and I would run—sometimes ahead, sometimes behind—to the highway and back, several kilometres. It was there that I saw a four-door sedan loaded by crane onto the back of a Volkswagen Westphalia that had been cut down to an open pickup. The car hung precariously in every direction and the old Volkswagen lapsed under the weight, such that its tires sunk to within millimetres of the wheel wells. I would have said, "This cannot be done." I held my tongue. After they were finished, I came to a similar conclusion: "It should not have been done." As I watched them drive away, I surmised that safety standards were non-existent in Kosovo.

I had to get in shape for my upcoming tour with the Israeli military, and Mark's parents needed a break to get their errands done. I was a nervous wreck each time I brought Mark home. He would take off ahead of me and disappear around the narrow street where cars travelled way too fast around blind curves. No matter how far we went, Mark wanted to go farther; he even wished to head out onto the main four-lane highway. Sometimes I would succeed in tiring him out, particularly when the broken pavement turned to packed sand and gravel. I would then have to pull the bicycle until he got tired and decided to sit. In any event, he played me like a harp.

Needless to say, I was soon fit for the army. My IDF assignments were to be easy by comparison.

The experience was wonderful. I got a taste of family life. I got to see Kosovo all the way to the northern Serbian areas. I got to build a model Noah's ark for the children's Bible class at church. I got to build a model Tower of Babel out of cardboard for the kids to tear down. I got to teach an English class while Kevin was away to the airport picking up the new Australian missionary family. I got to give an extended psychiatric consult to the local missionary administrator about a very difficult new believer.

Three mornings a week, I got to sit in a little café and talk across linguistic boundaries to seamen and soldiers and woodcutters and businessmen who came in for their morning beverage and snack. I was blessed to *be* and to serve in one of the most tortured areas of the globe, among heroes and heroines who had decided to live there in the name of Jesus Christ.

24

Mashuginah Goy Joins the Navy[66]

HAVING SERVED MY THIRTY-FIVE-YEAR SENTENCE AS A CLINICAL SOCIAL worker in community psychiatry, I worked nights to close off a career, downsized my life radically, and caught a plane with the intention of serving in Sar-El for another three months. The experience was unimaginable. Indescribable. It surpassed my wildest dreams! I lived a lifetime in those three months.

My previous two three-week assignments (in 2007 and 2008) had introduced me to the uniformed IDF volunteer experience, but three months truly made me part of Israeli society and Army life. Sar-El was the only place on earth where you could serve in the military of a foreign nation which was by definition forced constantly to be on alert.

My first assignment was Tel Hashomer, a large medical supply base as well as induction centre for new conscripts. It used a large, international Sar-El group. For the first time, I began to realize that Sar-El, as well as Israel, was positioned at the crossroads of the universe. We stood at the point in history and geography where twenty-five hundred years earlier the Jewish prophets Isaiah, Jeremiah, and Ezekiel had predicted that Jews from the four corners of the world would stream back to this tiny patch of real estate at the intersection of the world's trade, religion, and politics.

My dorm had two journalists from Atlanta, a member of New York City's finest, shot in the line of duty, and a brilliant Chilean linguist. Other volunteers included kids from France, Canada, South Africa, Siberia, Moscow, and the States, all with different motivations and plans with respect to Israel. There were also Aussies, New Zealanders, and Dutch—all heroic people, some with

---

[66] Originally published on Sar-el.org, Spring 2010.

unimaginable histories of tragedy and recovery. Many had amazing artistic, linguistic, and business accomplishments, as well as familial connections to the holocaust. There were Jews making the first stages of Aliyah, bright-eyed youth with careers and education headed for the Army while they learned from the unique people of this miraculous land. Observant Jews, atheists, Christians, agnostics, New Age practitioners, Hebrews, and Gentiles all came together, dressed in khaki with blue Sar-El epaulettes. They all had a wish to serve the most unbelievable military in history.

In the evenings, we discussed Israeli history, politics, demographics, and art. We swam in the Mayaon pools near Jerusalem, toured Mount Hertzl, and wept over the graves of the recent Cast Lead[67] and Lebanon operations. We spent an evening with a heroine of the 1948 siege of Jerusalem, Zipporah Porath. We passionately discussed the issues of Gaza and captured Israeli soldier Gilad Shalit,[68] and disclosed ourselves (our motivations and passions) to one another.

Pam gave me a choice for my next assignment, and soon Mashuginah Goy was off to the Navy.

South of Haifa was a large tech, logistics, supply, and transport base with a commander who treated us like royalty. He was a war hero who invited us to his board room three times and introduced us to his senior staff. Two mornings per week, we could run with the senior staff on the Hofa Carmel beach, since the commander held fitness as a high priority for his people. Base discipline was significant because of its security sensitivity—no photos, no computers. We served those Navy corvettes, missile boats, Mosquitoes, and submarines that kept Israel's coastline and airspace safe.

Bordered on the west by massive banana plantations and on the east by towering cliffs, the site was magnificent. When the surf was heavy, we could hear the distant roar of banana leaves being clapped and rattled.

The Sar-El group was amazing. There was a tenured American university professor and his wife. There was a Russian-American software specialist who ran his own business and had been beaten by the KGB and imprisoned for one year for possessing a copy of Solzhenitsyn's *Gulag Archipelago*. There was a former prima ballerina who had grown up in Iran; she was with her author and parliamentary aide husband from Britain. There was an Aussie businessman who had survived and thrived after a catastrophic auto accident. There were two Israeli women

---

[67] Cast Lead: A three-week military operation into Gaza in 2008–9 to stop the ceaseless bombardment of Israeli Negev towns and cities by rockets launched from Hamas terrorist emplacements.

[68] Captured on the Gaza border in 2006, Shalit, an IDF battle tank crewman, spent five years in the tender custody of Hamas while they negotiated the release of incarcerated terrorists.

living in Judea, a South African businesswoman whose children were prospering, and a New York businesswoman who had been living in San Diego and spoke fluent Hebrew. There was a multilingual Dutch woman, an electrical engineer from the States, and… me. They were all brilliant, accomplished, multilingual, multicultural individuals in love with Israel.

Our evenings were intoxicating. We discussed the history of the Cast Lead campaign and its politics, and heard the debate over the relevance of the Hatikvah.[69] The American professor delivered a presentation on how he had believed he was the only surviving member of a family line, exterminated during the holocaust. Over ten years' time, he had found over a hundred relatives living in Israel. It was a powerful and emotional event when for the first time I had a glimpse of the personal impact of having lost most of one's family to a ruthless, legal, extermination machine. Then we heard a British holocaust author, living and teaching in France, present his book about Jewish twins saved by the Kinder Transport. They had been raised as Christians in an abusive family home.

These creative, complicated, gentle, ingenious people treated me so well that I tear up to think about it. I was an outsider, a categorical representative of an institution that had persecuted their people for almost two thousand years. I was included, appreciated, and given a voice. This demonstrated that wonderful Jewish phenomenon known as "Hesed."[70]

The lone Madrika arranged tours of the Naval Museum and a spectacular high-tech winery in northern Galilee. As we descended through the Druze villages on our way back to the base, Hezbollah (literally, *Hizbu Allah*, or "party of God") launched a rocket into the area just to show their appreciation to the United Nations for the peace they were keeping.

I got into trouble in my assignment by climbing around on the high warehouse shelves to assist in the aesthetics of the arrangement of stored materials; an inspection of the base had been imminent. I was punished by being reassigned to the base maintenance and fire suppression commander. He was a young, vibrant, twenty-something petty-officer first class who had become an ensign while I was there (meaning that a stripe moved from his sleeve to his epaulette). I was invited to the ceremony. This young guy had driven ammunition trucks during the second Lebanon war while Katushya rockets flew overhead. He wore his war medal above the pocket on his white Navy shirt.

---

[69] In Hebrew, meaning "the hope." Put to music, it serves as the national anthem if Israel.
[70] "Hesed," from its Old Testament Hebrew root, means "loyal love" or "loving kindness."

We had to repaint all the fire hydrants and equipment boxes on the base with a glossy oil paint so they could easily be found, day or night. There were about two hundred items to paint and we had two days of forty-degree temperatures in which to do it. I loved my punishment and had no problem tolerating the heat. I got to be outdoors, with more work than I could ever finish. In fact, I had to recruit from the other Sar-El recruits, if their own workloads dropped temporarily. I watched F-16s do patrols and manoeuvres overhead. Blackhawks and Cobras flew by and I heard the comforting rattle of automatic weapons fire in the nearby range that swept up the mountainside. At night, I would hear local residents shooting wild boar.

When the blessed rain hit, it was wild! It blew out all the plastic-covered windows of our moadon,[71] but turned the beautiful mountainside green. We needed warmer clothing. During the rain, I was assigned to renovate the office of my newly promoted boss. I stripped, spackled, and painted his new office. That was in between pumping fuel oil to the hot water system and setting up for a fire suppression training session.

During that time, a group of Israeli Navy Seals (Shayetet) captured an Iranian arms shipment destined for Hezbollah. Then a munitions depot in a Hezbollah operative's home "accidentally" blew up on the Lebanon border.

I re-enlisted at this base, since my work wasn't complete after the first three weeks, and a major base inspection was upcoming. The next Sar-El group was largely comprised of Americans. I remained Navy while they served with the Home Front command under a gracious Druze commander. They repaired and replaced materials for civilian causalities of war and natural disaster.

Again, it was a stunningly varied group of businesspeople and professionals, more homogeneous in age but brilliant. There were accountants, pharmacists, artists, photographers, a Uruguayan-American linguist businessman, and several people with American military experience.

We visited the Hannah Senesh Memorial on the beach near Caesarea, as well as the Naval Museum. There, we had a wonderful interaction with a Parisian Golani soldier who had been injured in a high fall during training. He was recovering while on guard duty at the base. He was trying to get his points up to return to his unit.

We also met the young geniuses from the computer department responsible for missile, fire control, and threat alert systems. These young soldiers and Navy

---

[71] Essentially, a moadon is a recruit clubhouse, sometimes well-appointed, but sometimes *not*. Many bases don't have them at all.

personnel were magnificent. I was comforted to see that unlike the majority of Canadian, American, and Western European youth, they *knew* they were at war.

In our evening activities, we took a look at the Gilad-Shalit release from a new perspective, took quizzes in language, history, and culture, and debated between religious observance and secular business. Then there was the topic of the impact of the massive Russian immigration.

The remarkable gratitude and graciousness of the Israeli people to a Christian Goy who loved Israel with a visceral passion was remarkable. The indigenous sabra[72] cactus "prickles" were actually underdeveloped blossoms. Not only was the Sabra sweet inside, but it was necessarily tough, defended, and beautiful as a cactus blossom.

Tech and Logistics Base, Israel

---

[72] The sabra, the Israeli version of the prickly pear cactus, is tenacious and thick-skinned. It is a symbol for Israeli-born Jews, who are prickly, tough, and durable on the outside but have a sweet interior.

At the end of my second assignment at the Tirat Carmel base, Pam gave me another choice (bless her), and this, too, was spectacular. I had to serve in tech and logistics at Beer Sheva.

I had never been there and I was looking forward to it. At Beer Sheva, I experienced my first dust storm, yet we had beautiful, gentle rains on several other days. This was a different base, a different military culture, and a different Sar-El culture.

The Beer Sheva base was immaculately organized and clean, with good morale and more relaxed in its discipline. We were treated like royalty—relatively speaking, of course, by military standards. The nights were frosty and the days were twenty-two degrees.

My bunkhouse mates were again international, brilliant, and varied. My work partner was a genius Russian-American who had served missile guidance systems in the Russian Army. He had his own software development company now and a photographic memory, not only for technology but also for history and culture. Our dorm also had a retired lieutenant colonel from the U.S. Army and an Aussie businessman with an apartment in Israel. Of our group, we had a British agency translator, an Israeli "Oleh" couple who were travelling, an American artist and photographer, a chemical engineer, and a young Torontonian businessman. Again, we were Christians and Jews, observant and nominal, but with a higher proportion of "goyim" than in any other of the six groups I served with.

My job was in an open-sided warehouse where we dismantled, resorted, and catalogued Merkava tank parts into mobile containers for frontline repair stations. Around us were 1200-horse-power diesel tank engines, and the warehouse across the alley stored the 120-millimetre canon barrels. Our civilian supervisor spoke little English but was extremely experienced with Sar-El volunteers.

The Russian businessman had good facility with languages and had enough Hebrew to mediate between us. It was hard physical work, exacting and meaningful. When the containers were transported to the helipad by big forklifts, we would paint redundant Army vehicles that were held for parts so they couldn't be used for terrorist purposes. While the paint was still dripping, the forklift would literally come and snap it out from under our brushes.

Our evenings were vigorous, because the intellectual acumen in the room was stunning. The Madrichot were highly committed and delightful. We visited the award- winning Beer Sheva Palmach Memorial of the defence of the Jewish community from the Egyptian Army and Arab irregulars in 1948. Then we were off to Ben Gurion's Sde Boker and the Midreshet gravesite.[73] Our road passed amidst meditating camels, Bedouin encampments, and the spectacular desolation of the desert.

On base, the air was filled with Air Force activity. Nearby was a C-130 base that Sar-El had helped move from Tel Aviv. Because of it, the transport planes that I had served in 2007 flew overhead. F-16s and apparent F-4 Phantoms constantly buzzed by, as well as Cobra helicopters and Blackhawks. Beer Sheva's airspace was very active.

While on a hill overlooking Beer Sheva, the tank-testing fields behind us would yield the blast of a tested engine. A Merkava would soar over a ridge and down into the valley. M-16 fire was rare and intermittent.

I stayed mostly in Tel Aviv, however. Every Sunday, I got up at 4:30 a.m. and caught the train either to Haifa (when I was with the Navy) or Beer Sheva. The trains become troop trains on Sunday mornings and Thursday afternoons, as Israel's remarkable youth either headed off or onto bases all over the country. These beautiful kids carried automatic weapons and packs as big as they were, beautiful kids in their late teens to early twenties. The girls wore shoulder patches from every type of unit and ranks of all levels, carrying huge packs and firearms; they represented a sight so incongruous with our naïve North American and Western European view of the world that I was astonished.

But Israel is on the front lines of a war that the rest of the world denies is even taking place. Just as in 1930, they are hated for being Jews and blamed for every political problem on earth. They are conscripted into a war they didn't start and would ecstatically lay down their arms if they thought for a moment they would survive. They stand alone in a terror war that is different from any other in human history. They have to find humane ways to fight against people who hide behind, and celebrate the deaths of, their own women and children. When the Israelis defend themselves, they are condemned, because to the majority of the international community the only way there will be global peace is when they no longer have a homeland, sovereignty, and the capacity to defend themselves.

Israel Geva, the Air Force war hero who acted as coordinator for Sar-El, came and spoke to us on behalf of General Aaron Davidi, the architect of Sar-El. He told of the very unique situation in which Israel finds itself. The threat to Israel extends as a threat to the whole world, yet the world refuses to believe it. Israel has been forced by international dictators to give away the small amount of land

---

[73] Sde Boker Kibbutz is the Negev retirement home of Israel's first prime minister, David Ben Gurion, and the "place of learning" (Midreshet) is the spectacular gravesite where he is buried. (see: http://www.boker.org.il/english/).

it has, and immediately that land became a terror base from which to attack them. They saw it in Gaza, and soon also in Judea and Samaria.

In this untenable double bind, the soldiers, sailors, and airmen of the IDF see Sar-El volunteers appear. This diaspora of brilliant and creative Jews, and the Christians who support them, converge at the crossroads of the universe, putting out a hand to the Israeli Army to let them know they are not alone in the fight. So often the soldiers don't understand because it really doesn't make any sense: "You mean you spend your own money to come from your comfortable existence which we would like to have… to do grunt work in the army we would like to avoid having to serve in?"

One of the greatest challenges of retiring is the loss of one's occupational identity. These three months replaced my old identity with a new and much more meaningful one.

25

The Hurt Locker

IN THE 2008 KATHRYN BIGELOW FILM *THE HURT LOCKER*, **JEREMY RENNER** plays U.S. Army Sergeant First Class William James, an explosive ordinance disposal specialist in Iraq. A special qualification is required to wear the blast suit which shields one somewhat from the levels and numbers of improvised explosive devices (IEDs), and he has it. Because of Williams' basic character and adaptation techniques, he is especially equipped and fearless in dismantling lethal IEDs. He insists that all his subordinates respond in the same manner. Tormented and inherently rebellious, he anaesthetizes himself to his early and accumulating grief with the drug of war. His child, common-law mate, and those he comes to love in the theatre of war, are thoroughly encapsulated in the hurt locker. His intense focus, his life-and-death technical problem-solving skills, and the catastrophic danger requires it. He is addicted to the intoxicating adrenalin rush that buries the hurt locker.

Though an extreme example, the movie amplifies a common dynamic that drives drug, sex, work, electronic, and risk addictions. It is avoidance.

My hurt locker contains only a few scars inflicted by others. They're insignificant by comparison with what I have inflicted on those who I've loved and those who have taken the risk of loving me. Are mine sagas of drug abuse, bankruptcy, violence, marital infidelity, physical abuse, or neglect? No. They're subtle incidents of cruel words, profound insensitivity, adolescent egocentricity, and bad judgment. When I stop moving, stop working, stop taking risks, and stop obsessing about the next deadline, they erupt into my consciousness. They stab at my intestines and cause me to groan. I stop breathing in the wish I could undo the things I have said and done. But I cannot.

Born guilty, functionally an only child, I would sometimes lay awake and grieve at night, thinking about how my little tugboat felt while left outside on the shores of the tiny brook that flowed near my childhood home. I was exquisitely sensitive. But the pain of guilt didn't prevent me from inflicting further injury on others. My impulsive and impatient nature led to careless words and acts that I deeply regretted immediately afterward. The perceived pain I had inflicted on others turned back into virtual pain in my soul.

When I was in seventh grade, I knew a tall, sweet-faced girl who sometimes playfully pushed me. One day, I overreacted and pushed back so hard that she slipped on the ice, tore her nylons, and slashed her knee. I was too embarrassed and graceless to ask forgiveness and lend aid and comfort.

As I graduated to the idiocy of adolescence, the incidents increased in frequency and intensity. While listening to my deadhead friends, they told me it was cool to be hurtful and indifferent to girls who liked you. I cheated on my steady girlfriend while in a small Acadian town near Casey Cape; I later left her behind without deliberation when I headed to the West Coast. I broke the leg of my loyal fox-wirehair terrier while playing rough. Once I became adolescent, I neglected and ignored my mom, who dearly loved me. I didn't write nearly often enough to my dad, who would go faithfully to the country mailbox every day. I ruined a little terrier through exhaustion as he loyally responded to my calls to follow while I was on cross-country skis in eight inches of new snow. I married and emotionally abandoned my wife, a dearly beloved soft-lipped, blue-eyed girl. My brothers, along with my nieces and nephews, seldom heard from me throughout my life; they only saw me as a disappearing shadow.

But those are just a few.

Now that I'm "running on empty," there is the danger that the hurt locker will explode and the drug will run out. There is time to think, time to meditate, and time to ponder all I did and didn't do, time to feel the pain I've inflicted on many tender souls, the curse of the *Ghost Rider*.[74]

There are many acutely beneficial consequences to the hurt locker being unlatched. You can no longer run, and thereby must reduce one's "fuel" consumption; the morbidity risk may be diminished by the reduced velocity of life; the personal suffering makes one more attuned to the pain of others. Most importantly, one has to look into the face of God.

These thankfully are not the musings of a Marxist materialist viewing a failed

---

[74] In the 2007 film starring Nicholas Cage, sadistic criminals who looked into the eyes of the Ghost Rider were consumed in the flames of the pain they had inflicted on others.

revolution, but more the agony of a repentant soul like John Newton breathing, "Indeed, it is amazing grace."

The hurt locker is painfully opened and in tears laid at the foot of the Cross as sweet faces like incense rise on prayers for healing into throne room of God.

Time Machine

Johnny Yuma, from the 1959–61 ABC television series *The Rebel* kept a journal as he rode the Texas hill country and South Texas plains. I remember seeing it on my family's black-and-white TV in 1960. I was so impressed by how Johnny, haunted by his memories, would quietly pull the journal out of his saddlebag and begin writing in it by the flicker of his campfire after surviving another day. In 1962, I began doing the same.

In the film, journaling seemed to calm him. In reality, it calms me. He was tormented by memories of the Civil War. I was tormented by a world I didn't fit into. I had an exquisite sensitivity which made just about everything hurt.

By now, it and my photo albums would fill an entire room. When I open them up, I disappear from this world. My journaling wasn't disciplined, but then again, neither was I. Writing was cathartic. I picked up my journal like I picked up my guitar throughout adolescence—when I needed to vent, to express, to exult, or to wail.

When I look at those words, the handwriting that has changed so much, I am absorbed into the page... into another moment in time. Events rush to my consciousness after long absence. They explode in colour and sound. I escape into Einstein's multidimensional world of time travel.

I experience the horror of my marriage breakdown once again, and my heart stops. I climb Williams Peak and roll out on the crest to see Chilliwack Lake laid out before me; a large hawk rides the thermals through the saddle and brakes instantly, startled at my form on barren rock. I tour Europe once again, feeling the air and breathing in the aroma of rack of lamb near a Venice ristorante as gondola lights sway on the reflected canal and gondoliers sing arias.

I stare out a barred prison window to see a young man drop from the chain-link fence and collapse into a dusty pool of his own blood. I experience the shock of staring down the barrel of a gun, pointed in fear and anger. I remember a mother weeping in my office for her missing schizophrenic son. I see the killing fields of Kosovo.

I sit by the dry heat of the woodstove, listening to the crackle and snap of burning pine and fir. I sit in my rocker and see the reflection of the kerosene lamp in my window, the shades of night overtaking the pine forest. My heart dies within my chest as I see the woman I love walk through the security gate at the airport. I look over an embankment into Lebanon and stare at a mock village where I know Hezbollah terrorists are watching my back. From my bunk bed, I hear the roar of an Israeli C-130 rolling off the apron at 3:00 a.m. to do surveillance or a black op.

Then I look up, and…

Where am I? The maple and pine trees outside my mission home rustle in the waning summer breeze. The western glow of a setting sun turns them to silhouettes. Or I rise from the stone fireplace to take another log for the fire and drop it atop the deep bed of glowing coals as a cold moon drifts above the newly fallen snow and a deer sees the glow in the window. I pull out a tobacco pouch and stick the bowl of my pipe deep into the rich tobacco, watching as the flame from the match flares and wanes and flares and wanes with my breath. A cloud of Borkum Riff circles over my head and into the room, just like it used to with my dad. I hear my dad's voice and the strains of a Frank Sinatra piece: "When I was seventeen, it was a very good year." I remember when I sang it long and wistfully, at the age of seventeen, on a hillside above the river in central New Brunswick, my eyes not knowing what the Lord would allow me to see.

Now I know.

I have temporarily stepped out of the time machine.

Epilogue

Let us hear the conclusion of the whole matter: Fear God, and keep His commandments, for this is man's all. For God will bring every work into judgment, including every secret thing, whether good or evil. (Ecclesiastes 12:13–14)

Nothing is better for a man than that he should eat and drink, and that his soul should enjoy good in his labor. This also, I saw, was from the hand of God. For who can eat, or who can have enjoyment, more than I? (Ecclesiastes 2:24–25)

Solomon, the man who had it all, started out with the blessing of God. He then failed so badly that all allusions to him in scripture after that point carry a negative connotation.

"Meaningless! Meaningless!" says the Teacher. "Utterly meaningless! Everything is meaningless." (Ecclesiastes 1:2, NIV)

This teacher had all the wealth, science, logic, wives, concubines, and wine he could want. He introduced stunning architectural accomplishments to Jerusalem the Golden, had international diplomatic success, was considered the world's wisest man, brought peace in his time, and was mandated to build the most magnificent temple to the God of Abraham, Isaac, and Jacob.

Meaningless, meaningless…

> *I, the Preacher, was king over Israel in Jerusalem. And I set my heart to seek and search out by wisdom concerning all that is done under heaven; this burdensome task God has given to the sons of man, by which they may be exercised. I have seen all the works that are done under the sun; and indeed, all is vanity and grasping for the wind.* (Ecclesiastes 1:12–14)

But these are the words of the apostate, not of the man who in his youth asked for wisdom to righteously rule his people. He asked for wisdom over riches and not the necks of his enemies. He pleased God and was given, by God's grace, the riches anyway.

Mine was the apostasy of socialist revolution—a secular fantasy of heaven on earth.

Solomon's are the words of the man who made peace treaties with the nations around him by marrying the pagan and idolatrous daughters of pagan and idolatrous kings and priests. This is the man who allowed their idols to be brought into the City of Gold, the City of God, the Kingdom of Heaven. His conclusion to the matter is therefore as unsatisfying as his anguished cry, and so was mine.

He would have known that Scripture is clear that if you fail in even one law, you are guilty of failing in them all.

> *For whoever shall keep the whole law, and yet stumble in one point, he is guilty of all.* (James 2:10)

> *For God will bring every work into judgment, including every secret thing, whether good or evil.* (Ecclesiastes 12:14)

The thought must have terrified him.

But wise and knowledgeable as he was, Solomon didn't know what we know. He likely knew that the redemption was in progress, but he didn't see its fulfilment. He didn't know of the debt (his debt) paid in full, nor of a life motivated by love for the One who paid the debt with His own blood. He embarked upon his own secular fantasy and, unlike his father, King David, he did not remain a man after God's own heart.

Solomon was brilliant, and I am not. Solomon was rich and powerful, and I am not. Solomon did it all, and I have not. But Solomon was in bondage, and I am not. I am free, and Solomon was not. I am *"a deer let loose"* (Genesis 49:21).

I came a hair's breadth from entangling myself in the bondage that entrapped nearly a third of the world's population in the 70s and 80s.

Though I betrayed Him (like Solomon), lied about Him, and have not often abided in Him (like Solomon toward the end), the Lord has allowed me to *"eat and drink… that [my] soul should enjoy in his labour"* (Ecclesiastes 2:24). He gave me the *"peace… which surpasses all understanding"* (Philippians 4:7). He gave a loser like me a wonderful, exciting life, and accomplished it through direct intervention.

> *But God has chosen the foolish things of the world to put to shame the wise, and God has chosen the weak things of the world to put to shame the things which are mighty; and the base things of the world and the things which are despised God has chosen, and the things which are not, to bring to nothing the things that are…* (1 Corinthians 1:27–28)

God has sent me wonderful friends who are doctoral biochemists, schizophrenia sufferers, prominent research anthropologists, psychiatrists, gays and ex-gays, psychiatric epidemiologists, neurological researchers, ex-cons, murderers, senior diplomats, former sex offenders, victims of assassination attempts, ex-military pilots, and missionaries.

With limited personal resources and intelligence, He has allowed me to scuba-dive, white-water kayak, travel the mountains on foot and ski, live in the mountains, liberate innocent men from prison, and produce documents for commissions of enquiry and lieutenant colonels. He has allowed me to publish articles in academic and professional journals, in magazines and newspapers, and on the internet. He has had articles written about me and my work. He has allowed me to present papers and projects outside B.C., and outside Canada, and to to teach workshops in a medical school, colleges, and international conferences. He has allowed me to tour in Europe, Jamaica, Haiti, Curacao, Cuba, Israel, Macedonia and Kosovo, the United States, and Canada. He has allowed me to fall off motorcycles eleven times and not be seriously hurt and be in eight car accidents in seven years.

This was all quite impossible, given who I am.

I have never owned a house. I have never owned a car worth more than four thousand dollars. I have no wife and no children and have never had a salary above seventy thousand dollars (and only for a short period of time). Yet it seems I've had a much happier and more satisfying life than King Solomon, and only because of the saving power of the Word of God, the *logos*, Jesus the Christ Himself: *"And the Word became flesh and dwelt among us…"* (John 1:14).

> *Then they said to Him, "What shall we do, that we may work the works of God?"*
> *Jesus answered and said to them, "This is the work of God that you believe in Him whom He sent."* (John 6:28–29)

God used Solomon's tragic story to demonstrate how the truly great can end their assignments tragically, and how the truly weak can end their assignments victoriously.

All human effort to bring utopian visions into existence has carried immeasurable cost. In the case of fascism, it cost seventy million lives. The communist experiment has cost 120 million lives. The price of these experiments is always paid in blood, and most often in modern times the blood of Christians and Jews. Islam's genocidal record through their bids for global domination rings in at 270 million. According to Michael Horowitz of the Hudson Institute, the slaughter of Christians over the past twenty years is the number one human rights issue of our time, though it goes largely unreported.[75] That's the way Jesus said it would be. All pagan religions, including atheism, demand human sacrifice.

The blood cost for heaven has already been paid, but man's slaughter of his fellow man to bring heaven to earth, to pre-empt Christ's redemptive plan will continue, and it will get worse. The most revolutionary concept of all is embodied in the words of the hymn that says, "There is a fountain filled with blood drawn from Emmanuel's veins; and sinners plunged beneath that flood lose all their guilty stains."[76]

This constitutes a true revolution in mind. Put into action in the modern world, it constitutes subversive activity.

---

[75] Michael Horowitz introduction to Paul Marshall. *Their Blood Cries Out: The Untold Story of Persecution Against Christians in the Modern World.* Nashville Tenn. Word Publishers 1997.
[76] William Cowper, "There Is a Fountain Filled with Blood," 1772.

They wandered in the wilderness in a desolate way; they found no city to dwell in. Hungry and thirsty, their soul fainted in them. Then they cried out to the Lord in their trouble, and He delivered them out of their distresses. And He led them forth by the right way, that they might go to a city for a dwelling place. Oh, that men would give thanks to the Lord for His goodness, and for His wonderful works to the children of men! For He satisfies the longing soul, and fills the hungry soul with goodness. (Psalm 107:4–9, NKJV)

About the Author

BORN IN THE IDYLLIC MARITIMES IN 1946, ROGER NEILL LEFT HOME AT THE age of nineteen for British Columbia's Lotusland and got swept up in the cultural, political, and economic revolution which defined the late 60s and early 70s. He has a bachelor's and master's degree from Simon Fraser University. This was followed by twenty years of psychiatric social work in various capacities with the Greater Vancouver Mental Health Service. During his career, Neill published articles in mental health journals and presented workshops throughout the mental health system, community colleges, and the University of British Columbia. He also participated in presentations at the Canadian Psychiatric Association in Ottawa, as well as at an international congress on psychiatric rehabilitation in Orebro, Sweden.

This foundational training and experience prepared him for seven years with the Mennonite Central Committee in Jamaica, working with first the homeless in Montego Bay, and then the incarcerated mentally ill in the infamous prisons of Kingston and Spanish Town. An international story grew out of this episode. A coordinated partnership saw the release of a seventy-year-old man who had been incarcerated twenty-nine years for breaking a window while he was psychotic. Neill wrote multiple newspaper articles for the Jamaican press and appeared on radio and television talk shows.

His return to B.C. in 2003 brought him back to community psychiatry for six years with Fraser Health Authority. From 2007, he began serving with the Sar-El, a uniformed volunteer unit of the Israel Defense Force. His last placement was at an IDF post along the Lebanese border while President Ahmadinejad of Iran was in Beirut.

Retired now and living in Mission, B.C., Neill writes a blog on international affairs as they relate to the nation of Israel and the Christian Church (www.donningtheyellowstar.wordpress.com). His recreational passions centre around canoes, kayaks, wilderness travel, motorcycles, and guitar.

Coming Soon…

Enigma: Redemption in Jamaica
by Roger Brian Neill

COMING SOON IS THIS REMARKABLE STORY OF GOD'S MOVE TO FREE Jamaica's domestic refugees—the mentally ill—from dirty and dangerous streets and prisons to family and community. The Mennonite Central Committee placed Roger Neill in the prisons of Jamaica, and in a spectacular partnership of Jamaicans and North American Christians, miraculous things happened. The biggest international story from this time is of a man incarcerated for twenty-nine years for breaking a window while psychotic. But that is only one story of many in this fascinating autobiographical account.

Roger Brian Neill BA, MA, RSW

REVOLUTION IN MIND
AN AUTOBIOGRAPHY

http://rogerbrianneill.blogspot.ca/

REVOLUTION IN MIND
Copyright © 2014 by Roger Brian Neill
Author photo by Cindy Sommerfield

All rights reserved. Neither this publication nor any part of this publication may be reproduced or transmitted in any form or by any means, electronic or mechanical, including photocopying, recording or any information storage and retrieval system, without permission in writing from the author.

Unless otherwise indicated, all Scripture taken from the New King James Version®. Copyright © 1982 by Thomas Nelson, Inc. Used by permission. All rights reserved. Scripture quotations marked KJV taken from the Holy Bible, King James Version, which is in the public domain. Scripture quotations marked (NIV) are taken from the Holy Bible, New International Version®, NIV®. Copyright © 1973, 1978, 1984, 2011 by Biblica, Inc.™ Used by permission of Zondervan. All rights reserved worldwide. The "NIV" and "New International Version" are trademarks registered in the United States Patent and Trademark Office by Biblica, Inc.™

Printed in Canada

ISBN: 978-1-4866-0174-5

Word Alive Press
131 Cordite Road, Winnipeg, MB R3W 1S1
www.wordalivepress.ca

Cataloguing in Publication may be obtained through Library and Archives Canada.